FATHER & SON

finding freedom

Books by Walter Wangerin Jr.

The Book of God: The Bible as a Novel

Paul: A Novel

This Earthly Pilgrimage

Saint Julian

The Book of the Dun Cow

The Book of Sorrows

Preparing for Jesus

Reliving the Passion

Little Lamb, Who Made Thee?

The Manger Is Empty

Miz Lil and the Chronicles of Grace

Mourning into Dancing

The Orphean Passages

Ragman and Other Cries of Faith

Whole Prayer

In the Days of the Angels

As for Me and My House

The Crying for a Vision

For Children

Mary's First Christmas

Peter's First Easter

The Book of God for Children

Probity Jones and the Fear-Not Angel

Thistle

Potter

In the Beginning There Was No Sky

Angels and All Children

Water, Come Down

The Bedtime Rhyme

Swallowing the Golden Stone

Branta and the Golden Stone

Elisabeth and the Water Troll

National Book Award-Winning Author

WALTER WANGERIN JR.
AND MATTHEW WANGERIN

FATHER & SON

finding freedom

ZONDERVAN

ZONDERVAN.com/
AUTHORTRACKER
follow your favorite authors

ZONDERVAN®

Father and Son
Copyright © 2008 by Walter Wangerin Jr. and Matthew Wangerin

Requests for information should be addressed to:

Zondervan, *Grand Rapids, Michigan 49530*

Library of Congress Cataloging-in-Publication Data

Wangerin, Walter.
　　　Father and Son / Walter Wangerin and Matthew Aaron Wangerin.
　　　　　p.　cm.
　　　ISBN　978-0-310-28394-2 (hardcover)
　　　　1.　Fathers and sons--Religious aspects--Christianity. 2.　Wangerin, Walter. 3.
Wangerin, Matthew Aaron.　I. Wangerin, Matthew Aaron. II. Title.
BV4529.17.W36 2008
277.3'0830922--dc22
　　　[B]

　　　　　　　　　　　　　　　　　　　　　　　　　　　　　　　　　　　　　　2007049185

Interior design and illustration by Christine Orejuela-Winkelman

Printed in the United States of America

08　09　10　11　12　13　•　23　22　21　20　19　18　17　16　15　14　13　12　11　10　9　8　7　6　5　4　3　2　1

Contents

Book I: Father

PART 1

1

2007

I will return them to their homes,
says the Lord.

When I hug my son these days, I am conscious of his shaven beard, rough against the flesh of my neck; and my nostrils flare at the scent of the soap on his neck; and I'm but a sack of brittle bones within the absolutely ineluctable strength of his arms.

Matthew is thirty-six years old. With a greater ease than I had ever mustered at his age (had mustered for most of my life), Matthew murmurs into my ear: "I love you, dad."

This is the one who taught me how to express my love aloud without embarrassment. "I love you, too, Matt," I am gratefully able to say.

Nor does it trouble the man, my son, to lean back and look me directly and gently in the eye. Smiling. Popping his eyebrows, his black eyebrows like swallow's wings left and right, flights for either eye. The eyes themselves are black-coffee brown; they have a warm bedroom droop, an altogether reassuring gentilesse — and he can hold the affectionate gaze longer than I, even down unto the day of this writing.

Matt Wangerin barbers his own hair, cuts it so close to the scalp that the result is more shadow than bristle. Sometimes, while he holds his gaze upon me, I break the line of his sight by raising my hand and stroking the top of that head. I pet him, as it were, and thereby enter his being. The hand I remove tingles on the palm and the pads of my fingers. What have I just done? Well, it feels as if I've petted the smooth bark of the beech tree, tall, established and strong, planted by the rivers of water and prospering.

It is Christmas. Except for the years of deepest anguish, Matthew Aaron has made a point of returning home to spend this holiday with us, his parents and whichever of his siblings are able to come on by as well. With his nieces and nephews. Matt has never been married. His brother and his two sisters — these three have. Among them they've produced four nieces and three nephews, for all of whom "Uncle Matt" is a comet of infinite sparkle and adventure.

Christmas: and I've stepped out of the house to greet him.

When he's a tad self-conscious, he falls into that male African American rhythmic slouch and role. Even so has he come up to walk to me through sharp weather and hard snow, pursing his lips and flipping his eyebrows in a purely Matthean grin.

And then he hugs me.

Regarding that strength in his arms? Once when he was fourteen and his brother fifteen years old, I opened a bedroom door and caught Matthew squeezing Joseph's chest with enough force to suppress the older boy's breathing. Joe looked pale and a little frightened. Matthew stood behind him, arms enwrapping the rib cage, his strong fingers laced at the base of Joseph's sternum.

"Matthew!" I cried, angry at his uncaused and pointless aggression. Over and over the boy kept exhibiting his physical advantage by hurting his brother. Not out of malice, mind you; rather, out of something like an ill-controlled exuberance. Nor did Joseph ever blame him or tattle; Joseph has loved his brother from their first meeting together and has admired Matt's native talents.

"Matthew! What are you doing?"

I stepped into the bedroom and broke Matt's hand-grip. I took his two wrists and, as if they were braided rope, snapped his arms behind him.

In those days I was a full head taller than my son.

I barked, "You want to know what it feels like?" I was serious. At that particular moment I was not out of control. I had come to believe that Matthew lacked a capacity for genuine empathy, neither to know nor to care how another person felt.

"Come here," I demanded, spinning him so that his back was to my front. "You're going to feel what you do to people, Matt!"

He did not smirk, nor was he insubordinate. I remember these things with clarity. He accepted my punishing responses as natural to the scheme of these things.

Now it was my turn. With my own two arms I encircled his chest. I slapped and grabbed my wrists against his stomach. Then, never questioning my superiority, I began to draw my adult embrace as tightly around him as I could: a vise is your father!

Matthew may have taken the discipline seriously. But this did not turn out to be a serious discipline.

All of the following I observed in a flash: his ribs did not bend inward, not so's I could notice. Nor was his breathing in any way troubled—despite the breaths of exertion whistling in my nostrils. I was making discoveries, both about my son and about me. Under my forearms and under the flesh of each of his breasts, I encountered two imposing pockets of muscle which, when he flexed them (flexing too the sudden *latissimus dorsi* packed upon his broadening back), bid fair to break my hold! And yet the boy was willing to accept my behavior as a punishment of some sort. Or did he know that in that moment our roles had begun to modify?

On the chance that he had *not* recognized reversals in our dancing together, I straightway let him go. Perhaps I coughed in order to alibi the swiftness of the release (which was done before any signs of pain had appeared in his face). Surely I pretended satisfaction in the choices and the accomplishments of my fathering:

"Joseph, you okay?"

"Yeah."

"Matthew, do you get it?"

"Yeah."

"Well, good then. Good."

Now, out in the midwinter snow, it is his strength that reminds me of our times past; and grateful am I that his strength is granted also unto me, causing me to be strong again.

My son—the man—releases me and we turn to enter the house together: "Unka Matt! Unka Matt is here! Hey, Unka Matt."

It is almost exactly one year ago today, on the twenty-sixth of December, that I noticed a thick, sausage-long mass tucked along the inside of my left clavicle bone. At the base of my neck. I mentioned the thing to Thanne, then carried the news to our family physician, who ordered an X-ray which revealed, actually, three masses within me, one in the lower left lung, one under the sternum between the lungs, and, yes, that mass in my neck. The doctor who read the X-ray pictures termed them "suspicious," and a swift biopsy confirmed it. I had a metastasized, stage IIIB, lung cancer.

By the best of good fortune, all of our children and all of our grandchildren had gathered for Christmas.

Therefore, one evening after supper—after putting a movie on for the little children—Thanne and I explained my condition as best as we could to our children and our children-in-law. I assured them of my faith and of the peace which attends it; I also, with an honesty undiminished to this day, declared that whatever was to come of this diagnosis, even the dying, would constitute my best adventure.

But when we had all said everything we could think of to say, and when people got up to clear the table and wash the dishes, Matthew did not move.

He had been sitting to my left.

During the explanation, he'd dropped his face down into his two open hands. He had said nothing.

I reached to touch him. "Matt?" I asked.

Without a sound, but keeping his face obscured, Matthew got up from the table and went into the bathroom and shut and locked the door.

All at once I felt a loss which I hadn't even felt with the diagnosis of my cancer. Was it his sense of impending loss that had been communicated into me? Were our spirits so intimate that one defined the other? Or was mine the loss of his intimacy?

I paced. Finally, after about half an hour and a quiet discussion with Thanne, I called through the door: "Matthew, I want to take a walk with you. Will you come?"

Noises in the bathroom indicated acceptance of my invitation: nose blowings, toilet flushings, throat clearings.

He came out. We put on coats and went outside into a winter's darkness.

We walked in silence a while. Among the children, Matthew would, of course, have a somewhat unique reaction. He goes home to an empty apartment. His three siblings all go home with company.

"I don't know," I puffed into the night, "what's to come of this, Matt." Our breathings hung like spirits in the snap-cold air. Our shadows lengthened before our feet as we passed beneath the pole light by the barn. Thanne and I live on some twenty-four acres, a small farm, woods, hills down which everyone toboggans upon good snow.

"I don't know what's coming, but I promise you, son, it's not going to trouble me. As for you, you'll find your feelings as they come. But I'd like to give you something which might direct those feelings. Okay? Matt, I would feel so proud if you could accept the task of watching out for your mother. I think about Joe and Mary and Talitha; but it's *you* who has the freedom for" — *and you who has the loneliness to be filled by* — "taking care of your mother. Will you take the task? Is this okay?"

Matt: "Yes."

Then, you see, he stopped walking and I stopped walking, and the whiskery man hugged me long, hugged me tightly enough to suppress my breathing.

Matthew? Matthew?

I lacked the air to call his name aloud—but in my mind it was a kindly, unpunishing appeal.

Matthew? Well, you see, I have lung cancer. We shouldn't be squeezing the living oxygen out of me these days.

———

Last summer—a half year after the diagnosis of cancer, and a half year before this Christmas—Matthew welcomed his mother and me into his apartment, Atlanta, Georgia, by shaking my hand, then taking me into his ropey arms and hugging me. I felt his rough beard against a new patch upon my person. Not my neck, this time—I felt it on the white, unsunny skin of my bald head. An odd sensation. I was only just getting used to baldness, a side effect of chemotherapy. Bald of all hair anywhere on my person: skull, eyelids, the bushes in old men's nostrils and ear-holes, armpits—well, you get the picture.

I had just fulfilled a commitment made long before my diagnosis, which was to deliver two extended speeches in Gatlinburg, Tennessee. Then Thanne and I took the opportunity to drive the rest of the way to Matthew's place—where I would lie for several days in a trembling exhaustion. Together with my hair, I'd lost my natural energies.

Matthew (as he had promised me on the farm, upon a frozen earth) shared caretaking with his mother—each for the other, I mean, and both for me. He was a host, my son, a beneficent icon showing me his recent DVDs, grinning good health on these parents whom he loved: his mother. Me. Clearly he was delighted by our company. But I enjoyed something deeper than mere delight in his company.

For me in my extremity, my son's presence was a source of the conviction of the rightness of things in this turning world. Moreover, his personal, filial love embraced me personally in that conviction. I, too, was a rightness among right things.

For, given our history, this father and this son might well have gone completely separate ways. The truest insight regarding our relationship was that we would become strangers each to the other, if not actual foes maintaining a wretched hostility.

For there was a time when Matthew yearned nothing more than to get out of our house for good and for all.

And there was an equally sincere time when I bargained with God— offering to give up my son's love for me, offering to suffer his separation, his contempt, even his hatred—if only the Lord would intervene, helping him to survive this life. Better yet, O Lord, my God: *let the boy succeed.* Mine was a begging prayer, repeated often, just as one beats over and over against an imprisoning door. With all my heart I meant my offerings. This was, I believe, a measure of *my* love, that I would sacrifice his love forever.

And then there was indeed a day when my supplications hardened into reality, when loving him had locked me into a terrible loneliness.

But here: look!

I entered my son's apartment.

He hugged me gently, crushing none of my unbendable bones. In spite of the jolt my hairless and haggard appearance caused in him, he smiled that pursed-lip smile and whispered in an easy creed, "I love you, dad," whispered as much with moist warm breath into my ear, then rose on tiptoe to nuzzle my scalp with the jut of his chin.

An old man young in the love of his son.

And a son to this extent in love with his father: that when I carried home six or seven of his DVDs, Matt laughed over the chance to accuse me of blatant thievery. He turned it into a joke. This is exactly the same as turning wrongness into rightness. And he has kept his joke going for half a year by now. But you have to know our past in order to understand the marvel, the divine grace of this joke—for there was a time when it was I who made the accusation with an earnest grief, and he who was the thief.

2
1970

He shall cry unto me:
"Thou art my father!"

The first of our children (the first of our sons) was born to us. The second was adopted.

Even so for our daughters, the first one born, the second adopted—until we were finally a family of four children, and all things balanced. For one adoptee, there was another. For one of one of the genders, there was another of the same gender, a sweet crisscrossing, so we thought. And why not?

In May of 1970, Thanne, a perfect nine months pregnant, said, "Wally, let's go for a walk."

She was tired of the weight and the wait, and just plain tired too.

So we drove to an urban forest outside of St. Louis, parked, and walk-trotted at vigorous speeds, a bouncing journey intended to persuade the kid inside of her that outside was a better option, really!

That night, almost exactly at midnight while I lay reading *Sometimes a*

Great Notion in bed, my wife sat suddenly upright, breaking from a deep sleep into pure wakefulness.

"My water broke!" she announced. She hopped out of bed and scuttled off to the bathroom.

Me too. I threw back the covers, hopped with somewhat less energy out of bed, thinking, thinking, thinking, thinking: *Okay, what's next?*

I drove a little green VW bug through dark streets, Thanne bundled beside me. I had to stop at KFUO radio station, where I worked as an announcer in those days, to explain my absence, my inability to do the morning news. We would have news of our own.

We arrived at the emergency entrance of the hospital; were quickly separated while she was prepped and I filled out registration forms; were reunited in a small labor room (truly, at 1:00 a.m.!) where I began to help the mighty woman focus. When the contractions rolled under her, I held her shoulders up. I counted aloud the seconds of the muscles' fierce tightening. Thanne puffed and blew according to the rhythm which bore her above that tempestuous sea of pain—as if she were in a small and swampable boat. But she was never swamped. She kept a good oar in her hand. Her coracle spun, her eyelids squeezed hard enough to drive tears onto their lashes; she concentrated, concentrated, allowing me to pass out of her knowing a while. But never, not once, did the woman murmur in pain.

Recalling the year, 1970, you will know how gracious (because unusual) it was for a doctor to permit the husband a place in the delivery room, not merely to watch but to participate in the birthing event.

At (exactly?) 6:00 a.m. our doctor strolled into the labor room.

"Nurse?"

"Ten centimeters, doctor," she said. She pronounced the word *sauntarmeters.* This was the size of Thanne's dilation. The canal was wide enough for the head of the infant to enter it.

The doctor winked at me and led me away with him. We went together into the surgeons' changing room. He selected hospital greens to fit my frame (he himself being a smallish man, an eminently confident man) and we went side by side, after the rituals of hand-scrubbing, into the delivery room.

Thanne, her hair bound up and hidden, lay on a high, narrow table, her heels in two stirrups, a cotton sheet covering her from the shoulders down to her wing-spread knees. A round mirror was fixed above the stool where our doctor took his seat, arranging himself and his instruments between Thanne's delicate feet, her beautiful feet. This little mirror (something the size of the rearview glass outside the driver's door of my VW) was meant for me, though I suppose a mother might be interested in observing the drama in her nether regions. If she weren't so busy elsewhere. By it I was granted a sight of the doctor's hands and the parturition itself. The delivery.

I swallowed. The lights were blinding.

Each time Thanne gasped and crouched into a contraction, I supported her shoulders with both my hands, creating (I imagined) a schoolyard slide down which this mother could send power to the baby, now moving down the birth canal itself.

Go, Thanne. You're doing so well.

Sweating, mewing in her nose, strands of hair stuck to her temples, she pushed with a primal force.

Suddenly, "The baby is crowning," cried the costumed personnel. "Isn't that beautiful?"

I peered up into the VW mirror and saw something like a brown mud-daub bulging against the interior of my wife's most precious flesh.

I wanted (holding her warm shoulders), I wanted (blinking against the blear light and suffering my own bowel contractions), I wanted, I say, to cry out, *What's beautiful about that? About any of this!* But a sudden, swift activity interrupted me.

In one smooth gesture, the doctor cut Thanne's deepest self, enlarging (I know, I know) the birth canal to accommodate the baby's big head. I, however, I watched blood brighter than wildfire spring from the cut and pour down her buttocks. And I gasped. Immediately the flesh of her buttocks—no: *all* her interior flesh—went whiter than ivory.

Then, at *exactly* all 7:00 a.m., the little boy squirt into the room.

So much, so much was happening so quickly.

Not merely for me, for *him!*

Nurses swooped the infant from the doctor's hands; syringed his nostrils, his mouth; held the slippery, chalk-streaked and pale blue body somewhat higher than I thought they ought to—and then they dropped him. No! They did not drop him actually. But they lowered the babe with uncommon speed to his mother's chest—and he *thought* they had dropped him, throwing wide his tiny arms, popping open his boiled-bean eyelids, creating a baby-shout of terror, all of which went straight into my heart, so that I too was convinced that they had dropped him.

In that moment precisely, I began to love my son.

He was me most intimately. I read his first expressions, his primitive gestures as if I were reading the moods and messages of my own soul. I feared for his safety, would immediately have exchanged my life for his, would not, at the same time, know how to live *without* his life in mine. I loved him with a wholly new sort of loving, an urgency I'd never known before in all my experience. I was twenty-six years old.

And in that very same moment, I became myself a new entity. I became a father. Certain instincts arose and seized me, instincts completely foreign, untaught, unprepared-for, though each one of them existed (I could tell) for the sake of that blue thing now breathing pink hues from an oxygen tube hissing near his translucent nose. Instincts for the survival of my child. Verily, I distended my own nostrils in a manner I'd never known before. I became conscious of a smooth electric field, bare millimeters above the surface of all my skin. A laminar of gentle wind enveloped me. With my son I had been bequeathed purposes, new rhythms, new definings of my person—all of which I am convinced Thanne had experienced first, during the months of her pregnancy, and had again experienced this same day, during the contractions and her rhythmic breathings above them, for the sake of, and in the name of, (as we came to know the pretty person) Joseph Andrew Wangerin.

Even so.

And all that followed seemed written in a script somewhere, the performance of which we fulfilled with a giddy ease.

Thanne nursed the baby.

I went forth *(Hail, the conquering hero comes!)* to sound out by trumpets and to beat upon drums the glad message, a boy unto us has been born!

———

And then, almost exactly one year later, the question became: *Can I love the child not born of my loins as much as I do the child that was?* A parent's question. Perhaps what a mother might ask, though I think that Thanne knew the answer ever before there was a question in her mind. But for me, indeed, the serious uncertainty of a father.

And then again, *Will my present fatherhood be large enough to embrace another? Or must a whole new sort of fatherhood be shaped to fit the adopted child?*

3
Choices I

Thou art our Father,
though Abraham does not know us
and Israel does not acknowledge us;
thou, O Lord, art our Father,
our Redeemer from of old is thy name.

I thought that I had chosen fatherhood. Parents assume they *choose* parenthood by *choosing* to bring a child into their families.

Well. They do, and they don't.

We may ourselves choose the concept—to open a door to another being. But not until we are in the midst of the very existence do we truly know what parenthood is. And what *sort* of parenthood our persons shall establish with the little person will be unique, the result of several unique personalities intermingled with each other. These things we do not choose. I was altogether too ignorant actually to choose fatherhood. Rather, fatherhood chose me.

In the event of Joseph's birth, fatherhood chose me!

And only in becoming a father did I even begin to understand what it meant, what it was, what would be required of me, and who I was/am within that identity, father. And what the transgressions of human iniquity would cost us, both parent and child. Frightful!

Nevertheless, the God of the Hebrews chose. Chose the whole scenario. Chose the entire sweep of the parenthood/childhood relationship, both the good and the terrible. For God acted with full knowledge!

And the choosing continues also into our era. Read the intentions of God the Father, in the Gospel of John: through "God's only Son" to draw us into a second birth, granting us to be born *anōthen* (meaning both "from above" and "again")—by which we are made his children.

How can this *not* move us to a deeper, more ineffable wonder?

Fatherhood caused love in me. Observing my child caused love in me; observing, moreover, my child in his fresh innocence caused love in me.

God, on the other hand, loved first; loved completely *before* choosing fatherhood. Love chose us. Love caused fatherhood, *sui generis*, of itself alone. Love found its object and thereby made it (made us) belovely.

Against that standard consider the rest of this book.

And take hope in this: that *behind* the rest of my story is the Father who can catch the gravest fault and call us all to the image of his own fatherhood.

Or how could I reveal such intimacies as I will give you here?

4
1971

Like grapes in the wilderness,
I found Israel
Like the first fruit on the fig tree
in its first season

I.

Ruthanne Bohlmann was born tenth in a family of fourteen children. In my eyes, a marble figure and sparkling and salt-of-the-earth as well. She was the farmer's daughter, elementally pragmatic and wise, prepared to walk a hard road evenly, with motherwit if not with money for solving the difficulties of poverty. The Bohlmanns as a whole were a self-sufficient family, producing together—and on their own—the food they sold and ate: vegetables, milk, pork. They raised soy beans, field corn. Gertrude and Martin never owned the land, not even the house. But they survived well enough!

Imagine, then, the frugality which their daughter brought to our marriage. No rage for money here. Nor for glamour, nor for material things.

I was not raised on the farm. I was raised in the household of a Lutheran minister — who, in time, became a highly regarded educator. Therefore, we had known something of poverty too. My father's congregation in North Dakota supplemented his small salary with potatoes and cabbages, lefse and stollen, sugarbeet greens, the services of Dr. Kohlmeyer for the birthing of Mrs. Wangerin's babies. Though my family numbers half of Martin and Gertrude's, ours could be considered large as well. I'm the oldest of seven.

The both of us having experienced a clutter of siblings, then, we both hungered to raise a clutter too.

On the other hand. We were conscious of the uncontrolled consuming of the resources of our natural earth. And though the heedless destructions of the '60s scarcely equal the rip-roaring, wholesale ruination of this present millennium, even then we recognized these behaviors and their dangers: the dangers of an individualistic, self-serving *(I got my rights!)* society.

Among solutions back then was to restrict the growth of the population. We didn't want to scold others regarding the issue. For us, however, it was a "Moral" decision. We felt that in good conscience we might swap two for two. That is, as we were two, we could bear two new mortals into existence. Hence, Joseph.

But then, as we approached Joseph's first year, Thanne yearned a second child. She wanted Joseph to have a sibling close to him. I joined her. And given our convictions, it seemed right and proper that our second child be adopted. (I don't need to repeat here all the solid arguments about children growing up without parents, do I? We all know them. They haven't changed over the years.) But, since Thanne and I seemed to bear children easily, we decided not to seek the healthy sort of infant which those who could not bear children might most desire.

We chose to ask for a child categorized as "hard to place."

Thanne's younger sister had been born with Down Syndrome. Dorothy. This pure child slept in the same bed with Ruthanne and Carolyn and Mary, her back fitting perfectly in the cave of Ruthanne's stomach. Between my wife and her sister there grew year after year a wordless love.

I, too, loved Dorothy, from the years of our courtship, even past the day of her death.

"Hard to place." There it was that love awaited us.

A sunny-faced and confident pair, we drove north from Evansville to Indianapolis early in June 1971. Baby Joseph was left back home in order that we might both give our full attentions to a first interview with a counselor for the Child and Family Services of Indiana.

II.

"Yesterday," the counselor said. "Only just yesterday a child was born and immediately turned over to us for adoption."

She was smiling. She believed we understood the force of her announcement. Perhaps Thanne did. I did not. Even now I tremble somewhat at the swiftness with which she was judging us a fit family for a "hard to place" infant.

"Oh, I mean that only as an illustration. How many children are seeking the security and comfort of a home like yours."

I was teaching at the University of Evansville and had a steady, assurable income. Moreover, because the chairman of the English Department was willing to cosign our loan, Thanne and I were in a house of our own. And we were Lutheran, as was this agency. We were youngish and educated. We seemed to be realistic, not a stunned, young, romantic couple. All of these characteristics put us high on her standards of potential parents. Hence, I suppose, her too-easy reference to an actual and living infant: "One that would be just right for you."

She had asked earlier: "What do you wish for such a child?"

We had answered: "Only that he or she should be happy. And we will love the baby. We will make it happy."

Today I hear our younger selves so blandly, so innocently repeating so common an expectation — utterly ignorant of what "happiness" must in the future mean, believing sweetly that love alone will accomplish the "happiness" — and I remember how ignorant I was of life when I first asked Thanne to marry me. *We can work it out. We can work it ou-out* — whatever "it" is. Such silly people, not even to know what "it" is.

Nevertheless, our counselor initiated not only the paperwork for the adoption; she initiated in our hearts already (though distantly) an anticipation for this "hard to place" infant, born just yesterday.

"Hard to place?" I wondered. "What makes the baby's chances of being adopted so low?"

"Ah," said the counselor. "Well. You see, he's bi-racial. Now, then. When's a good time for me to come down to Evansville to do a household inspection?"

III.

My office at the U. of E. was in a Quonset hut — actually, a long, low wooden building constructed near the end of World War II as quick housing for administrative activities. The room, my room itself, was ten feet by twelve feet, containing a desk, a chair for students, a bookcase. I can't remember whether I had a filing cabinet; surely, there was something for the remembering of classes past — and I was already writing short stories and poetry and plays in those days.

My desk faced the single window in this low office; the chair beside it faced the door. In that chair sat our counselor, having only just arrived in the city, parking nearby, knocking on my wooden jamb, entering, smiling wondrously, bright red her complexion, perhaps from the heat of early July.

We discussed my position in the English Department, the appreciation of my superiors for my instruction, my own plans to complete a Ph.D. in English studies. She was highly satisfied.

Suddenly she scrounged in her purse, drew out a small leather folder, flipped it open and showed me the contents.

My heart leaped from calm seas into terrible swells and screaming winds.

What she was showing me was a photo of the infant born the day before we'd met her a month ago in Indianapolis. It was a tiny boy zipped into a red pajama suit, slight hair on his skull, starkly beautiful, dark brown eyes, intelligent and sharply watchful eyes, a milk-chocolate skin, arms thrust out as if to tear down trees.

"No," I said with a fierce sincerity. "I don't want to see this."

"Why not?"

"Because already I am feeling love, and I shouldn't, I shouldn't feel this if he is not going to be our child."

"Oh, don't worry. This visit is just a formality. We're more than joyful that you came to us — that we can put this beautiful baby in your care."

IV.

Matthew Aaron Wangerin was rigid as a wooden board when we carried him home from Indianapolis. I drove our green VW bug. Thanne held the boy. This was August 1971. I recall the dusty green of the trees, the woods on the west side of the highway. They seemed something like a refuge in which Native Americans and sad young mothers and Walt as well might enter, crouch, and dwell in coolness and in an unconscious peace.

Matthew's scent was acrid enough to be noticed. His arms and legs moved with unconscious strength, making fists of both his hands and his feet. Thanne kissed him. He did not turn away. She said, "I wish I could nurse him" — a comment that left me partially outside the moment and the swift attachment this mother and this child were experiencing.

When we brought the baby into the house where friends were babysitting Joseph, we were greeted with joy. Thanne showed Joseph his "new baby brother. Do you like him?" Joseph (wearing a honey-bee brown-yellow pullover) immediately and without hesitation puckered his lips into a small round O, and kissed Matthew somewhere near that baby's mouth.

5

1971 — 1973

Yet it was I who taught Ephraim to walk;
I took them up in my arms

I.

Matthew was a missile.

Nothing could contain that baby's brown, bulleting, exuberant, heedless energies. Not even the binding of his feet.

From the very beginning we had recognized that the bone structures from his knees on down — the shin bones, the ankles, the fanning metatarsals inside his feet — had in a common conspiracy turned so severely inward they would not be able to support his walking. Under an orthopedist's scrutinies, then, we purchased a flat plastic brace punctured with a widening scale of holes; into these holes a pair of tiny shoes were bolted, and periodically rebolted in order to accomplish a slow adjustment: toes in, toes farther and yet farther apart. All day long bright Matthew wore the booties that dragged his brace. Week by week we bent his soft bones straighter. But day after week after month, the little boy's feet were fixed, his legs forced to flex together, never separately. How could an infant locked in such stocks be expected to crawl by the natural shuffling of his knees? How could he crawl at all?

But Matthew did! And the brace itself? *That* became his weapon!

By mighty strokes of his arms — and by a kind of worming contracting of his torso — the boy pulled himself through the house fast as a locomotive, loud as a tractor, joyful as Vesuvius. Matthew didn't smile or chuckle. He grinned and spat and yelled.

Ah, but he also cried at night. Every night (I'm not exaggerating). Starting about midnight. Matthew wailed in wild misery despite our holding him, bouncing him, rocking him, kissing him, walking him. With the strength of my arms I could silence the child. As the Lakota immobilized their infants in bands and blankets upon a cradle-board, so did I embrace him in all his parts, his heels and butt in the palm of my left hand, knees bunched into my stomach; my right hand pressing the whole of his back, my fingers his neck and the base of his head, all of him against my own broad breast. Perhaps such fierce stability alone could console him. I held him hard. Pacing through our little house. My arms beginning to ache.

Dreams? Can one so young be victimized by nightmares? Or did his physical chemistry torment its own interior tissue? — a tiny body divided, victimizing itself?

He was adopted. I didn't have within me natural instincts to recognize his experiences by the tracking of my own. I *knew* the meanings of his brother's tones and twisting expressions; I read them according to the dictionary of my own past, my own nature. But Matthew was adopted. His tones, his gestures were as a foreign language to me.

When I released him from the pulsing, sweat-smelling compressions of my body, laying him back into his crib, he'd give a shuddering hiccough and throw himself back into his urgent, inexplicable anguish. I confess. I grew angry at his persistence, my failure, the genetic wall between us.

Picking him up again, I squashed him more than I should have. To this day I wonder whether he, whom I could not read, read me. Did he take into his mute spirit that anger communicated by my arms? Did that anger affect him years and years later?

When I returned to Thanne in our warm bed, she said with genuine sorrow, "I wish that I could nurse him."

Ah, and there's a telling point: *nobody* nursed Matthew. Ever.

His birth-mother was a sixteen-year-old child herself. She was the offspring of a white parent and a black one, but the white went away and the black parent only remained to raise her in a black community. Her complexion was light, "high yaller," as it was called in contempt; certain features tended toward the European. Perhaps she had "good hair," hair that was not kinky, smoother, thinner. Whatever the details, the poor girl suffered a continuing, unhappy prejudice among African Americans.

She herself conceived in concert with a black man. Their baby, then, would be three-quarters black. Making him, for all intents and experiences, altogether black.

Before his birth, that father too vanished from her life. For several reasons (1971 being one, an African American aversion to abortion at all being another) the teenager decided to bring the baby to birth and then to give it up for adoption: specifically, by her clear request, to a white family. I think she expected her baby to be as light as she. And, given her youthful inexperience, I think she thought the white community would go easier on this baby than the black community had on her.

Dear soul. So young! So long injured by the evils of society, yet so thoughtful for her little beloved, that every one of her decisions was made on the baby's behalf! This, of course, was to our benefit, Thanne's and mine and little Joseph's. Truly. But I wonder whether she has come to realize how universal is human cruelty, neither better nor worse from one group to the next.

And I wonder how she is doing, now in the fifty-second year of her life. Is she living still? God's peace, woman. Though no one nursed him with the milk of her mothering, in this you were not wrong: your son has done right well.

II.

The new kid's characteristics, both easy and difficult, raise the question in a new parent's mind—the same question friends are too delicate to ask aloud: can a father ... can *I* love the child who came to us by adoption even as much as I love the child who came through the sweetness of our loins?

Yes!

And it took absolutely no effort on my part. None. He was here, and he was ours, and he was my beloved, profoundly.

Joseph's terror at nose-pokes, the cold air, the sight-blinding light of this world, and then at "falling" from the nurse's hands did (once in a hospital) cause in me a terror the equal of his. In exactly the same manner, Matthew's suffering of unspecified prejudice (in Evansville food markets as in St. Louis diners) caused me to suffer within me an equal thump of the prejudice directed at him. On his behalf. On Matthew's behalf. Without his knowing it. Without even our friends' knowing it. But I knew it. And the swift withering of my bowels proved the immediate force of my love.

I loved this boy as much as I loved his brother. But because he was a different boy *(not*, please, because he entered our family by a different door), I loved him with a different love, something shaped unto his peculiar self. As the next years went by, this variousness of loving occurred for each one of our four children. Parental loving may be explained in terms general enough to embrace every sort of child. Yes. But the miracle of our realistic and individual lovings is that each actual relationship—each outpouring from a mother's or a father's watchful heart into the hearts of each of their children—conforms to the character of that child.

Even so is the quality of the love of the God who declares himself "Father" for each (and each, and each) of the individual persons walking the earth, both past and present. *That* love knows us all. Embraces us all, equally, everywhere, everywhen, at once. That love may also be known by us all, as smooth as the cobalt sky. Yet it breathes by singularities a blessed *spiritus* into the nostrils of us each, a sacred exhalation unique unto every particular name and soul.

Then, out of the dirt of the earth, the Lord God formed a human frame. He breathed [inspiravit] into the nose-holes the breath of life [spiraculum vitae], and the dirt became a living being.

Unique is every one of the Father's lovings for every one of his children. Nevertheless, *he* is the same from everlasting to everlasting, one God, one Creator, unchanging heart to heart, the Lover of us all.

III.

The house into which we brought our baby Matthew sat on a high ridge above the Ohio River: Newburgh, Indiana. Between the sliding glass doors of its back room and the edge of that clifflike ridge were perhaps ten yards of grass. Standing right at the edge, one looked down a steep drop but walkable on stone steps down. At the bottom of these steps was a plateau wide enough for my first gardens.

During the dry summer months the river subsided, running lower than the plateau, revealing rock and scree and old root and the gouging effects of its multilayered and spiraling currents. By late summer, early autumn (when I was harvesting little more than winter squash and pumpkins, a few last brussels sprouts) the river had recoiled into the form of a narrow serpent some twenty feet below the plateau. Early in the mornings — or else in the evenings after a day of teaching — I would descend directly to the water's edge and cast a line. Black crappie, catfish, something called a buffalo fish. We knew little of waterborne toxins in those days. I cleaned and we ate the fish. Beyond that, I took a deep, contemplative pleasure in sitting at the low bank, the water scarcely murmurous, my somnolent companion.

Joseph loved the river even from his own beginnings, kicking his pleasure when he was small, singing it when he had learned to stand on two feet. Joseph pressed his forehead against the cool of the glass doors, peered across our patch of a backyard, and watched as enormous barges navigated the river's lazy turnings. The tugboat's horn caused him to pop his knees in a pretty dance. At night a passing transport would turn on its bright long sword of a reaching spotlight, then switch the lightsome beam back and forth, shore to shore across the waters as nimbly as if flicking a wand. *Bam!*—the light would hit the backside of our house. Joseph gasped and laughed. It didn't hurt—though it should have. And then, when the rains in Pennsylvania, Ohio, Kentucky, Indiana raised the river, raising the barges upon it, Joseph's fascination grew more silent for growing more intense. Of course: the barge-light had risen dead level with the glass doors and with the eyes of two little boys. But while Joseph banked his awe in a cautious quietness, his brother exploded, driving his brown body, despite its plastic brace, straight toward the sliding doors as if to drive right through them.

During the rainy seasons, the Ohio River uncoiled, swallowing power and swelling like Leviathan, that beast of uncreation. Swiftly up, its whirling surface reached and exceeded the low plateau, enriching the soil of my next garden. More slowly, but inexorably, Leviathan kept rising, lipping my stone steps one by one, turning its malignant attentions to the next level of life, our backyard. It swept westward no louder than before, maintaining always a supernal mighty silence, as if its motion were oiled or ethereal. Yet its massy weight, its immeasurable length rolled forward in an outraged passion, faster, deeper, wider than three miles between our glass back doors and the fields of Kentucky on the other side. As if they were the amputations of Armageddon, things drowned and deadened, sailed westward with—and upon the back of—Leviathan, silent, bobbing, spinning memorials of the fierce upriver floodings: bushes torn by their roots from the ground; branches, limbs, the rolling and root-dressed trunks of whole trees; clapboards stripped from old walls, sections of roof, and unframed doors; cats clawing for purchase on those doors, rodents blind in dying, the white bellies of numberless fish; now and then a small domestic animal....

And while Joseph held his peace before that headless, endless, terrible torso, Matthew threw himself forward; clattered his brace against the glass doors; grabbed curtains and yanked himself up the better to feed on such swollen energy outside. Matthew opened his mouth and uttered quick, pistol-shot yips of wild delight.

But soon that plastic brace was coming off his feet for good. He whacked it on our furniture. He put dents in wallboard. Besides, his bones were hardening straight. Everything in him yearned to be upright. Yes: and when it came off, when on his own swift feet he could run, what then? My Lord, how the child delighted in danger! It was his siren song, hearing which he cast off caution and every inhibition, and pitched his football body headlong toward the waters.

As a hedge against disaster, then, Thanne and I built a chain-link fence around our small patch of a backyard. We had two gates installed, one by the side of the house, one at the head of the stone steps, that I might descend to the lower plateau in order to garden and to fish. Good. Matthew could go outside in health and play his own games and not destroy himself, our overenthusiastic kid.

Soon thereafter I would lead both boys into the protection of a well-fenced yard. I would turn to face the house while one of my sons faced me at my knees, grinning upward, knowing what was about to happen. Suddenly I'd stoop, as suddenly lift the kid — Matthew — beneath his armpits, his body thick and firm as a flour sack, swing him high and release him, tossing him straight toward heaven, and forth he would go, shrieking his joy. He would sail a brief, eternal moment — his eyes wide, his breath a great swoop of inhalation — then turn and tumble back to the earth, would fall into my arms with an absolute trust and a skyborne laughter. Danger averted! A little boy tough inside the trust that outfaces every harm, happy, contented in his father's arms.

Did Thanne worry, watching us flirt with the crackings of little skulls? I can't help but believe it. Yet, if she said anything to me then, I can't remember it. Exuberant times. Youthful assurances. A father's protections.

What, asked the counselor, *do you hope for your baby?*

And we answered, *That he be happy. That he be able to fulfill his dreams.*

And what will you do to accomplish this?

Ah, that's easy. We will love him.

As if love alone, affections deeply rooted and blossoming, were enough. Yes.

Yes, but less than six weeks after the brace came off and Matthew was walking—boom-booming his foot-falls, hitting floor with his small, pink heels, swinging his glad head left and right, charging out the back door and into the yard—that boy was *climbing* that chain-link fence meant for his protection!

I looked out a back window and saw his feet tucked into the fence spaces as if tucked in little stirrups. He himself leaned his chin on his two arms, which were laid along the top rail. He was peering westward, toward the mud-brown river, that sweet and sleeping horror.

"Thanne," I said, "come and look."

We were both stunned sober. Not yet knowing Matthew wholly, our planning had not taken Matthew wholly into account. Our devices were shortsighted and failing.

He and risk and vast floodings were closer friends than we could ever have perceived in an infant.

"Look at his eyes."

He was fascinated, drawn to an uncontrollable, terrifying element of Nature—which would be no Mother to him. These sleepy waters were the Destroyer. Yet he didn't know. He did not, in his childhood games, know the infinity he played beside.

As if my soul gazed down from a great height and from a position far inland, I suffered my son's proximity according to two lines written by William Wordsworth:

[I] see the Children sport upon the shore,
And hear the mighty waters rolling evermore.

"Ode: Intimations of Immortality," ll. 170 – 171

IV.

In the autumn of 1972, when Matthew was achieving his seventeenth month of life and Joseph the fifth month of his second year, we discovered that Thanne was pregnant the second time. 'Twould be the third child come unto us. Time to reassess.

Through the winter into early spring—even as Leviathan began its third ascent toward our backyard—Thanne and I stole time to discuss certain decisions. We named out loud the calamities we now knew to be lurking around the present property. We talked about the future generally. By the end of June 1973, our family would number five in an unaccommodating house, two tiny bedrooms, an awkward C-shaped arrangement (all persons and purposes having to pass through the kitchen), a kitchen too minuscule even for the cooking, a utility room in the passageway between house and garage, and a foundation that had been riddled with termites when we bought it, now exterminated, but breeding suspicion in our spirits regarding problems not yet revealed.

And the river.

We decided to seek other lodgings.

6
1988

Out of Egypt I called my son.
The more I called him,
the more he went from me

Matthew is sitting in front of me in a reclining chair the color of crushed strawberry. Thanne purchased the chair last Christmas, a gift of comfort for my study here at home. I have an office at church, too. But that accommodates the broader range of my ministerial labors. This room (which was once a dining room) is reserved for my more private and personal work. I've been publishing books of some consequence since 1978; here is where I write, research, revise, maintain my correspondence. The library shelved on three walls around the two of us, Matthew and me, consists of reference books and works of a literary bent. The library in my office at Grace Church tends toward the theological, exegesis, commentary, counseling, education, social justice, homiletics, and so forth.

The two windows on the fourth wall, directly behind me, look out upon a pitch-black midnight. Autumn. A weeknight, for Pete's sake!

It would not be improbable to hear a gunshot outside. We live in the inner city.

"At your age," I speak the words through my teeth, spitting every "T," repressing an animal urge to shout: "At your age," I say, "you ought to know better."

My son has entered his senior year at Bosse High School.

He just got home. Midnight. Two hours past his curfew.

And no, he is not "sitting." He's sprawling, legs thrust forward like open calipers, hands fisted in his jacket pockets, the flat of his back lying on the sitting place, where his butt should be. It's his neckbones, not his hips, that bend in the angle between the seat and the backrest. His lips are pinched into a tight round circle. Infuriating me the more, his eyes are shut.

I myself sit upright on the straight-backed wooden chair which I've pulled over and placed immediately in front of him, between his stretched ankles, trying to fill his vision with my face, my emotions, my exactitude.

Would he but open his eyes.

The room is softly lit, a single incandescent bulb within a yellowing shade. The rest of the house is quiet. Sleeping. Except, perhaps, for Matthew's mother, lying awake in our bed. Well, and it is possible that Joseph too lies wakeful and worrying on his brother's account. The girls are asleep. The rest of the city is asleep.

"Where were you?"

He shrugs. He produces a bulldogish grunt. He articulates nothing. Neither does he open his eyes.

"Answer me, Matthew! Where have you been for the last two hours?"

My son, filled to the base of his brain with worldly experience, inhales a great breath of air through his mighty nose, then blows it out, a long, long, exasperated and weary sigh. Apparently, I am to receive this breathy expulsion as an answer.

But I would argue my state to be the wearier between us two, and my exasperation to be the lengthier. I know what *I've* been doing during the last two hours.

I can never sleep when Matthew hasn't returned by the curfew we've agreed upon. Everyone else indoors, everyone else in bed, at the stroke of ten, I go into my study and try to work while I begin to wait upon my son. I am already prepared to be angry. This happens all the time. *All the time!* But, to pass the time and to occupy my mind, I set myself a small, do-able task. Its work consumes twenty minutes, maybe a half an hour—though constantly inside of me, there exists a low-level roaring, like a distant surf, which, as soon as I finish the task, rises to flood my attentions: *Wher-r-r-re is the boy? Wher-r-r-re has he gone?*

From this point forward into the night, I have no ability to concentrate. I'm helpless before my emotions. I am angry. *Can't he see what he's doing to his mother and me?* I pace. I try to restrain the pacing by forcing my feet to tiptoe. After another ten, fifteen minutes I hit the floor heel and toe. Soon I am hurtling back and forth in my study; and from the study into the living room; finally, over and over again, from the study through the living room to the front of the house where the windows face Chandler Avenue and the library across the street. I peer out, looking for a familiar, dark, athletic figure. Surely he is (in my mind's eye he always is) mere strides from the house, trotting homeward. But over and over again I find nothing under the street lamp. I see nothing. No one is coming.

At this point I'm fighting hard against the next stage of my emotions. Anger is clean, sharp-edged. Anger is the easier mood to handle. I fight to preserve it, but every night in which the boy is more than two hours late coming home, I fail.

Now I begin to suffer a wild panic on my son's behalf.

It isn't only *wrong* to amble the inner-city streets after hours, in the darkness; it's downright dangerous. People get shot. Stripped. Tossed aside. Too often have I been called to the emergency wards of all three hospitals when members of my congregation, African American, have been brought in from knife fights, gang fights, overdosings, gunshot wounds; when members have been accosted, whipped, rolled, looted and left to die; or, sadly, next day, when the church-going mother telephones me to say that her son is in jail, *himself* the thief, the shooter.

I know the streets which my son thinks he knows. I know the cold authority, the easy brutality with which white cops patrol these black streets. If Matthew is in trouble, those appointed to "serve and protect" will neither serve nor protect a strong black male, seventeen years old.

With panic has always come what is for me a treacherous dilemma.

I will go out to find him, I've said in the past, and then I have. I've found him alone on the basketball courts installed up at the projects, shooting through hoops with chains for netting. Or else I've found him standing there and watching young men, more powerful and older than he, playing a violent, body-slamming sort of game. His face, Matthew's face, filled with longing. When he'd happen to notice our car curbside (it was a little white Reliant) he'd rush over to it and to me, afraid that I might embarrass him in front of giants he hoped one day to join.

I knew of several places where he might hang out. But in fact, I did not know all his haunts. For one night in the spring of this year, shortly before school let out, I drove everywhere, walked many places, and could not find him. While I was gone he came home and found himself locked out. I arrived just as he was leaving the front porch of our house, prepared to trot eastward into Bayard Part. And gone.

Now, therefore, I must wring my hands and do nothing, go nowhere to save him, suffer my anguish passively. Because I don't know whether, finding the home locked against him again, he might take off with a greater petulance into nighttimes darker and dangers deeper than those already tested. He knocks to be let in. He doesn't ring the doorbell, which might awaken others. His knock is soft. Perhaps its lightness, Matthew's hesitancy, signals some uncertainty on his part. Or guilt.

I open the door. Panic in me subsides. His face, his strutting manner of walking, the fact that he is alive and fine — these ignite in me a hellish rage. In my lowest voice I command him: "Go into my study. Take a seat. Now."

He goes. He slouches down in my new reclining chair. He knows the drill as well as I do, without truly *knowing* anything.

"Matthew, snap *to!*" I spit-hiss between my teeth. Open your eyes. Tell me what you've been doing outside till now!"

His eyebrows rise, their temple-ends highest, like the wings of a swallow stretching. They drag his eyelids upward, open. The whites of his eyes are bloodshot.

"Have you been drinking?"

That snaps the lock. He looks at me. He answers me. He says, "I'm tired. I don't drink."

Well. Most likely he's telling the truth. He's been on Bosse's varsity basketball team since his sophomore year, plays point guard for the "Bulldogs." In all this time, he has been careful concerning his body, its quickness and its instincts. Matthew truly believes that basketball will be his ticket out: *Hey dad, I'm not gonna cost you a cent for college. I'm gonna get a basketball scholarship. Watch!*

"Not drinking," I nod. "Well, then, what *have* you been doing?"

"Um," he closes his eyes again. But he doesn't cut off the conversation. "At Andrea's," he mumbles. Andrea is Matthew's girlfriend. More accurately, he is her boyfriend, since she's made all the moves so far. A schoolmate of his, she is a genuinely intelligent, delightful girl. "Fell asleep watching TV," he continues. "Didn't wake up until, I don' know—till just now; sometime. Came home."

The explanation is a fistful of twigs. I could snap each detail offered to me. I *want* to crush the whole in a rhetorical tide of logic and accusations and woundedness and fury. Ah, but what good would it do? He knows, you see, the drill.

And he has used the "Andrea" excuse often already, with good success. She lives only a few blocks north of us. Her family is faithful, happy, and serious regarding righteousness. To me my son seems sultry with the young woman, off-handed, never altogether attendant upon her. Nevertheless, Andrea supports his story of their nights together. She says she tries to wake him, then just goes to bed herself. No matter if he wakes on their sofa in the morning. Where's the harm?

Instead of walloping him with ineffectual rhetoric, then, I take my stance on a superior platform from which I try probing his mind.

Here is my platform: "Matthew, right now I am the smartest man you know. I know about this city and this inner city and the streets and the hospitals and the jails. I know about the future, both yours and mine. I read all the time. I write. People look to me for wisdom."

And here is the probing: "What do you want, Matthew? Go down deep. Tell me truly. What is your heart's desire? Please, let's work for it together."

He sucks air again, then sighs, causing a whirlwind in the broad caverns of his nose.

He poofs out his lips in a large kiss of contemplations. *Oh my son! You have so noble a head and such natural beauty!* He opens his eyes and looks directly at me. This is meant to convey the earnestness of his forthcoming answer. Red eyes must mean tremendous tiredness. He wants to go to sleep.

Matthew says, "Lemme alone. I just want to be left alone."

"What does that mean?"

"I wanna be free. I want to do what I want to do."

He closes his eyes again. That's it. That's what he wants.

Really: I *am* smart about our futures. His heart's desire makes me want to cry.

Unto my son I say, "I will, Matthew. The moment you graduate with good grades from high school, I will let you completely alone. I promise."

I pause. I am being as truthful as I can possibly be. During this, Matthew's final year in high school, his mother has come to the end of her rope.

You take him, she has said to me. *I can't do this anymore. He is yours.* You *see to his education.*

And I have agreed. The boy is now essentially mine. Thanne loves him no less. Indeed, it is the tender, enduring love in her which has been rubbed so bloody-raw. But among the three of us, Thanne is the one most weary—and she will sin less, engaging our son the less.

"Matthew," I say, "in the years to come you will need me. But I will keep the promise I am making right now, tonight. At graduation I will set you free to live the life of your own choosing. Listen to me. Listen to me! I'm saying 'at graduation.' With good grades! And you can hate me throughout the school year, if you wish. I can't control your feelings. What I *will* control between now and graduation, however, is your schoolwork. Get ready. I intend to be your master! I will push you, I will discipline you, so that you earn good grades. That's my goal. Your good grades. Because I will not have you shutting that door at least—the door to higher education."

I sit looking at Matthew awhile.

He is immobile. He may even be falling asleep.

Unto my God and in my heart—perhaps even in my eyes—I say: *Father, I make a vow to you. Let my son succeed at school and then at life. Watch over Matthew with your greater power. Take care of him when I can't and as I can't. And this I offer in return: I will live without his love. I will give up his loving me. I will endure his hatred, his separation from me, even unto forever. Just, please, take care of him.*

7
January 1972

Guard him —
as the apple of your eye.
Hide him —
in the shadow of your wings

It's 1972. Matthew is in the eighth month of his life.

Thanne carries him in arms, half-running. And I, holding Joseph's nearly-two-year-old hand in mine, follow her across a cold St. Louis street. We're making for a breakfast diner and rushing on account of the traffic and the weather.

We're attending a conference at St. Philip's Lutheran Church, which sits in the middle of a governmental housing project. A region almost altogether black.

Meetings will begin in the hour.

We've little time to eat.

The sky is a hapless grey. Snowing. Arriving in front of the diner, Thanne nudges me and points to a small child with a richly oiled complexion.

She stands in a parking lot, facing heavenward, sticking out her tongue to catch the white flakes. A tender scene. We smile.

Patrons of the diner are crowding through the doorway. We wait our turn, but finally have to press into the line if we are to find a table at all.

We are a tiny family of four, swamped by fell currents of people.

Behind us a young black woman lifts up her voice.

"What?" she says, as though baffled. "What? What are they doing?"

Then she releases a long, contemptuous, hissing breath.

"Yeah! Lord, I know what they're doing." And with real rancor she fairly shouts: "It pisses me off! They've adopted that little boy. White crackers stealing our babies. And stealing culture *from the kids!*"

We do not turn around.

8
1973 — 1974

Look down from heaven and see,
from thy holy and glorious habitation.
Where are thy zeal and thy might?
The yearning of thy heart and thy compassion?
For thou art our Father—

I.

Early in June 1973, daughter Mary Elisabeth left the calyx of her mother's womb to enter the world and our family, roly and poly and pink—and filled (it has since proven true) with a perpetual cheer. She and Joseph shared white-blonde hair, soft as spiders' filaments on the air. Joseph tended toward introspection and long, involved and whispered stories. Mary, on the other hand, lived outside herself, trusting in the kindness of strangers and the essential simplicity of all things sensible. His whiteness was pale. Hers was as pinked as a peach.

And they loved equally their brown brother, with admiration and forbearance, both.

Joseph had been given a wooden toy shaped like a small carpenter's workbench. Drilled through its top were six holes to hold six round pegs, and then a seventh hole into which a peg could be pounded with a wooden hammer, driving it through the bench to pop out the low hole at its side. Even now I see Joseph kneeling by that toy, wearing that shirt striped brown-and-yellow like the bee. Carefully he inserts a peg in the seventh hole, where it sticks inside a rubber collar. He grips the hammer and swings and misses. Two hands, and misses. When he does hit the peg, it takes several little whacks to get the peg to appear like a pig's snout in the hole below.

Suddenly Matthew is at his side, shouting delight at this tiny enterprise. He takes Joseph's hammer in his left hand; with his right he sets a peg in the seventh hole; and then, both hands working at once, he hits the peg, the peg shoots out, even as his right hand has already picked a new peg and set it, so that the left hand in one swat shoots out the second peg—and so forth until, in several blinks of an eye, he has cleared the top of pegs altogether.

With admiration (you see) for the brother who does all things physical so easily and so well. With forbearance for the brother who will also barge into the midst of things, snatch the hammer and do the thing he (Joseph) was capable only of *trying* to do, the older never blamed the younger.

Mary, watching her brother from a blanket on the floor, laughs a hearty, husky laugh. Just to watch him causes her gladness.

Nor was her baby estimate wrong. Matthew's behavior caught the eyes of several neighbors too. One delicate child, young as he, would often stand in her yard facing ours, fascinated by the boy's quickness, his laughter, his volcanic joy.

When encountering new people, even from infancy, Matthew has always fallen quiet, suddenly becoming a mute observer at the edges of things. He needs to assess the rules, I believe, to gauge the natures of the people and of their relationships, before committing himself. It may have been Joseph, then, who first spoke with this child and went into her yard to play. But soon enough, when some uncertainty had been satisfied within himself, Matthew too went over to play. Sedate at first. Amazingly polite he was (but what did we know, not having seen him mix it up with other children his age before?). He came to like this porcelain-pretty child.

Zorn was her family's name. Ashley was hers. Between our two sons, it was upon Matthew that her friendship most was fixed. He felt a proud Daytime Strutter, having earned his first personal friend outside the family Wangerin. He gave her gifts. Strawberries.

II.

From Newburgh Thanne and I had moved into another house not bigger than the first, but better. The new home had two tiny bedrooms and a third somewhat more accommodating; between these, an L-shaped living room and ceilings less than a foot above my head. The kitchen was larger than the last, its back door opening onto a kitchen-wide back porch enclosed with windows on all three sides. The house sat on two acres of country land, woods to the north and the east, neighbors to the west and the south, the Zorns, the Tuckers and, at the southern end of the lane, the Heerdinks, for whom the lane was named.

Two acres, high for the house and garage and yard, low to hold the annual flooding (the shallow and peaceful flooding) of Pigeon Creek which wound through the woods. Two acres. Space, then. Happy, uninterrupted spaciousness in which the children could play—and Matthew could run, race, rush, dash and laugh the day long.

Thanne and I planted a garden twice the size of my first efforts on the plateau above the Ohio River. This earth was a harder clay, more spent than the enriched soil on the Ohio; yet it produced right well—and good that it did, since our growing family needed the vegetables, while my university paycheck was low and did not grow according to our needs.

There were three plum trees along our driveway.

There was an empty chicken coop on the place near the rear of the high ground. I saw in that another source of inexpensive food, fresh meat, fresh eggs. Our first summer there, I swept it out and patched it and prepared it for the hundred chickens to arrive in the following spring. My brother-in-law, who cut meat for a city grocer, taught me how to slaughter a chicken, then how to butcher it clean.

The chicks came in flat boxes. Little yellow hatchlings. Little peepers so ignorant of life that I had to teach each one how to drink. I caught a tiny head lightly between my thumb and forefinger and directed the beak into still water; an instant in, an instant out, tipping the small beak upward until I felt the quick clicking of a chick-swallow. Do that again. Do it again for each of the hundred. Next, wet my finger; scrounge it in cracked corn; hold the corny fingertip against the point of each beak; let them tongue it, peck it, and taste; then show them where the feed trough sits. Return them to the incubator for the night.

I taught them how to live. Thereafter I helped them to thrive. They learned. And all thoughtlessly they attached to their mother, me.

My children called it the "chicken poop." They did not love it. It stank. And the roosters, when they grew (but before I butchered them one by one for supper) would rush at the backs of the children's knees and thrust their heads forward to bite the soft flesh in their beaks. Mary cried at that and experienced her first genuine hatred. Joseph (truly) philosophized their natures, male and female distinct from one another; but he would not approach them. Matthew, on the other hand, used them to test his personal bravado—coming close to a rooster, baiting a rooster blind, then dashing free of beaks a-biting.

And there was a strawberry patch. When we moved into the house that first June, 1973, we found a fresh, magnificent carpet of green, four rows wide, nearly ten yards long. Among the leaves there lingered still some smallish red fruits, which we ate fresh. At the end of the autumn I scattered straw across the whole patch of runners and standing plants, and retired indoors to awaited spring pickings.

It was that second year then, 1974, when we began to take pleasure in the produce. And Matthew began to anoint his friends with gifts.

The strawberry patch. I raked loose straw away but left the straw beneath the new-grown leaves in order to keep their roots moist. With a building excitement I watched the white, five-petaled stars of flowers reach toward sunlight. I knew at once when they started to transform themselves into small hard green "berries."

Whether Matthew had kept watch with me, or during the times when I wasn't home, I don't know.

But one day he stood on the small ridge behind the garage and gazed down upon that beautiful green carpet, softening his face into a kind of awe. He was just beginning to notice the shy red fruits among their mothering leaves. I was watching him. This he did not know. Neither did I know the plan forming in the cauldron of his mind. Therefore I was not quick enough to stop him.

Matthew's lips peeled back into a white, tiny-toothed smile. His eyes started flashing. He pressed the edge of his tongue between his teeth, uttered a single spit-laugh, then charged top-speed down the incline toward the berry patch. "Matthew! No! Stop!" All his senses zinging. Every nerve delighting in the day. My sinless child as new to nature as Adam at his second breath! The mighty ounce launched himself bodily over the long runway of strawberries, landed on his tummy and, even before he had stopped skidding, was filling his mouth with fistfuls of the sweet fruit: laughing and eating and dripping red juice from his chin, a bloody pulp squashed adown the front of his shirt from his throat to his belly.

Shall I be angry at the waste? Shall I be exasperated by the ruination of year-long preparations and the loss of important produce? I am torn in two.

But ah, my hedonist! My baby Bacchus! How much I had to learn from him in those days. Not only of joy, but also of straight, uninhibited kindness.

It was close to these moments of his own rejoicing when he got a bowl from the kitchen, went out back, picked and then carried the fattest, reddest, sweetest fruits across the yards to his friend, Ashley Zorn. In my mind's eye I still can see them sitting together on her back steps while she eats the offering, one berry at a time, and both their mouths are sparkling red in the sunlight, smiling.

III.

Between those first two years on Heerdink — after preparing the coop, but before the chicks appeared; after strawing the bed of strawberry plants, but before Matthew's slick ride down the broad course of it — I went to stay and to study during the autumn at Miami University in Oxford, Ohio. Having taught at the University of Evansville since 1970, I focused solely on the completion of a Ph.D. in English.

By December I'd nearly finished the course work, passed the language exams, chosen the topic for the dissertation.

But then, short of *writing* the dissertation, I stopped that study altogether. Another profession had been pursuing me like the Hound of Heaven.

In my absence Thanne had borne the responsibility for three children and every domestic labor required to keep a household healthy and well. She alone. How the woman had survived those months is beyond me. She organized. She established times and tasks for the children. One weekend she drove our VW bug all the way to Oxford, the two boys on seats, baby Mary sleeping under the rear window. The family enjoyed a weekend together in a cabin in Kentucky. The days were bright and pure. She drove the distance home again. She carried the children to church. She shopped. She nursed her daughter. She survived.

Finally, at the end of my school term, it was in a light snowfall that she returned to gather me up and to bring me home again. She arrived in the afternoon. She spent the night with me, the two of us alone. We walked small streets in a cloud-dark evening, hours after the streetlamps were lit. Their shaded lights caused gentle cones of snow to brighten in the air. I was not yet smart enough to recognize or else to measure the depth of my guilt for having burdened my wife the way I did. I was just happy to be with her, and to take her hand, and to walk that evening's walk.

As we drove home again I spoke quietly, solemnly: "Thanne," I said looking straight ahead: "I believe I should take the call."

"The call?" she responded, as soberly as I.

"An odd thing. While I was studying literature, I became convinced that it is a call from God."

We rode in silence.

Thanne said, "Which Wally believes this thing? The Wally who listens? Or the Wally who talks?"

She wasn't wrong to make this distinction. When we married, we moved to St. Louis so that I might earn that Masters of Divinity then—but after a year and a half I'd already broken away (for reasons I couldn't make clear even to myself) and moved us to Evansville to teach. An unfinished student.

And the call about which we were talking was as an assistant to the pastor (David Wacker) with a decline in pay and the requirement that I *get* the degree and get myself *ordained*—even while working full time as head of Church Education, head of Youth Activities, counseling, preaching, visitations for Redeemer Lutheran Church.

I glanced at Thanne. "The listening one," I said softly. "This notion has been pressed upon me. I haven't been able to run from it."

"Listening," she continued, still gazing forward, "to God?"

"Yes. Yes, I think so."

"Not to the praises of nice people?"

Wacker had been using my brain as his library and his commentary for his every sermon through the last year. My insights showed up regularly in the pulpit on Sundays.

"You should finish seminary," he used to say. "You should become a pastor."

And then: "They love you, Walt. They love Thanny [sic!] and the kids."

"No," I said to Thanne. "No, it's rather that I love them. I love Dave. But truly: it's God who has led me to my 'Yes.' Listen. Let me explain—"

We'd passed Loogootee on highway 50 westward, then turned south-by-southwest onto state highway 57 at Washington. About a half hour yet for talk.

"I was reading the Vulgate Bible in the Latin," I said. "Late one night I came to this verse in Romans, chapter eight: *Quicumque enim spiritu Dei aguntur, ii sunt filii Dei.*

"I translated the sentence fairly well, but interpreted it, perhaps, idiomatically: 'Whoever are led by the Spirit of God—they are the sons of God,' causing me to think that my holy childhood of God is proven by (may even be effected by) my permitting myself to be led by the Spirit. See, Thanne? What I want almost more than anything else is to be a child of the Father. And it seems the Spirit of God the Father spoke to me, saying: *Let my Spirit lead you, Walter, and you shall be my child.*

"And I, unable to think of a more spiritual highway by which the Holy Spirit might guide me than into the ministry ... I said, *Yes.*"

———

During my first year as Wacker's assistant, a small, black, inner-city congregation—Grace Lutheran Church—asked whether large Redeemer would oversee their ministerial needs while they studied a difficult question: whether to close their doors forever.

They were worshiping with twenty to twenty-five people.

Redeemer agreed. I was given the task. In effect, I became *the* pastor for a while.

IV.

On the other hand, it was during that fruitful summer of 1974 that our own pearl, as translucent and lovely as the rose of India, came into our family, making us six.

Several months after Matthew sat eating strawberries on the back steps of the house of his friend Ashley Zorn, and Mary at fourteen months tumbled around our house, walking and falling in equal beats, and Joseph began, already in his fourth year, to pencil-draw with a surprising eye for perspective and balance, Thanne felt the stirrings of new motherhood inside herself. No, she wasn't pregnant, though those stirrings were similar to these. Rather, she viewed — she *felt* — our family to be unfinished.

She said to me something like: "Everyone's lonely till they have a match. Only Joseph is complete."

She meant that Joseph already had a brother *and* a sibling born into the family as he was born.

Well, we were discovering both the subtle and the gross differences between the adopted child and the one to parents born. With one's offspring there is an immediate inter-knowing one of the other. Having cried, when I was young, the way my child now cries, I can instinctively interpret the cry. I speak the same inner language. From the very beginning my blood-child's gestures and spontaneous expressions are compatible with mine. But I must by external, intellectual efforts learn the foreign language of my son, must do so long before he is capable of teaching me, must learn it when he knows it not himself.

And when we sat down to dinner, I could look at Joseph or Mary and see myself in them, see Thanne there too — so gentle the blending. But when I looked across the table at Matthew, neither Thanne nor I were in that face. I would blur my vision in order to imagine (*try* to imagine) the lineaments and the features of his two birth parents within him, to seek their ghostly apparitions lurking behind the child. But, of course, I could not. They remained elusive. My son had lost his history.

Matthew, Thanne's stirrings were saying, should not be singular.

He should be able to share his experience with another adoptee. Thanne was thinking of adopting.

And Mary was an only daughter. No childhood sister yet for her, whose importance Thanne had learned by growing up with the love of Dorothy, a dear presence in her every nighttime bed. Perfect companionship. Thanne was thinking, then, of adopting an infant girl (if we had a choice in the matter). And as Joseph and Matthew were exactly a year apart, wouldn't it be nice, her abdomen murmured, if Mary and her sister were likewise about a year apart?

I agreed.

In August, two months after Mary's first birthday, mother Ruthanne telephoned the Child and Family Services of Indiana.

She spoke to our familiar counselor.

She said, "We're thinking of adopting another child. Hard to place? Yes. Except — she ought to be an infant so that the birth order isn't broken. A she? Well, yes. If it's possible."

Before the end of that conversation, the counselor said to her: *And we have just the child for you. When can you come?*

Thanne hung up and stared at me.

She put her hand to her throat and whispered: "Oh, no. I just got rid of Mary's infant things. Crib and clothes, you know. Diapers. Toys. What am I going to do? I have to get it all back again."

Which was as much as saying to me, if not yet to the counselor, "Yes. We will adopt this baby girl."

You must honor the divinity of the timing. The agency had just, suddenly, without warning, received the child, already eight months old. Since she was already recognizing her birth name, they believed it would damage her to be shuffled through a series of foster homes. And since they had already vetted us, Thanne and me; and since the official, legal steps of our adopting Matthew had gone forward without a hitch; and since they were proud of the work we had done with him, they could think of no course better than that we would say "Yes" and take the child back to our house … in two weeks.

Thanne said she never had so fast a pregnancy.

And I had begun to work among African Americans in my ministry. Yes, indeed, there was something divine about these convergences.

Hard to place? Well, this baby was the issue of a white mother and a black father. "Bi-racial," as the world continued to call it—long before African American activists began to question the practice of placing black babies in white homes. Long before they condemned it as a racial intrusion, the snatching of their children into the domineering, arrogant, presumptive white world.

After a brief first interview, within some tender, hidden, mothering chamber of her heart, Thanne comprehended this child's condition. It was she, then, Thanne who knew best the name which must accompany it:

"Talitha," Thanne declared.

This is the word Jesus used when raising Jairus's young daughter from a sickness unto death to life again. *Talitha cum*, Jesus said, taking the hand of the twelve-year-old who lay pale upon her pallet. *Little girl, I say to you, arise.* Immediately the girl got up and walked—and he, like any blessed grandmama, told her parents to give her something to eat.

As did her brother, Talitha Michal entered a family which spoke and moved according to a foreign tongue. But for her the hurdle was higher than it had been for him, because a great deal of shaping and learning—yes, and of suffering—occurs in those first eight months of an infant's life. Talitha was the more sharply conscious of our divergence from the community wherein she had awoken first, from which her birth-mother had just sent her out.

Moreover, for reasons we could not know, she was already a child of anxieties and, paradoxically, a gaunt figure of almost hollow passivities. Men with moustaches seemed especially to frighten her. I was such a man. The moment she first looked at me, there in a small room of the agency in Indianapolis, Talitha burst into tears of a wild-eyed panic. Quickly we learned that Thanne could hold and hug and comfort her. Thanne became the one who eased the yoke upon this baby's terrified mind, Thanne who bent down to her and fed her.

For my own part, from August into November, whenever I drew near to her, the child's eyes would widen, and she would tear the air with wailing. Poor baby, poor little pearl, such danger all around her! And lo: more dangerous than anyone else was her father.

Therefore, as did the Holy One of Israel for his wayward children, I had to wait to be gracious to her. I sought ways to exult myself—not, surely, to frighten her, but to show her a mercy in which she could put her trust. I crept past her at measured, proper distances. I did not try to pick her up, never to carry or to cuddle her. I did not change her diapers. It was only when she slept, lightly, moistly snoring, that I permitted myself to touch her, to stroke her soft dark hair, to kiss her.

But I watched. I watched her all the time. Better yet, it was love that watched her, which is a finer eye than these two lamps blinking in front of my face; for love can find the slightest gaps and can interpret the most delicate of responses.

Passive. Into the autumn Talitha Michal would lie on her back, blank, disengaged from the life and the lives around her. She let the boys fawn over her, but she scarcely acknowledged them, not even Matthew's boisterous energy flying over her, bare inches from her stomach. A cool, beautiful, light-skinned enigma, she lay in the midst of indoor activities and knew not how to join them.

When little teeth appeared it became evident that our youngest had a terrific overbite. Something we would have to deal with in the time to come. But for now, a luxury: it caused the child's pink lips to make the shape of that mythic, sweet extravagance, a cupid's bow. Her eyebrows were black etchings perfectly balanced in skin the color of pulled taffy. Her gentle head itself bore the form of Egyptian refinement, set upon a narrow stalk; a broad forehead protected dark eyes and their endless lashes; a round skull which tapered down slender cheeks to an elegant chin at the point.

Just gazing upon my petaled baby lying in sunlight on the living room floor made me want to weep.

V.

Bright with exultation, Thanne met me at the door and said, "Talitha played. Wally! All by herself she started to play."

We stepped into the living room. Having been born on the ninth of January, Talitha was entering her eleventh month.

"How?" I said. "Why?"

Thanne was grinning. "I was at the kitchen sink," she said, "when I heard the jingle of the toy, the plastic ball the kids roll around. There. There it is. See it?"

Red and blue and twelve sides to it, I gave the toy a nudge with the toe of my shoe. Its myriad bells jingled. Talitha turned to it, her eyes, her head and her hand.

"For a moment," Thanne said, "I didn't think about the sound. Then it dawned on me, the other kids were outside. Talitha was here alone. I went to the doorway and looked into the living room. I saw her. She was on her stomach, pushing the ball first one way and then another. Wally, she's never initiated play before. Not on her own. I was so happy, my eyes began to blur with tears."

VI.

In the middle of the following month, the last of the year 1974, an oddly generous rainfall swelled the brooks that fed the Pigeon, causing that creek to spill beyond its banks. Water flowed over the ground within the woods north and east of our place, rose maybe two feet up the trunks of the naked trees, and nuzzled the borders of our own property. This was nothing like the gross Leviathan of the Ohio, down whose mighty mud-vein the silent floods of four states poured. Pigeon at flood sat fairly still. It gurgled round roots and dangling twigs. I was not afraid.

Suddenly, all in a single night, the weather changed. Temperatures plunged into the teens and stayed there, fixing and freezing by swift degrees all the water around us. Great skims of smooth ice turned, over the course of several days, solidly blue and slippery beneath patches of an encroaching snow. For neither had the precipitation ceased. It fell as a powdery snow and kept on falling. At night the wind got up and blew. Whiteout. A blizzard. Something altogether new for the children. In the morning they put on their coats and boots and stocking hats and went outside to slide on their heels, to laugh when they fell bump on their bottoms—and I did not deny them the joy.

I followed them out.

I slid too. And fell with bumps rather more dire than theirs. What was I then? How old in those days? Thirty? Thirty years old! The husband of one, the father of four. Joseph, the oldest, was four years old, Matthew three, Mary fully one and a half. Talitha short of a year.

Single file, four of us stomped out a huge in circle in the snow: a snow-pie, in which we added crisscross trails and smaller concentric circles.

"Now!" I cried, and we broke into various speeds, dashing about in heavy coats, my right hand foremost, playing tag: "No going outside of the lines!"

Matthew bulleted the pathways faster than anyone, laughing, spitting foam from the tongue caught between his front teeth. Bright eyes! Oh, his smooth and beautiful face! Why *wouldn't* he want to be "it," since he could race faster than us all?—"it," though, only for the flash of a moment before he tore through snow and tagged another—

—then waited dead still (impossible challenge!) for someone to tag him back again.

"Come on, Mary! Don't you see me here? Come on!"

Schools closed. In fact, Evansville's street department had lost the city's plows and wouldn't find them again until the snow-melt. I could, however, drive into town and work at either church, Redeemer or Grace.

But I took extra time with the children. We built snow forts and threw snowballs at each other, the boys on one side, Mary and me and sometimes Thanne on the other.

And with Joseph and Matthew I built a wondrously huge snowman, upon which both of them climbed, and from which they threw out their arms in a wide triumph, while I snapped a picture.

Blessed, bright and happy days!

Thanne telephoned me at my office at Redeemer. "Matthew," she said through a throat constricted, choking. *What's the matter, Thanne?* "Matthew and Joseph," she said, then paused to compose her voice. Finally: "Matthew and Joseph got caught on the ice—"

I thought I was beginning to recognize the choking.

"What ice?" I asked. There wasn't much ice left. A thaw had come.

"No, listen," she said. "I got a call from Mrs. Heerdink. She heard children yelling in the woods. She said she thought it was our boys yelling—"

Thanne hit a hiccoughing crack in her voice.

"Thanne? You all right?"

"It *was* our boys. They were calling for me. When I ran outside I heard Joseph calling, 'Mommy,' but Matthew was hollering, 'Mop! Mop!'"

Ah, such a tough kid was Matthew in those days. He thought "Mommy" was for sissies, but he hadn't quite gotten the hang of "Mom."

"MOP!"

Well, and there was good reason for him to act the toughie just then. The boy was genuinely scared. And in an instant I knew the meaning of the constriction in Thanne's throat: she was laughing.

Before the ice had begun to melt, the water beneath it had retreated into the banks of the creek again.

"They had gone walking on ice in the woods," Thanne squealed, seeing the picture before her eyes. "No support underneath the ice. It started to crack and to break like glass. Poor things, they made their way toward a large tree, to the nearest tree trunk, and there they could stand,

and there they *were* standing when I found them, on the circle of ice attached like a shelf to the tree trunk, holding onto branches, frightened
out of their wits."

"*MOP!*"

My brave boys.

Thanne was laughing at the sight. I felt uncomfortable.

No, no, no, after all these woods were not without their dangers.
What had I been thinking? Country living was no more safe than the
city. Hunters sometimes prowled our woods, banging at small creatures
or at the larger deer, or (why not?) at the sudden flash and dash of a
fawn-fast child.

And I read of cattle caught in open fields when the blizzard-wind
drove the snow so blindly that they turned their haunches toward its teeth
and lowered their great heads and did not move. By morning the hoar-
frost of their breathing had grown hard as iron, attached to the earth,
trapping their snouts in columns of ice. Silent, obedient monuments of
dull patience, bowed down, awaiting farmers and food or else, slowly,
immovably, death.

And in that same night of the battering wind outside, I caught the
conversation of our boys in their beds:

"Joe? Joe?" Matthew's piccolo voice, filled with awe at nature's enor-
mity. "Joe? Is it goin' t'blow the bafroom away?"

"No, Matt." Huskier, older, he had the answers. "No, 'cause how
would we pee then?"

"Oh."

And maybe this next event happened in another year, but in my mind
it is associated with *that* year and the end of *that* unhappy snow-melt —

Besides the Zorns, there were other neighbors west of us. Among
them were the Trauer's, soft-spoken, common-sensible, and most impres-
sive to our three children because they owned a horse named Captain.
Their horse's shelter was three sided and small, half the space to accommodate Captain's stall, half to house the tackle, brushes, feedbag, and an

enclosed bin in which the feed was stored. The front of the shelter stood open to the eastern weather, and therefore toward our place as well. Joseph would lift a finger to indicate quiet; Matthew would tip his head to one side, keeping still; they were listening to the ragged sneezes and the whinnies of their great-hearted friend.

All three kids would often troop over to Captain, carrots in their hands. Mr. Trauer had taught them how to lift the carrot on the flats of their palms so that the animal's teeth would not nip off their fingers with the food. So they told me.

"Dad, can we go over?"

They assured me that they knew how to be safe by Captain.

The Trauers lived in a cramped, older home. They intended to build a new house on their acreage, but for now it served as land on which the gelding could graze. During the week of our exuberant snow we saw the creature use its forehoofs to scrape through the snowcover to fresh hay and the dried grasses below. It snuffled the earth, yanked grass, seemed to shake it by large shakings of its whole head, then nodded while it chewed.

Here's horse flattery: Matthew and Joseph had learned to mimic Captain with a pretty accuracy, blowing air between their flapping lips, nodding their heads and pawing the ground with their boot-toes.

"Can we, Dad?"

"Okay. But be careful."

In the midst of the grazing acreage Mr. Trauer had begun to dig a large hole likely for the foundation of their new house, whenever he could get around to building it. Or maybe it was meant to be a small pool from which Captain could drink. Probably, it would serve both purposes, since the cavity was usually half-filled with water, and Captain did daily lower its muzzle to drink. That December, during the rain, the water's level had risen closer to ground-surface than at any other time I could remember. And with the water in the woods, this water also froze. Until, again, the snowmelt—and the slow subsidence of fluids from under the ice.

I can imagine a thirsty Captain putting forehoofs on the lid of ice on the Trauers' pit, then striking hard in order to find a drink. I can imagine next how that slick surface split, knifing outward from the hoof-hits, radiations of breakage which weakened the floor on which the horse was mincing forward. At a sudden, wholesale shattering, I can imagine the great animal's plunging through the hole, then turning and thrashing, striving to climb, but only smashing ice while miring itself more and more in the mud-pit below. And there was blood on the ice-edges. Blood on the moist ground. And Captain's bellowing denoted more than fear: a fearful pain. Which the children heard even inside the house — to their own terrible distress. For the horse had fractured its left front canon bone, which in turn had pierced the skin. Captain howled and could not stop beating high ground with a broken leg.

Never thinking of their coats, the boys dashed out the back door. Through the cold they raced to the Trauer's place, then froze, horrified by the sight, the horse struggling helplessly, its eyes white and rolling with panic, its great neck snapping upward and bowing as if to bite the ground to pull itself up again.

Somewhat slower than they, Mr. Trauer arrived at the hole just when they did.

"Busted," he whispered to himself. He turned and started back to his house. To the boys he yelled, "Go away."

They didn't. How could children watch so close a disaster? But how could they *not* watch it. They were mute before the calamities of the universe. Mute and mindless and immobile.

I had taken the time to get my coat. I was just crossing our backyard when I saw Mr. Trauer come out of his house, carrying a very large rifle.

"Go away!" he roared at the boys. "Get out! Get *out* of here!"

And I: "Joseph! Matthew!"

This was a good man. These were quiet neighbors, kindly to us. But Mr. Trauer neither could have nor should have spoken gently to my sons, who were unprepared for the next incident that December day, close upon the end of 1974. Moreover, I heard grief in the rough weeds of his voice: "Go home."

The boys broke their stances and, as if on fawn's unstable feet, stumbled back to our house. We entered the back porch, the three of us. Joseph sat down with quiet tears in his eyes. Matthew held himself as hard as marble, all his muscles taut, his mouth compressed, his eyes fixed on mine, paralyzing me with his paralysis. Neither could I then, my eyes on his, move. Matthew's heartbeats were quick as a small bird's.

And while we stood thus in the porch, we heard the gunshot.

Just one. Loud. Mr. Trauer's old .257 Weatherby.

Matthew flinched and broke posture. His eyes reddened.

"I knew it," he whispered. "I knew Mr. True was going to do that."

9

1975

Father of the fatherless, protector of widows
is God in his holy habitation.

I.

Early, early in the difficult year, *anno Domini* 1975, the sun broke through and shined — and lo, how its best beams shot forth upon me from a face light brown and beautiful, a head as ancient and North-African as that of the Egyptian, Isis.

Love watched my yearling child. Love watched closely, with a razorly eye, seeking her language, which would be foreign to her father. Long before the baby girl could speak in the tongue of the one who loved her, he had to learn hers, that love might speak at all.

She cried. This was surely one of her more forceful vocabularies. But it never asked a thing of me. It was uttered in fear against me. Or else it touched upon a past altogether hidden from me — as when her bare butt touched the porcelain of our pot, and she leaped away, screaming as one just burned.

What, O my child? What in your experience has turned coolness into a searing heat?

Frowning, smiling, questioning — the whole host of subtler facial expressions: these came later and yet later; and when they did, they were blunt, unrefined, illegible at first. Oh, the poor child! What happened during the first months of your life?

Thanne feared the baby had not been held in the crook of a mothering arm and fed at the nipple, scenting the pretty sweat of a tender breast. Again my wife murmured her impossible yearning: "I wish I could have nursed her."

Talitha sucked her thumb so vigorously, it drove the bony roof of her mouth high into her sinuses, obstructing her nasal breathing. Yes, and what did *that* word say?

"Wally, I wish that *someone* had nursed the infant."

And then came the supper in spring when we all six sat at table, eating. I at one end of the table, facing Thanne at the sink-side end; Joseph to my left; Matthew to my immediate right, within quick reach when he tilted his chair too far backward; Mary beside him, around the corner from her mother; and on the other side of Thanne, sitting still in a highchair, Talitha Michal.

This is how stubborn Matthew was in those days.

I said, "Eat your beets."

He didn't.

I repeated the command, clarifying that it was a command.

Still, he didn't. Nothing was left on his plate except the offending dark red vegetable.

I threatened: "Until you have eaten those beets, Matthew, you cannot get up from the table. And if you wait long enough, I'll put you straight to bed myself."

He put the beets in his mouth.

But he did not chew.

He sat there, sucking beets, for nearly two hours. Two hours. But he didn't get up from the table. He sat in a clean kitchen alone.

I returned. In exasperation (have I used this word before?) I said, "Spit them out."

He spat them.

And behold: he had sucked every beet into a whiteness pale as a cuticle.

"Get up," I said. "Go play."

I suppose we both could claim victory. He'd taken the nutrients after all. But he had "eaten" nothing. And in his mind, he alone left the table triumphant.

Talitha was a mess. Arising now into our world, she would smear oatmeal all over her face. She would turn bowls upside down on top of her elegant head. And so she sat, that vernal evening at dinner, with dollops of stickiness matting her hair and forming jujubes on her cheeks. Egypt, suffering the plague.

She happened to glance at me. Just as she did, she twitched her black eyebrows — quick up, quicker down.

Love watches. And, even before the brain has chosen, love responds.

We still were looking at each other, I did the same, flicking my eyebrows up and down, once. Immediately the child was looking at me, *looking* at me, hooked by my minimal gesture. She must have known that it had been in response to her! She must have remembered her own quick twitching. It must have been to her *more* than mere unconscious twitching. For next, slowly, the child raised both eyebrows high, held them, then lowered them.

I did exactly the same.

Which caused her to hold as perfectly still as an owl on its midnight branch. She was thinking.

This time I took the initiative. Every other feature in my face as transparent as water, I raised just one eyebrow. My right eyebrow. Which began to quiver by the strain —

—and suddenly Talitha grinned.

She reached a gummy finger to her left eyebrow and pushed it up, removed the finger and felt it drop. Tried again, and actually giggled at her failure.

I had found the language of my beloved! It was eyebrow language. And oh how we began to chat then. I could by nature lift just the central portions of my eyebrows, steepling them, as it were, in the mask of tragedy. I could somewhat semaphore them, while she bent her efforts to match me. I said, *Pass the salt.* She laughed and answered, *Oh, daddy, you know I can't reach it.* I signaled back, *I know.* And we were swept on waves of mutual giggling.

In time I tested the truer communication. I said, *Talitha, I love you.*

And she, by the steadfast gaze into my eyes; she, by permitting my close approach, my knuckles brushing her mealy cheek; she said, *I love you, too.*

That, compacted by my brief retelling of a long experience, was the beginning. Little Talitha crept from her cell and got up and walked.

In order that our children should apprehend their differences in love rather than in division, I named them for their colors. Joseph we called white. "Vanilla," we said, though Matthew received that nickname in high school for the great quantities of the drink which he drank. Matthew, earlier, was our baby brown: Chocolate. Mary, because her ready laughter turned her fresh face pink: Strawberry. Talitha, Butterscotch. More classically, and more often, I called Joseph, Erasmus; Matthew, Diomedes of the Loud War Cry; Mary, Monica; and Talitha, Isis.

II.

Sometime between May and June, the third summer of our living in the house on Heerdink Lane, when the strawberries were just coming into fruit and Matthew was about to celebrate the finish of his fourth year in this chancy world, I received from Thanne a sobering telephone call at my office in Grace Church, inner city, Evansville, Indiana.

If Thanne was choked this time, it was not laughter. She felt a wild fury. And she was deeply aggrieved.

About a month earlier, Mrs. Zorn had visited us in order to talk about our boys. Especially about Matthew. Plainly, without emotion and without seeming to blame us — the two of us, I mean — Mrs. Zorn told us that our younger son was out of control. I did not argue with her. Sometimes when I came home in those pretty days, he would explode their prettiness by attacking me from behind. Literally, in perfect silence he would launch himself from some piece of furniture and fly and hit the tops of my shoulders with his whole body, attaching himself there. I shouted. Sometimes I would topple forward, while he rode me down like a cat on my back. He caused such a tension in me that I ground my teeth and trembled.

Mrs. Zorn said that she had begun to worry for the safety of her delicate daughter, Ashley.

Therefore, she said, she was putting an end to their friendship. She would thank us hereafter if we kept the boys to our own property. If they came to hers, she would close Ashley in the house and lock the door against them.

Neither Thanne nor I argued with her. We felt burdened, though: however could we train our bright, busy, affectionate child in proper behavior? And we felt monumentally sad: how often would he lose friendships on account of his heedless energies?

That same day I spoke to him to tell him of the new restriction.

"Matthew, you have to think of other people first," I said. "Or this is what happens. People go away. We stood in our backyard. He gazed through the new, invisible wall. I gazed down on him. "Son, give before you take. Walk before you run. Listen before you talk, and whisper before you shout."

He murmured with genuine sorrow: "Now but she don't have a friend too, either."

"I guess not," I said. I hadn't thought of that.

"My fault," he said.

Then, at that particular comment, I held my peace.

Now Thanne was on the phone. "It's Matthew," she said. "It's Mrs. Zorn. Come home." Her tone was soft by means of a fierce restraint. It shook.

I tried to ask, "Why, Thanne? What—"

"Come home."

"I know the boy is hyperactive—"

"Please, Wally! Just come home!"

End of May, beginning of June. The weather was sweet with apple blossoms, the breezes balmy. All four of our children were outside so that Thanne and I could talk inside.

The beaming sun was about to be shrouded by the imaginations of the human heart, "only evil continually."

"I know the reason," Thanne said, sitting at the kitchen table and clasping her hands together. "I know why Mrs. Zorn separated our children."

"Yes. Matthew is—"

"Wally, don't talk. Listen to me. Matthew picked strawberries this morning. He put the best in a bowl. Without my knowledge, he carried them over to the Zorn's and knocked on their back door. And he told me later why he went. Our son went to fix the friendship—because, he said, he was the one who broke it.

"Mrs. Zorn threw the door open with such force, it knocked the bowl from his hands. She was not nice. It was worse than scolding. She raised her voice as if he had come over to rob them. To cut them with a knife. I heard her. She saw me. And now I know the real reason why she has shut our son away from her daughter.

"This is what she said. She said, 'Black and white don't marry!'"

It took several moments before my eyes went moist. Anger. Sorrow.

"I'm going over there," I said.

"No need," Thanne said. "We just won't have anything to do with them anymore."

It didn't matter what Thanne said. I could not stay in our small house. I walked out the front door and up the lane to the Zorn's. I knocked on their front door.

Mrs. Zorn — whose first name I would despise if I could remember it — opened the door to me. She smiled and stood back, welcoming me through the living room into her kitchen. We sat down at a table, just as Thanne and I had been sitting two minutes ago. I had yet to speak a word. She knew I was a minister. And though she was Catholic, she held ministers in some regard. She offered me coffee. The woman who had just excoriated both my son and my wife — she offered me coffee! Please, God! How can such absurdities exist?

I refused the coffee.

I said, "Matthew is my son."

She acknowledged as much, giving me a sympathetic smile. I truly believe that she would next have reached consoling fingers to touch the back of my hand.

"Matthew," I said, "will always be my son." I wished my voice were steadier. I was shivering. "How you treat my son," I forced the whisper, "is how you must treat me. How you treat me is how you treat my son."

"But," she responded with a bland assurance, "you and that boy are not alike."

"Why not? Why wouldn't we be?" I knew what she meant. But I explained to her what I thought to be the ignorance of such a statement. "He's white too," I said reasonably. "He has a grandfather as white as you. Adoption agencies classify him as *bi*racial. Two races."

It was on account of her next words that I felt a sudden, crimson, outraged shame for having revealed such personal and private information regarding my son.

For now the woman spoke with a real but detached and an altogether superior pity. "Ah, Reverend Wangerin, I do feel so sorry for the boy!

Not one thing or the t'other. Caught in the middle. It can't be natural. And it can't be easy. But you and your wife? Oh, how much I admire you for giving house and home to the little thing."

———

On the Sunday when Thanne brought our four children to Grace Church for their first experience of a service in that place, Matthew stared at the twenty, thirty black adults now surrounding him. Shy, he stood back a while, considering.

Then, "Mop," he whispered, tugging on her dress. "Mop, tell those people to take off their masks."

III.

By November 1975, I had completed all my coursework at the seminary in St. Louis. I was ready to receive Redeemer's congregational call, and then to be ordained into the pastoral ministry.

Between 1973 and 1975 the Lutheran Church–Missouri Synod had fallen into internal hostilities. An entire seminary (minus five faculty) was, in effect, fired. Given no more than two weeks' notice. Dismissed either for heresies or for insubordination.

The newly jobless professors formed a new seminary—from which I received my diploma.

When I was deciding, however, whether to follow my professors into "exile" or else to stick with a church-approved seminary, I laid the matter before Redeemer. "The Lutheran Church–Missouri Synod," I prophesied, "will make life difficult for us when it comes time to call and install me."

"No problem," both the congregation and Pastor Wacker answered. Neither knew how unscrupulous and legalistic the Missouri Synod could become. We smiled in ignorance.

A year later the president of the Indiana District had begun appearing before Redeemer (a moderately wealthy and large congregation, anchored in southwest Indiana). He taught them how heretical were the opposers and the destroyers of the true church. Redeemer, the congregation, began to believe him. Worse, threats were made regarding the congregation's properties.

All this became very personal.

The district president charged my seminary with heartless, ruthless liberalities. "Gospel Reductionism" he entitled the heresy against which he inveighed. By innuendo, then, he blamed me for introducing subtle but devilish falsehoods into the congregation (poor, unwitting people) by my (charming) teachings and preachings.

And "personal" grew even more personal for me particularly.

Near the end of my second year at Redeemer, the executive counsel met to decide, among other things, the salaries of the congregation's personnel. Wacker didn't mention mine to me.

Late in November, then, I asked to see the budget myself.

He obliged.

My name had been removed. There didn't even exist a line item referring to an assistant to the pastor.

I swallowed. Wacker sat quietly, hands flat on his desk. But he himself had begun to fear the accusations of the Missouri Synod against *him!* His rostered position. His pension.

"Listen," he said to me: "Redeemer isn't ready to handle the bump, Walt." A friend speaking to a friend of inarguable facts. "I'm afraid it would split the congregation in two. And which side would get the facility?"

Wacker: "Walt, I have to do what's best for my charge."

And I: "When were you going to tell me? After the budget had been approved?"

Wacker sat silently.

I said, "You can't do this."

He looked up. "Please, don't make it any more difficult—"

"David. I'm speaking with cold clarity. *Legally* you cannot do this thing this way. If voting members of the congregation appointed me in the first place, it must be voting members again who have the authority to release me. You can't hide the fact you're turning me out."

"Turning you out, Walt?"

"You, or the council chair, must bring the issue before the whole congregation."

Wacker consented.

There was scheduled a meeting for the discussion and for action upon my relationship with this particular community of Christ.

During the previous two years, I had become the sole preacher at Grace, whose worship always ended a half hour after Redeemer's. By the time I arrived at Redeemer on the Sunday of Redeemer's general meeting, therefore, it was already in session.

I entered the assembly hall from the rear. I saw where Thanne was. I didn't go forward. The discussion was intense, intensely personal and emotionally difficult—for everyone.

A parishioner would rise and take the microphone and declare: "We love Walt. We truly love him and praise him for the work he's done among us. But a synod is a synod. That word means [more than one parishioner explained, having learned it from the district president] to 'walk together.' To 'walk as one.' How can we disobey the Missouri Synod? Why do so many people in the synod have to break away?"

Another: "I grew up in Redeemer. I don't want it to change. I want my children to be confirmed here, to marry here, to baptize their babies here."

Whether such passionate assertions argued against the tumult I'd visited upon this congregation or not, I couldn't know.

Martha, elderly, one of my Sunday school teachers, absolutely capable of strong opinion and stark clarity, stood up. "Yes, we love Walt. And Walt loves Jesus. There are very few people here at Redeemer who know the Bible better than he does. And you all know how well he speaks and preaches. I vote for him. What'll we *be* if we're the ones who throw him out?"

And so forth.

They didn't know that I was standing in the back.

The vote went heavily against my ministry at Redeemer.

People were subdued when they stood and shoved back their folding chairs. There was a certain murmurous talk, but in low pools, as under people's attentions at a wake.

And then they saw me.

One couple stormed toward me, the woman openly weeping. The man said, "How could you *do* this to us? How *could* you?" He was angry. Because he loved me and felt torn apart.

Thanne found me. She came to stand by me. Many people embraced us.

And some said, "What will you do now? How will you support yourselves?"

Many members — most, in fact — skirted the place where we stood. I'd rather have everyone do the same. It was for that reason I had stuck myself into that doorless corner.

Thanne and I climbed the stairs to the nursery. We retrieved our children.

Matthew said, "What's-a matter?"

We drove home.

PART 2

10
1979

Thus says the Lord who made you,
 who formed you from the womb and will help you:
Fear not, O Jacob my servant;
For I will pour water on the thirsty land,
 streams on the dry ground,
 my Spirit upon your descendants,
 my blessing on your offspring.

This one will say, "I am the Lord's,"
 another will write on his hand, "The Lord's."

Who is like me?
Who has announced from of old the things to come?

Fear not. Be not afraid;
 have I not told you from of old and declared it?
Is there a God besides me?
There is no Rock; I know not any.

I.

On Saturday afternoons my father would lie prone on his bed, his eyes closed, grinning and groaning (and drooling!) with pleasure. There was giggling too, but not from him. And the sounds of four enormous mice.

At the right time, Dad would roll over onto his back, put his hands behind his head, and ask, "You ready?"

And so began his side of the covenant.

Oh, how fast we clapped ourselves against his sides, *our* hands behind our heads too—four mice, four sons, four boys ages four through eight. "READY!"

Then our father would say, "Once upon a time, Ambrose ..."

The tale began. His story ballooned in the bedroom, itself growing the size of the whole room, and invited us in, where we soared higher than the mountains with "Ambrose," a dull-sworded loon of a knight, who clattered about in armor too large, too loose (little David?), and too rusty, fighting dragons each with its "tail in a sling," stumbling, bumbling, surviving, and finally rising triumphant.

Hoo-ey!

Those afternoons have left an everlasting impression upon me, on my imagination, surely, but also on my mind *and* on my heart. All my senses had been in play. The bright blue and scrubbed autumn skies of Grand Forks, North Dakota—that and the spacious bedroom for a setting. Sight saw the hard bars of the sunlight sawn apart by venetian blinds; sunlight setting tiny fire to the dust motes floating on the motion of the air. Touch felt the cage of my father's chest, swelling and diminishing, the scratch of his beard, the fabric of his T-shirt and the coverlet. Smell received and retained Dad's personal sweat-scent. Hearing thrilled to the sound of his voice, wordless, a cello's murmurous echo within his torso. My whole self, then—my mind (suspense) and strength (endurance) and heart—was engaged in the ritualized event. Moreover, feeling my father, hearing him, rejoicing in his spinneret intelligence, the rush of exciting narratives, I experienced as a palpable thing my love for him.

And it had all begun with a covenant, a definable something of relationship in which both parties have something valuable for the other. Important! This isn't the service of one (important person!) to another (helpless person). For as Dad would tell the story, we had already granted comfort to him.

Before the story, while still he lay on his stomach, we had massaged him, rubbed his back, scratched it ("Oh, yes! A little lower, Wally"), had pummeled around his neck and shoulders, had walked up his spine. And I, if I could catch him off-guard, could also enter the man's spirit: by tickling the bottom of his foot, at which he would produce a mild laugh: *Heh, heh, heh, heh.*

Our part of the covenant.

———

Now, then: what my father had done for me, granting certain earnest but evanescent sentiments a habitation and a name, I wished to do for *my* children.

And I did.

At night, while they lay in the darkness of their bedrooms tightly tucked in bed — when Matthew was less inclined to bolt about — I told them stories. I sat to speak. I ritualized the tender event first by announcing, "Another story of Orphay and Dice," then by taking time to light my pipe (how did they see my face as it emerged from darkness? — a flickering mask in the match-light?) I tamped the fire. I drew the ambrosial smoke, causing the bowl to glow, then puffed it into the bedroom air. With creakings of my belt and rustlings of my fabric, I positioned myself on the chair, leaning it back on two legs, hoping these sounds would communicate to the children my motion and my ease. Then I began the story.

Ritualistic fire. Ritualistic time and place and behaviors, since ritual by its repetition establishes order and security and trust. Moreover, it lifts a thing above the ordinary, elevates that thing halfway to sanctity, accords it a mystic power.

It was my notion to excite my children's senses, fixing sight and sound and scent in their memories ever thereafter. The tobacco's glow, a moving red dot in bedroom air; the tobacco's aroma, satisfying and lingering in their nostrils even into adulthood; my baritone voice, softened or sharpened by emotions; my whipstitch fancy, the waterfall of pretty language, and the delightful ride in my story's car: these would, I prayed, become the vehicle for naming, containing and exercising our dear relationships: trust and love.

Just as my father had done.

Moreover, I constructed particular tales for particular children, building each upon that child's personality and repeating it as often as my son or my daughter had need of it. (Several of these, once the child outgrew it, have been dressed up for publication: *No Sky, Thistle, Branta and the Golden Stone, Elisabeth and the Water-Troll.*)

I peopled one long-running narrative altogether with African American characters, "Dice" and "Orphay," the child-heroes, "Mordred," the cruel villain, and "Hadies," the holder of the dead, whereunto Orphay descended with talents of vigor (Matthew) and music (Joseph) to save his burnt-umber girlfriend.

In those days there was a remarkable dearth of literature for African American children. It was the 1970s. I strove to fill a literary vacuum — the lack of black materials, though there *were* the wonderful picture books of Ezra Jack Keats — by weaving the stories we could not buy with filaments of my own imagination.

Too, at the best parts of my stories, when we revered this character or that one, I defined that hero by using the word "adopted":

Dice, dark-skinned and lovely, Dice as delicate as the whorls of an Adriatic sea-shell, had been ADOPTED by her mother Sephony and her grandma Deemety, women of power both over the earth and under it.

Some such language I sent forth through clouds of aromatic pipe-smoke, though perhaps in vocabulary less grandiloquent. Nor did I mention that Sephony/Persephone "under the earth" was the wife of "Hadies," King of all shadows also living under the earth.

Even so: as I had been shaped in the fires and on the anvils of tales told to the young, I sought to shape my sons and daughters. I fashioned for them a world equally as difficult for children white as for children black: this to approach the troubles they had already begun to know and to suffer in the external world around them; this, at the same time, to persuade them that trouble, though real, need not kill them in the end. I meant to prepare them for the malice of humanity. I meant as well to persuade them of their own resources for meeting such malice. Therefore, I fashioned a world as equally advantageous to children black as to children white: this to grant them the genuine (albeit imagined) experience of finding within themselves personal resources for overcoming these troubles; to learn, too, the strength of community *and* the presence of a Father more steadfast, more effectual, and ever more merciful than I.

It wasn't against Mrs. Zorn herself that I tried to build my family's fortress. It was against the unexamined, unacknowledged, and therefore unconfessed malevolence of almost all created people on this planet. Levies against the drowning flood of the rivers. I threw up storied and stony walls against that smiling villainy which (with mighty self-justifications) rips human relationships apart: against, I say, that criminal arrogance which chops people from people even as one might chop a serpent into parts, killing both the parts and the whole; against that self-love which condemns certain "others" to squalid isolations, which condemnation, as the caged and starving antelope knows, is as much as to kill them outright.

Prejudice (especially that of the powerful over against the powerless) is one example of such damnable, self-serving human wickedness. But prejudice is not its only manifestation.

In the beginning, with the ax of self-aggrandizement (with, truth be told, the Thor-like hammer of self-deification) we chopped asunder the cords of love by which the Creator held us to himself. But since he was the source and we the beneficiaries, it was (and is) a continuous act of self-destruction; but we were (and are!) too busy coronating ourselves to notice.

The serpent said to the woman, "You will not die. For God knows that when you eat of it your eyes will be opened, and YOU WILL BE LIKE GOD."

So when the woman saw that the tree was good for food, and that it was a delight to the eyes, and that it was to be desired to make one wise, she took of its fruit and ate.

That mythical, most real rejection of the Lordship of our God was (is) not unlike the murderous destructions of the primary gods by their children in pagan accounts of the beginning of things. Arguably, we were (are) like the (god-ish) grandchildren of Ymir, killing him, butchering him, throwing his brains high into the sky to become our clouds; like the (god-ly) offspring of Uranus, killing him; the (god-like) descendants of Tiamat, murdering her and forming a visible world from her bulk and the chopped-up pieces of her corpse.

In *our* narrative of the creation, however, it is not God who dies. (Not yet!) It is we ourselves. For in our desire to "be like God," and by our subsequent rebellion against the Creator's sole and universal Lordship, we divorced ourselves from Providence, from provisions of loving, from every resource by which creatures can continue within creation. On that day (which is always and ever *this* day) we began the long, delimiting process of dying as surely as the vine, hacked from the branch, must die.

But of the tree of the knowledge of good and evil you shall not eat, for in that day you shall die.

Countless cruel separations are embraced in that narrative, each of which is suffered in our lifetimes as yet another dying. Countless mortal sunderings have followed upon that primal one: divorces, wars, exploitations, oppressions, thefts both rugged and refined, murders high and low, the despising by children of their parents, the abuse by parents of their children, slanders, covetings. Oh, Christ, I want to quit this list of shattered commandments! It is too burdensome. It is too long.

By my stories (so I wrote above) I was building a fortress for my children, throwing up a wall for them against the bland malice of minds like Mrs. Zorn's. So I wrote — but now I must confess that the "fortress" metaphor is not completely accurate. Truly, I was not seeking another sort of isolation for them (as have families and religious sects of all ages); I wanted rather to grant my children an experiential preview. By my stories I meant to introduce them *in a way both companioned and controlled* to the truth of the human race. In the ritualized glory of my storytelling I meant to give them, within the good order and the love of their bedrooms, the actual *experience* of humanity's mad propensity for estrangement, for power, for dominance. Soon enough my children would encounter these evils face to face. But yet before they did, I hurried to teach them to swim in safe pools before adolescence and their terrible desire "to be free" tore them from my arms and pitched them headlong into the rolling and shoreless ocean.

But the ritualized story need not be confined to the invention of one father's mind. With greater force, it may come to the children from entire communities. With saving power, it comes of the creating and then covenanting Father, who called his children out of Egypt.

And so it is that, during the seder meal of the Jews, the youngest child asks aloud: "Why is this night different from all other nights," this night of only one sort of bread, unleavened; this night of bitter herbs only; this night when we dip the bitter herbs twice; this night when we all recline?

The child's questions are answered by the Haggadah, the narration — the verbal *telling* of the *story* — of the Exodus of Israel, the salvation of the people of the God who led them out of Egypt into the wilderness. Thus, annually, in the safety and the good order of their own homes, do Jewish people young and old re-experience the world and its horrors, the Lord and his salvation, in the place and the time and the rites of a sacred story told again. Their traditions are — as are they themselves! — revived in the tale's retelling. Herein they may re-experience the primal relationship with the Lord; herein reassert their own identities, known ever in relationship with the Lord. Herein, among the consolations of family and community, they may encounter again the world's hostility, its rancorous cruelty—but herein as well, over and against the Enemy, find reaffirmed the strong right arm of the Lord, the merciful kindness of the Lord God, his perpetual watchfulness and his clemency.

In the *story*, you see. In its telling.

A form which Christians also use for the communication of their faith: retelling annually the birth of Jesus with manger scenes and angels, his subsequent ministry, his passion and death and resurrection once a year; telling the tale in ritual settings less intimate than the seder meal, perhaps, and in time-frames stretched out between the start of winter and the start of spring, and in narratives too often too folksy, too personalized and sloppy against the crisper accounts of the Gospels. Nevertheless, despite our present carelessness with this Holy Story of Salvation (amidst armies of stories meaningless and venial) we still do introduce our children to humanity and to divinity, to *Immanuel*, Christ ever beside us, in the tellings of our sacred tales.

II.

Declare before the Lord your God:
"A Wandering Aramean was my father …"

Whereas I could spin no firmer context for my children's protected development than with the quick filaments of my imagination, the Lord God spins with iron bands and flat realities. And just as his words are deeds, so do his tales occur on the physical plane of our lives, and as palpably as the weather. The Heavenly Father can change my children's contexts as I could not, cocooning them a little while in communities of care and blessing.

Like this:

Shortly after my dismissal from Redeemer Church (that congregation of size, with sway in city economies, its membership completely white, middle class and upper-middle-classy), the leaders of *Grace* Church (little, black and inner-city) came to my small office. They had telephoned ahead to set up this appointment, so serious was their business. And the meeting was conducted with sober formality.

This was in December 1975.

Mrs. Allouise Story, a thin wheat-colored folder upon her lap, wasted no time in chit-chat. She said, "You will graduate the seminary in several months, yes?"

Yes. To the satisfaction of the faculty at Seminex ("Seminary in Exile") I had finished my vicarage and all my coursework. But I wouldn't receive the diploma until 1976.

"As I understand the procedure," she continued, "it is only with a bona fide call from an individual congregation, yes? that you can be ordained into the ministry? Into general ministry, I mean. Is that right?"

So far as I knew, it was. No one from the Missouri-Synod would ordain me now, of course. But that tiny upstart collection of congregations, the Association of Evangelical Lutheran Churches, and its Bishop for the Great Rivers Synod, Rev. Herman Nuenaber, had offered to ordain me when I had received and accepted a call.

"After the ordination," I said, "could come an installation as pastor somewhere. To the people who have called me."

"Now, I'm not saying I understand all this," Mrs. Story asserted. "Seems all backwards to me, tight as a ditty-knot —"

I nodded.

She continued: "Let us be that people." She lifted the slim folder from her lap and handed it to me. "Read it prayfully. Don't answer now. Meditate. Talk to Mrs. Wangerin."

She noticed my fingering the edges of the folder. "Oh, go ahead on," she said. "No need to wait."

I opened the folder upon a single sheet of paper. It was an official Call Document, issued by Grace congregation to Walter Wangerin Jr.

Will you be our pastor? I did not hear the question. I saw it in the twin drill-bits of Mrs. Story's eyes. She gazed at me, not blinking. The gaze communicated some regard for me, but more than that, an expectation that I would consider the question with a dreadful integrity.

Finally Allouise Story smiled, stood up, and with the others departed, leaving me to my own considerations.

III.

*". . . . and he went down into Egypt
and sojourned there . . ."*

In the summer of 1979 the Wangerins moved for the third time since arriving in Evansville, Indiana, June 1970.

We had found a wonderfully accommodating home just five blocks from Grace Church, the best house of all our houses before or since: four bedrooms upstairs, a large living room with a workable fireplace downstairs, a family room, a wide and workable kitchen—and a dining room which we converted into my personal study. And we could afford it. For two reasons. One: I had just sold the paperback rights of my first novel, *The Book of the Dun Cow*, to Simon & Schuster, whose purchase price was an unexpected windfall. Two: the house was astonishingly inexpensive. Of course. That tiresome triple-"location" dictum of real estate agents cuts both ways; properties too close to the inner cities are not considered desirable.

We moved in with the help of our parishioners, African American all. We made a huge noise. Laughter and welcome and bonhomie and singing and "church" right here on the street. The house was situated on a northeast corner of Chandler Avenue, the gracious oaks and gum trees of Bayard Park to our east, Evansville's East Branch Library north, directly across the street from our front porch door.

Matthew had a little two-wheeler, a rebuilt black bicycle which lacked anything unnecessary to locomotion, no fenders, no gears, a drive chain so loose that it regularly rolled off its sprockets, forcing the boy to come off the bike, to squat beside it in order to rehook the chain again. He, accustomed to our frugality, took these odd measures in stride.

Watch that child!—racing all around the house, charging into Bayard Park and back again, hooting with happiness. Pay attention to the freedom and the joy apparent in all his bodily expression. Here for him God had opened a different sort of context: African Americans whose exclamations of gladness and love were as boisterous as his own.

At the old place on Heerdink Lane, when he and Joseph first received their bicycles, Matthew had built a wooden ramp at the bottom of the backyard slope. He'd laid the top edge of an ancient, out-house door upon a box turned upside down, then grounded the bottom of the door in the angle between the slope and the lower flatland. That door—his bike-ramp!—met the downhill slope at an angle of a hundred degrees.

Matthew had retreated ten yards from the edge of the slope, had cried, "Watch, Dad! Watch!" (my first alert to his anticipations) had leaped on his bike, crouched, pedaled, pedaled furiously amid shrieks of his own laughter, pedaled to a fine blur of speed, shot over the slope, sailed briefly on a downward arc in silence, and hit the wooden door dead-on.

The bike bounced backward. The boy continued flying, performed a graceful somersault in the moveless air and landed—*Whhhomp!*—on his back.

My son had lain still, blinking into the sunlight.

I too stood paralyzed at the back porch steps.

Thanne came out. "What—?"

Little Joe, fingers fluttering at his lips, whispered, "Oh, no. Oh, no."

Mary said, "Get up, Matt."

Matthew, in the distant tones of wonder and discovery, breathed softly, "Wow."

And then did not say, *What a high!*

But such punishing consequences seemed never, never to school the lad in caution, not to take a dare. They had in fact the opposite effect. Dares he dared himself to worse and worser disasters.

By mid October 1979 Joseph was in the fourth grade. Matthew, the third. Mary in first grade, Talitha kindergarten. Matthew's mother had learned from the members of Grace how to pick his hair into a pretty afro. We had been by then about three months in the city. A radical change from the country. Change for the good, as God would have it: neither Thanne nor I knew yet how to read, much less to teach, our children the subtler signs of racism. Change, also, for the bad.

A Saturday afternoon in autumn. I sat in my study, reading, gathering thought for my sermon the following day …

Suddenly Joseph punched through the front door and dashed straight into my study. He panted in anguish. He couldn't stand still.

"Dad! Matt's in trouble. Please, come! Hurry, come! Let's go!"

We went out the front door. Joseph led me into Bayard Park. He pointed: "There. See?"

At the northern border of the park, I saw two figures: Matthew, short, straight, bending backward in order to see the lanky teenager now shouting, stomping, making threat-signs in my son's face.

Joseph: "He's going to hurt Matt!"

My blood went hot. I sped into a jog. The closer I came, the more I understood the problem. Both had been riding bikes. Matthew's was lying on its side, one pedal upward. Around that pedal the spokes of the teenager's front wheel were bent and broken. His was an expensive twelve-speed affair, bright in the sunlight and new. The front wheel formed a figure eight. But Matthew's stripped black bike was aimed in the proper direction for his side of the street. The skinny screamer's, on the other had, was aimed against the traffic.

"—gonna slap, slap, *slap* you!" the teen was screaming, clapping his hands. "You owe me, boy!"

Matthew was immobile, his eyes and eyebrows twitching between fascination and fear. He knew of my arrival; he drew a deep, trembling breath; I felt his spirit lean my way. But he could not tear his eyes from this outraged, wavering serpent before him.

"Owe me for the whole bike! Two thousand dollars!"

Ridiculous.

But to Matthew, the difference between the country and the city was fathomless. He was running into a buzz-saw of new rules. What was he to do? *Was* he wrong? *Did* he owe?

I cleared my throat. I said, "Listen—"

Matthew drew another deep breath and stood four-square. I believe he expected me to resurrect and reinforce the failing rules, to make these strange streets straight again.

I said, "Listen—"

And immediately the teen rounded on me. "Stay outa this, cracker! You got nothing to do with our business. Go away!"

Matthew's eyes grew the wider.

I said, "I have everything to do with this. This boy is my son—"

"Aw, spit. Aw, *spit!*" The teen spun himself into histrionic gestures, beseeching heaven to laugh at such absurdity.

I raised my voice. I made it commanding. I comforted Matthew and Joseph thereby—but what I said distressed poor Matthew all over again.

"Shut up!" I shouted. "Look!" I pointed. "Look over there!" Somewhat confused, the teenager looked. "That's our house. We live there. My family! There! This is our neighborhood."

"Aw, sh—"

"SHUT! UP!" I roared, a larger, stronger, overbearing man. I pointed westward in the direction of the church. "On the corner of Elliot and Gum there is a church called Grace. You know Mrs. Story? Mr. Thomas? Mr. Fields?" He nodded, uncertain. They were all school teachers. "You know Mr. Coleridge Churchill?" He nodded quite clearly. Yes. He knew the principal of the elementary school where he must have once attended.

"They are members of Grace. I am the preacher. You know Gerald Summers? Officer of the law? Him, too. Now, *you* listen to *me!*"

In a voice more controlled I told him that he had driven into my son's bike. I said I knew that as a fact. I knew that Matthew had been winding the bike chain back onto its sprocket when Mr. Show-off came cycling down the wrong side of the road and drove his front wheel into Matthew's pedal, an "inoffensive and stationary object."

"What?"

"It's your fault," I said. But I was in the neighborhood as a Christian pastor. I didn't want to be stirring up antagonists. Therefore I added — to Matthew's audible distress: "And it is somewhat our fault. So, take your bike on home to your mother. You ask her how much it'll cost to fix it. Not to buy it new! Just to fix it. Then come to that house [pointing], and I will give you half that money."

Thus my solution.

No one was happy.

The freckled, red-haired, knee-popping teenager picked up his speed bike and walked away with a thunderous frown, mumblin'.

Matthew picked up his bike and walked it between Joseph and me as we turned into the park and started for home. The chain dragged. We shoe-shuffled through dry leaves, the lobed oak, the five-pointed gum. The ground had only a grim sort of grass cover. We crackled twigs and snapped dry sticks as we went.

But then I heard a moist note rise from the mouth of my Matthew. It was like the vibration of a flat reed in the wind's sudden bluster, as if he were saying "The" without the "E": *Th-th-th-th-d! Th-th-th-th-d!*

Matthew had not stopped walking. I looked down. He was staring straight ahead. But the edge of his tongue was squeezed between his small, separated front teeth, his eyes wide open and shining with tears. He was fighting the urge to cry.

I stopped. We stopped. I knelt beside him.

"What's the matter?"

"You tole," he said, still staring straight ahead. "You tole that boy where we live."

"Oh, Matthew, I won't let him hurt you!"

But this is what happens when fundaments fail, when basic moral laws are suddenly unmoored and left to drift on the uncertain seas: even natural and physical laws are mistrusted. The whole world becomes a strange and dangerous place.

I had not, as Matthew had expected I would (for hadn't I done this all his life long?) re-established the moral laws in which he had experienced order and had trusted in security. These laws had reassured him of a persistent protection *even against his own wild desires*, against the lawless inner compulsions by which he could hurt people and ruin things. Matthew needed the laws. Losing them, he lost the very structures of common daily life.

At which point the boy began to outgrow the strength of my stories and the rules maintained within them. He stood not on the edge of the small slope in our backyard, ready to pedal like "Evels Knievels"; he stood, rather, on the high edge of a black canyon, too dark below to know what sort of landing awaited the child who fell.

Such passages in a young life, when all the good walls crumble and fall, make real an existence of lawlessness, make possible a future choice *for* lawlessness.

"Did God give you a law like this one, saying, 'You shall not eat of any tree of the garden'?"

"Dear me, no. We may eat of the fruit of the trees of the garden. What God said was, 'You shall not eat of the fruit of that one tree in the middle of the garden — neither shall you touch it! — lest you die.'"

*"No, no, no, no, no. Don't believe it. By such expedients God wants to keep you weak and keep all power to himself. You won't die. Rather, you'll make yourself equal to him — and **then**, when so exposed, what will that selfish Law-Maker do?"*

Late that same night, some time after midnight, while I was pacing in my study, desperately seeking my sermon, I heard a basso rumbling of the movement of furniture through my ceiling.

Matthew.

I climbed the stairs and walked to the end of the hall, to my sons' bedroom door. Which I opened.

Two of the room's windows faced out on Bayard Park. Against those windows, in silhouette, I saw blocky black lines of a fortress. Matthew had moved a dresser, a toy box, several chairs against the bottom sills of the windows. He crouched like a soldier in the trenches, peering over the furniture into a park gone silver under moonlight, my little boy, a-shivering.

"Matthew?"

He jumped. An agonized return: "What?"

"What are you doing?"

After a moment, hunkered down and breathing hard: "I'm waiting for that boy. He said he's going to kidnap me."

Ah, child!

So it is that, when spiritual laws no longer hold, neither do laws as elemental as gravity. Breaking free of the first law sets one free of the second — and boys who threaten younger boys apparently can fly.

———

In time it would be my Matthew who would take the wings of the morning to dwell in the uttermost parts of the sea, soaring toward *anomia*, skimming the winds of lawlessness. That day cannot be unrelated to this.

11
1977 — 1986

My heart recoils within me.
My compassion grows warm and tender.

I.

Now we must take our story backward in order to carry it forward by an unbroken sequence from the childish disobedience of spontaneous joy to that harder-eyed, calculated, Adamic disobedience of willful premeditation.

Here is Matthew during the summer of 1977, playing in the glassed-in back porch of the Heerdink house: he moves his entire body like the bionic "Six Millions Dollars Man," slow motion, step-step-stepping toward the foe, uttering his version of the sound effects of incredible speeds. "*Chn-chn-chn-chn—*" he intones, a little, brown Steve Austin, filled with loyalties to that hero of his. "*Chn-chn-chn-chn-chunnn!*" An eerie warning for whatever might suddenly smash when his bionic body finally strikes something.

It wouldn't be so nerve-wracking if I weren't also in the porch, crouched over a 1925 Underwood, revising that first novel of mine, *The Book of the Dun Cow*, which was already under contract with Harper Junior Books. Matthew loves me. He likes to be near me when I'm at home. And I like him by my side.

I say, "Matthew. If you want to stay here, you have to ... Play Quietly."

And he tries. And he believes completely in the possible success of his best and better efforts. But the Knave within his royal soul cannot be altogether repressed, and "quietly" becomes a slower, tauter, more desperately restrained animation of the bionic boy: (*"Chn-chn-chn-chn...."*)

Which, when it unsnaps *(BOOM!)* shatters my calm and puts my teeth on edge.

"If you do that again, son, I'll have to put you in your bedroom. Can you Keep Quiet?"

Earnest face, convinced of his abilities: "Yessss."

He lies down on his stomach to draw something. Something bionic.

I bend over the typewriter and wrestle my attentions to the book at hand, rereading a page of the old manuscript, screwing fresh paper into the Underwood, typing fresh paragraphs, scarcely hearing—

BOOM!

"All right, Matthew, come with me."

I take his hand. We go into the kitchen. I lead him around through a tiny hallway through the door, into the room he shares with Joseph. He is five, going on six.

I sit him on his bed. I point to the door.

"Do not—do you hear me? Do *not* touch that doorknob until I say it is time for you to come out."

He nods.

I close the door and return (hallway, kitchen) to the back porch and sit. I write a sentence. I write a complete paragraph. I begin to lose myself in the work, inhabiting the regions of my imagination, relaxing, working. It feels so good.

But then I hear a sound I have not heard before and, immediately upon that one, the sound of destruction.

HI-EEEEEEE-YAH! Matthew, his voice and his body hurtling.

And then: *Caa-rrrr-ASHHH!*

That sound I know, but I don't know what.

I rise. I pass, stunned, out of the porch, through the kitchen, into the hallway where I find Matthew's door still and solidly closed. But in the wood of the door is a hole smashed through, and through the hole hangs my son's left foot, shoe and all.

I pull the door open. At the same time I am pulling my son, who lies on his back, across the floor by the connecting link of the bones of his leg.

He is smiling. Proud, I'd say. Proud of himself.

"See," says Matthew to me, neither guilt nor accusation in his cheery tone. Triumph: "Never touched the doorknob, Daddy. Not one single time."

II.

While we lived on Heerdink I did not know of Matthew's growing obsession for comic books. A boy of loyalties he was, of purposes single-minded and unrelenting. As he had attached himself to the "Six Millions Dollars Man," so he became attached to comic books, as many as he could find, wherever he might find them.

One evening during our first year in our next house, the "city" house, I stood in the boy's bedroom, preparing to pray the bedtime prayers.

Joseph on the top bunk, Matthew on the bottom. Above, a Quaker silence; below, the rouncing search for a proper position. My salt and pepper sons. The salt one given to a sometimes paralyzing caution, tending toward interior feelings both high and very low, this son suffering guilts not his own but of his brother's making. The pepper one (or better, in those days: the fine filbert son) given to outrageous physical and moral risks, his feelings ever exterior and declarative and, in the days of his emergence, guilt-free. Both of them still willing to be serious in their bedtime praying; both of them, despite their unlucky exchanges of law and lawlessness, of the raven's freedoms and the wren's shrill fears — both of them in love with each other. My wondrous sons: they are not Jacob and Esau. They are David and Jonathan.

We folded our hands. We began a familiar prayer:

> *Jesus, Savior, wash away*
> *All that has been wrong today.*
> *Help us every day to be,*
> *Good and gentle, more like thee....*

My "good and gentle," uttered with a supplicant's force to the *Heavenly* Father on behalf of this twisting, spit-spraying, rocket-delivering Matthew. In order to put force behind the phrase, I lowered my head, lowering my sight as well and noticing that the bottom drawer of Matthew's dresser, partially open, showed a shining paper and colorful covers.

I bent to pull his drawer the farther open. Muscled arms and thighs, I saw. Capes and masks and flying people. Hair so black it was highlighted blue, and fonts that fairly shot from the pages: *Zazzzz!*

Comic books.

The drawer was filled with comic books.

"Matthew." Pause for investigation. In wonder: "Where did you get all these comic books?"

There must have been half a hundred magazines here.

Honest (still the honest kid), he said, "Fum the li-bary."

"You took them out?"

A burst of light in his brown face. Evidently, I'd hit upon exactly the right words. "I took them ... out," he repeated.

I narrowed my gaze. The room was lit by a single incandescent bulb. His darker face in darkness could conceal his expressions.

"You took them," I said, dropping the *out*.

"Yeah-ah-ah," watching me.

"You're going to return them."

"Um...."

"Matthew!"

Startled: "Daddy!"

"You are going to return them."

"Yeah-ah-ah?"

"Go to sleep."

Every magazine in that drawer had been ink-stamped with the identity of its truer owner, the Evansville Library System; particularly, the *East Branch Library*. Directly across Chandler Avenue from our house. Under the watchful care of its librarian, Carolyn Outlaw.

I wasn't completely ignorant. My enterprising son had enriched himself with comic books he never intended to return. That last clause defines the act. *Stealing*. He had taken them home as his own. He had stolen them.

Steal to me is a witching word. It has the same resistless, spellbinding power as the word *lie*. When I was a child my mother could use either word like a sorceress to fix me to the wall, for she despised these sins with all her stomach and believed that one sin would inevitably lead to the other, and both would drive her child into "perdition."

It was *my* stomach now which suffered revulsion—yes, and fear as well, for the sake of my son. Even after my discovery he was as cool as a pagan. What then? Was he headed to hell? The less scared he, the more scared me.

It was required of me that I do something to save him from himself. That I change the soul of my child early, while it was still malleable. Matthew must learn the law.

Carolyn Outlaw stood tall and strong, unbending, a monument of biblical morality. Her spine was not of mortal bone but of rectitude; her eye flashed divine lightning; smoke and fire (it seemed to me) did issue from her nostrils when she delivered the commandments of God. To anyone mis-minding them. God was her God. She was his prophet. More than a Moses, however, Mrs. Outlaw was the mountain Sinai itself, the very Shekinah of the Almighty.

I had seen her approach dope-smokers parked in their low-riders on the street between East Branch and our house. Fearlessly. Unhesitatingly. Her arms folded beneath the *Shaddai* of her mighty breasts, her word a low insistence. When she stepped back from the vehicle, its occupants gunned the engine and fled.

"Miz Outlaw," I said to her, "have you noticed an absence of library books lately?"

"Well—"

"Comic books, I mean?"

"Yes! Indeed! And not just a few. All of them."

"We have a problem. Would you be willing to talk to my son Matthew when he returns with the goods this afternoon? All of them?"

And so it was that, fifteen minutes after school let out, the father and his son went forth from their porch, crossing Chandler in a mutual silence. The little boy short, an innocent muff of Afro hair around his head, two eyes tremendously huge and peeping over the top of two high stacks of magazines; the man visibly nervous on behalf of his son.

Together they ascended the massive library steps which were conceived as a kind of altar to Public Reading by its distant creator, Andrew Carnegie.

Inside, the boy lifted his slippery stacks to the checkout counter. They spilled left and right in front of the Sinaitic Carolyn Outlaw, who caught them in her large hands and regarded the child reprovingly over the twin tablets of her cheekbones.

Not deigning even so much as to glance at me, she said, "Excuse us, Reverend."

I was dismissed. I crept outside. I paced back and forth through ten minutes and through fifteen before Carnegie's monument to human nobility, more and more anguished for the sake of my son under judgment inside.

The big library door pushed open.

A little boy with a nimbus explosion of sunlit hair descended the stone steps. He stood on the sidewalk. I took my place beside him and we crossed Chandler to home again.

"Did Mrs. Outlaw have something to say to you?"

Matthew nodded.

"Did you understand what she said?"

He nodded.

"Matthew. Did she talk about ... stealing?"

He nodded. And it seemed to me that his eyes popped wider, like a sunstroke, suddenly.

"Will you ever steal again?"

Slowly, with deep meditations, he shook his head.

In the wordless caves of my bosom, I hazarded the sentiment: *Thank you, Jesus.*

———

We bought the house on Chandler from the city of Evansville. Its Department of Metropolitan Development (the DMD) had rehabilitated the structure in order to exhibit what home owners in the Central City might themselves accomplish with Federal Community Development Block Grant monies (CDBG monies), which offered 2 percent loans for home improvement. During its two years as Exhibit A, the DMD kept offices in the house, and kept the building open from nine to nine. Clients came and went daily, using the house at 831 E. Chandler as something public and of the people.

Then Evansville offered to sell the house by sealed bids.

The paperback rights to *The Book of the Dun Cow* had just been sold by Harper & Row to Simon & Schuster. If we were to serve the city, it was required that we also live in the city. Thanne and I calculated our personal bid according to two figures: the amount of the check which we would receive from Simon & Schuster, and the lowest price established for the bidding. We sealed a bid and sent it without much real hope of its succeeding; for our bid was exactly one hundred dollars above the city's basement figure.

The city functionary who telephoned us with the remarkable news that our bid had been accepted ... well: his mood was less than happy.

"How——?" I asked, amazed.

"Yours," he said, "was the only bid."

Hummm.

But even after we had moved into 831 E. Chandler (with the help, the food, the song, the glad enthusiasm of the members of Grace Church), Central City people kept ambling by, ringing the doorbell or just sitting on our porch steps, both front and back.

And sometime after that move, we took ownership of a boundless, coal-black border collie who could not *not* run. Lincoln was a licorice streak with driving desires to dash at birds, to herd squirrels and little children, to explore the misty blue distances as well as the garbage cans that lined our alleys.

We received threats, communicated by our immediate neighbor: "They say they've got the solution. Next time they hear cans crashing in the alley, it's a gun they'll take to that dog. They intend to shoot the beast."

We built another fence.

This one was not the low, chain-link restraint against a climbing child, saving him from precipitate falls and the disasters of flooding waters. This one was wooden, a row of pikes each top cut to a spike, a six-foot palisade surrounding the backyard.

The fence announced our personal ownership of the house.

The same fence tried to keep another climber——another spirit yearning to breathe free——*within*.

But Lincoln learned by a hard dash to snap its latches and its gateways open! Breathtaking was this jet-black dog, white flashes at his chest, breaking free, swallowing air inside his jowls. Excited. Displaying a palpable, physical delight in the mere *dash* of dashing.

"Lincoln! Lincoln, come!"

And he would turn and look at me. In fact, he would, with a bark of exultation, kick dust and race straight for me, laughing, rejoicing — but, at the last minute, would veer from my open hands and pass me as a nasty blur.

I put bolts on the gates, unbreakable, unpoppable — thereby putting bruises on the dog until he ceased to hit the latches at all.

So he learned to climb the fence. He charged a pile of firewood to sail over the palisade of pointy posts, howling his own most jubilant Ode to Joy.

"Lincoln!" I ran after him. I called him and I called him. He seemed to love the very game of it, at distance prancing like a stallion, then lowering his head, transforming himself into a long black grease-streak on the air, and: *gone!*

The more I called to him, the more he went from me.

But how do you command a creature whose aptitudes are in his legs and not in forethought? To him the whole world was an invitation to break out and join in doggy play. To me, that world was hateful and dangerous and, when crossed, would shoot you.

And indeed, soon enough the hard rules of the world ensnared our carefree collie.

One evening we, the Wangerins, returned from a short trip out of town to discover that our neighbor (the man who spoke of gunshots canceling family pets) had built a separate fence in the center of our backyard. It went nowhere, starting at an isolated post and ending at a tree. But the brief fence was stout and very strong. And to it, by a long, tough cord, was Lincoln tied, the dog that once could fly.

In those years my annual salary was less than $10,000. Although I had no book agent (Thanne taught herself both to read and to negotiate publishers' contracts) we did, every third or fourth year, experience the small windfall of a publisher's advance against royalties for the books which I wrote and which they sold.

It was perforce a frugal life we led. I think our children did not want for the necessaries (even if they wanted dearly the things upon which to build a flouncing, or else a strutting, reputation).

Matthew's fenderless bike was stolen from our front porch. But a word put out on the street brought the bike back again, mysteriously, without visible human locomotion, even to the spot from which it had been snatched.

We never ate in restaurants nor drank at common watering holes with arches or bells or kings or cowboy hats above them. We had but one TV, black and white, the knob-cranking kind, before which Matthew would lie on the floor, watching football games, cranking the channel-changer with snaps of his wrist. "Watching," did I say? No, *memorizing* sports events, especially football games; memorizing and, by the twitchings in his body, mimicking the moves of various players; on the chalkboard of his mind drawing the strategies that won those games. My son educated himself in those departments where his father remained an oaf and no teacher at all.

Our children—having dozens and dozens of cousins—wore hand-me-down clothing. We ate "musgo." *What didn't go yesterday must go today.* When Thanne got ("such a!") deal on ox tongue but neglected to identify the new variety of meat on our plates, we tried, we tried to chew it and to swallow it. And as my father had been paid in potatoes and lefse, sugarbeet tops, pole beans, tomatoes and sweet corn, so did we receive payments in kind. Phil Amerson helped us install the appliances I could not. Good people babysat for free. Others loaned us the use of their vans (when we drove to Colorado), took our boys to stock car races, gave us cast-off toys.

Thanne eventually found work with an Evansville law firm.

And during the summer months I earned extra money by teaching at various seminaries in the states, Denver, St. Louis....

In 1978 Thanne and I were invited to dinner in the house of a wealthy physician and his wife. They had several children, one of whom, a daughter, had been adopted. It was an old house restored. Tasteful, ordered, reverential to the past but glad for the amenities of the present.

After dinner, while all the children played elsewhere in that house, the physician and his wife became very serious with Thanne and me. They had a question, they said, which the two of us might answer. Soon, however, it became clear that what they had was an answer, for which they were seeking our approval.

Their adopted child was incorrigible.

She would not obey. She would sneak about the house at night, pilfering food and coins, breaking into private drawers. She would lie. When disciplined she would grow physical and fight or run, would put herself in danger, and the family, and especially (and here they paused with the gravity of the thing) the boys born to them. What should they do?

Well, they had made up their minds.

I confess to being overwhelmed by wealth. I feel a supplicant in such places and therefore not very bold. Thanne, without the least antagonism, argued for their keeping the girl, since she had been shuffled through so many foster homes before. I can't recall offering any advice of value. But of this I was aware: these parents had already made up their minds. They would—and they did—return the child into the foster system before the summer was over.

When Matthew and I had first tossed a football back and forth in our yard on Heerdink, I marveled at the boy's ability to throw a hard, spiraling pass directly for my midsection; his ability, too, to loft the ball in a perfect arc, its points fixed, balanced and leading. This was instinct. It had been bred into him, for I could not have taught him the skill. And this was one of the surprising joys of adoption: my son could do what I could not; moreover, I could now *seem* to do what I could not by living within my son, and throwing footballs vicariously.

Once while he and I were in the family room watching (with our respective levels of insight) a Pittsburgh Steelers game, Matthew reached up to dampen the sound and said in easy sentences: "No offense, Dad, but we play better than you."

Then he turned the sound up and rested his head on the palm of his hand, his arm akimbo — while I allowed myself to parse his sentence for all its meaning. His *we* did not include me. It separated himself from me. This father and this son belonged to different categories. Matthew cannot have been referring to families. Couldn't mean gender. Not religions. He *could* mean a difference in age, but there were still men of my age able to *play better* than me.

Ahhh. The one thing left was race! For though Bradshaw was white, the greater part of the team was black, and Matthew had just observed a mid-field reception of unspeakable grace by … a black man, and that man had outpaced a white man to the ball's drop, and then had, rescuing his footing from a near fall, continued into the end zone.

At some time when I wasn't looking, Matthew had come to realize that I am white and he is black. And he truly meant no offense in the observation. It didn't sunder the goodness of our relationship as father and son, for he had said, "No offense, *Dad*— " But with him and between us, racial differences were observable and discussable.

On the 20th, 21st and 22nd of October, 1982, when he was eleven years old, I took Matthew with me to a cabin in western Kentucky, the two of us alone. I was about to repeat what I had offered Joseph the year before: the Father-And-Son *(sex!)* talk.

At eleven each son had just begun their sixth grade years. Stuff was coming at them from schoolmates and from countless other unknown sources regarding the body and the genders and mysterious desires. Thanne and I planned these weekends as mini-vacations with our children, each child and one parent alone, when any number of things might be done or discussed.

The cabin was another "payment in kind," since its owners gave us the use of it (and of their fishing equipment and their outboard motor boat) for free. Joseph and I had roared over the lake. Matthew and I moved (oddly) more sedately.

I recall the morning of the 22nd, our last day away, when the autumn winds were strong and steadfast, rushing so loudly in my ears I could scarcely hear my son. Across the water from the shoreline where we were walking, there stood a magnificent maple tree. It put me in mind of a royal head, the leafage, its hair, a fiery reddish orange. The wind was tearing through the maple's branches, blowing a stream of flaming tresses crosswise into the air.

I had said to Matthew, "Does it trouble you, that you're black in a mostly white family?"

He walked a few steps then spoke. But the wind tore his words out of my ears. I touched him in order to stop him, then knelt by his side.

"What did you say?"

Without looking at me he said: "I don't give it two thoughts."

———

Two summers earlier, in June of 1980, I was asked to teach a portion of the first summer school term at Seminex, my alma mater. I agreed. If the family wished to come to St. Louis with me, the seminary said, it could offer us an apartment free of charge. One of its friends and *his* family would vacate the place during the period of our need. Well, and the major draw was this, that the seminary would pay me in money, not in kind. To these offerings too we all agreed.

It was a spacious apartment with a fine view of the broad and beautiful park across the street: green grass, macadamized pathways, swings and benches and seesaws. There the children were free to play the daylong through. And we went to the arch. And they—that is, Joseph and Matthew—went to a drugstore around the corner. This was not free. Nor were we aware of their regular expeditions thither—

—until we had returned home to 831 E. Chandler Avenue.

In the course of an unremarkable day, I happened to discover another (altogether new) stash of comic books, but this time in a place more secretive: high inside his closet. These were fresh magazines, almost unread, preserved in a box, each within a clear plastic slip-cover.

I went to breathing hard. My neck prickled. Not under the heat of the summer, but for the furnace of fears within me.

As the boys were getting into bed that night, I opened their closet door, lifted down the cardboard box, and spoke to Matthew.

"Where did you get these?"

My tone must have cracked—or whip-cracked. Once to sin this sin may be construed as an act of ignorance. But twice is to act in spite of the knowledge that it *is* a sin. This is a willful disobedience. But not only against one's earthly parent. Against the heavenly Parent. And the consequences thereafter can be dire indeed.

"Where, Matthew, did you get these!"

"From," he said, "from—"

He allowed his gaze to wander all around the bedroom, as if seeking the chute that blew out comics of its own accord.

I was losing control. I had no patience for his slow selection of some new lie. I fairly shouted: "Matthew! These are new. You don't have the allowance that could purchase as many as these. Where did you get them? Do *not* be a liar in front of me!"

"Yeah, Dad," he said. "Ummmm. From—"

Suddenly his brother could stand it no longer. Near tears he said, "From St. Louis. From the drugstore."

"*Mat*-thew!" I stared at him.

He lowered his head.

O Christ, let it be in remorse.

He murmured, as if in a kind of wonderment at the answer just unfolding before him: "Yeah. Yeah-ah-ah-ah. From the drugstore."

O God of our fathers, and of our mothers too: what should I do with my son? This wasn't a mistake. Could it be the true, emerging character of the boy? How could I change it? How could I save him from himself? I knew, I knew, dear heaven, I *knew* the uncompromising ways of the world; worse, against young black males the world struck with a gut-emotional, unconsidered, prejudicial and more furious force than at others. I had seen it. Already I was visiting young black men in prison, the responsibility for their incarceration only partly theirs! The system lay like a crouching cat in wait for them. What should I do? How could I even now begin to save my son?

I chose dramatic means.

Despite the lateness of the hour, I commanded Matthew to go barefoot down the stairs, into the living room, to sit on the sofa there. He did.

I picked up the box containing his every new comic book and followed him down. But I knelt down between the sofa and our fireplace, crumpled up the top comic, felt in my pants pockets for my butane pipe-lighter, lit the comic on fire, and threw it into the fireplace.

Matthew watched.

One after the other in the large room illuminated by fire alone, I burned Matthew's comics. His eyes reflected the flames. I knew thereby the focus of his looking. I wanted his heart to go there, too.

Therefore, while I sent super heroes *WHOOSHING* toward perdition, I talked. No: in language stern as Deuteronomy I *preached*, by threats and blessings, the Law.

The statutes of God are established in love for us. To save us from the suffering of wrong-doing. There is right. There is wrong. (*WHOOSH!*) And though doing the right may not preserve a person from suffering, it won't be that terrible suffering of guilt, whence there is no exit. But doing the wrong will surely crush a kid underneath the punishment of the world—of the white world, mind you. (*WHOOSH!*) And on account of guilt the kid will one day have to bear some blame for the punishment, will *not* be able to stand strong in righteousness.

(*WHOOSH!*)

Thou shalt not steal, Matthew!

Matthew, please don't steal.

Oh, my son, stealing will bring down upon you both the irons of the law and the despair of the lawless soul.

I never mentioned (*WHOOSH!*) hell.

But I hoped that the hammering heat of the fireplace and the vision of painted pictures so swiftly burned to ash might cause the boy to experience what was not named.

Did Matthew understand?

Well, he nodded. He blinked a skim of moisture onto his wide, white eyes. And he swallowed. I took these small signs as grounds for further praying:

Thank you, Jesus.

———

But Matthew was Matthew, certain things unchanging, merely developing. As loyal as he had been earlier to "The Six Millions Dollars Man," Matthew kept loyalty to the bright, impossible, primary-colored heroes of the comics.

He stole again.

By some unintended command, Thanne discovered a file that Matthew had begun to keep on her computer. It surprised her, since, at a stroke, the entire screen began to flash black then white then black, two words flashing always the opposite hue of the background. These words, in capital letters, one set directly above the other, shouted: BAD MATT! BAD MATT!

Within that folder were lists of comics, carefully kept.

We went looking. And we found that the child had graduated — not to morality, but to finer, more calculated dodges.

Ah, my son, my son.

Thanne always prayed, and to this day prays, that we will meet all of our children in heaven. In those days I had begun to pray that we would never meet a child of ours in jail. The probabilities were increasing daily. And the sorrow was that it was I who sank into the despair at the prospect, not my son.

My son. He had not changed. What was there left for me to do?

Whether my mother's punishments had actually changed me or not, I cannot finally say. Well, there was change. But whether for the better or for the worse, even so blunt a judgment I am unable to make. Beatings are not spankings; and even spankings are so complex an interchange that minds more capable than mine continue to debate the issue without coming to consensus.

But what else was left for me to do?

I would punish my son myself.

"Matthew."

"Yeah, Dad?"

"Go into my study. Wait for me. I have no choice. I … You need a spanking."

He went. He closed the door. We both waited.

I paced on the living room carpet, committing myself to a cleanly, reasonably devised procedure of punishment: nothing should be done in anger; but neither should I for pity foreshorten my arm and muddle the effect. I would use the palm of my hand to spank him so that I should in my own flesh feel what he felt; five swats on his bottom, no more (which in my childhood memory led to unmanageable furies on my mother's part) no less (which tenderness might undermine the dreadful necessity of the Law).

And so, and so.

I entered my study and closed the door behind me. Matthew sat small in a large chair, his face cast down, his expression mute in mystery. What was he thinking? Where was his mind? What language did he understand these days?

I sat. As clearly as I could, I repeated the law, the deed which broke that law, the consequences of such deeds. Did he understand?

He nodded, but he did not lift his eyes to look at me.

I called him to myself. He came. In two arms I lifted him and laid him belly-down across my knees. We were almost the cartoon of a spanking.

I raised my right hand. I brought it down.

The instant I connected with Matthew's bottom, a hundred emotions converged within me: His muscles contracted in pain. His entire body went as rigid as a board. He made no sound. But by that rigidity I knew the pain, and his pain straightway became mine—even as I felt the stings in my own palm. Our nerves were a single system. I stiffened even as he did. I felt tremendous guilt: my son! My son!

But I counted the spanks, two, three and four and five.

I stood and carried him back to his chair.

His face was shut. His aspect one of cold refusal. He did not cry out, he did not complain, he did not show anger. He sat.

And because I had despised my mother's waiting for my tears and then her voyeuristic staring at my crashed, defeated countenance, I left the study altogether, closing the door behind me. His crying ought to be a private thing.

I went through the living room into the kitchen—and then I burst into tears.

Oh, this was more than I could stand. I bowed my head and covered my face and made a wet boo-hooing mess of myself.

Thanne came. She looked at me. I draped my body over hers and sobbed until I could control my emotions again.

I went into the bathroom and washed my hot face with cold water. Dried it. And finally returned to my study.

Discipline cannot be finished at the administration of pain. If I had touched my son to hurt him, I must absolutely touch him again in kindness, to comfort him.

So I sat a moment and repeated all over again the necessity of that punishment, repeated myself almost word for word for, now, the third time: the thing that had been wrong, the thing that should be right.

And at the end I said, "I love you. I love you, Matthew." I arose and walked toward him. "I will never not love you." Then I bent down and embraced him and held him tightly to myself.

To my knowledge, my second son did not steal comic books again. And I thought it had been the spanking that persuaded him toward such moral restraint.

I was mistaken.

Some years later, while Thanne was driving the four kids back from shopping at the mall, our teenagers were discussing certain secrets of their childhood, things they thought their parents had never known.

"Sugar sandwiches," Matthew announced. "At night I snuck into the kitchen. *Poured* the sugar on slices of bread, and ate them whole."

The topic of comic books arose. Thanne mentioned how long the thievery had continued. That was one secret of which we were surely aware.

But Matthew said softly, "I haven't stolen any for a long time."

"And we know why," Thanne said.

"Why?" Matthew asked.

"Because Daddy spanked you."

"Oh, no." Matthew fairly sang that long *O*, lengthening it: Nooooooo.

"Then why did you stop?"

"Because Daddy cried."

12
1986 — 1988

Make haste, beloved!
Be thou the antelope!
O be that younger stag
    who prances the looming ridges,
    rampant on mountains of spices!

I.

Having begun to serve Grace Church in 1974, by 1985 I'd been pastoring the people of that parish for more than a decade. During those years my desire to write (never weak, not since exercising my talent in high school) had increased to a professional obsession. I could not *not* write, devoting my mornings to the typewriter until twelve noon precisely, producing (on account of my wish to bring something to completion every day) chapters short as hiccups. My ability to publish books (four solid volumes by then) likewise had increased. And in spring and early summer a publisher came wooing me with a multi-book contract, which could cover the next several years' work.

Both internal motives, therefore, and external opportunities argued for a shift in my daily duties, more application to the writing and less to the parish.

I would continue to serve Grace, but in a much diminished capacity—and altogether *pro bonae ecclesiae.*

Losing Grace's salary, my family's income would drop, its regularity suddenly becoming bumpy. Thanne still worked for the law firm; but that was slim pickin's for a household of six. We would have to rely on the honoraria I earned by lecturing, and on the hope that the actual sales of my books might begin to pay past their advance on royalties.

Thanne and I sat our children down to ask their opinions. Should I accept the multi-book contract? Could they live on less again? I promised that I would write the sort of books they liked, if they'd be willing to give me the ideas.

Matthew said, "Superheroes."

Thanne said, "A love story."

This summit was somewhat rigged, of course. First because none of the children was able to understand what "living on less" could possibly mean. The burden fell heavier on Thanne than on anyone else, for she was the one who handled the budget, and her creativity ran more in the order of conservation, thrift, prudence: *"Provide. Provide."* Her children had played happier with blocks than others' whose toys yapped and growled and wheeled about on batteries.

The second manipulation was altogether my own. I made an offer. Each child could choose a trip, wherever he or she in the next few years desired to go. I would, if I could possibly swing it, take them there, myself and the child alone.

They didn't forget.

Each remembered till all four had accompanied me on one journey or another as I traveled to speak or read or lecture on someone else's ticket: Talitha to San Francisco, Alcatraz; Mary to New York and a reading I did off-Broadway. Soon enough Joseph and I flew to Chicago where I taped a television show for its PBS station, Channel 11. We walked the following day to the Goodman Theater, where we saw the annual version of *A Christmas Carol.*

But Matthew was the first of all to take advantage of my promise. After much research and planning and preparation, on Saturday the 22nd of February in the new year 1986, we drove together into Chicago to watch a Bulls basketball game. Michael Jordan was playing. Michael Jordan was the reason.

What we had not planned for, however — nor could have planned for — was a command appearance in another sort of court, scheduled on the 18th, the Tuesday of the same week when Michael Jordan flew the key and stuffed the ball without biting his tongue off: Matthew, under another sort of judge for flights he should not have taken …

———

A day when there is no school. Certainly in chilly weather, perhaps a Saturday, though it might be one of the days of Christmas vacation. I don't know. I am not fixing the day itself in my memory and shall never be able to retrieve it again hereafter.

"Mr. Wangerin? Mr. Wangerin!"

I hear boys' voices outside my home study. I step to the window and look, but I can see no boys.

There is a small basketball court in our backyard, its basket attached ten feet above the ground on the garage wall. The siding there is freckled with shoe-prints as high as six feet, since Matthew and his friends use it for practice. My son, despite a soaring vertical jump, hasn't yet begun to stuff the ball in a single airborne flight. Often he (and others) toe the garage wall in order to gain the height a singular leap cannot.

"Mr. Wangerin!" They're shouting now — and suddenly I notice curly red hair bouncing up behind the back of the palisade fence.

Jerry Copeland. He can't get in.

I throw on a jacket and go out to him.

It was upon this court, in fact, where I learned to my shame—and my shock—that I still harbored traces of racism within me. For either of our daughters could play with their friends in the backyard and I'd not give them the slightest attention. Joseph could with his white friends shoot horror videos out there, and no never-mind from me. But when Matthew and his black buddies began to shout and tumble and slap and shoot and harass each other, why, I flatly could not write a line. Constantly I went to the windows expecting to see some deviance, some grievance performed. I knew instinctively that these boys would without blinking break my possessions, and that bits would be missing that evening—could I remember what bits exactly I'd left lying around. *Hi, Mr. Wangerin*, the boys might call out to me. I would smile and lift a hand, as if I were some royal personage, or else the Pope, blessing constituents.

It was Jerry Copeland's sweet spirit (and the dumb pride that would announce to Thanne or me some new infraction: *See, Mrs. Wangerin? I'm free! A fake ID!*) which caused me one day to examine myself—I mean the soul within myself. The white pastor of a black congregation; the white father of African American children—he is not clean. He who preaches the evils of prejudice, who abhors it in all its manifestations, must confess his own complicity.

Ah, Christ!

I open the gate. There is an old car idling in the alleyway, three of Matthew's friends inside, Jerry Copeland outside and backing away from the swinging gate.

He is mortally contrite. Actually: afraid.

"They got Matt," he says.

"What do you mean?"

"The cops—"

"What? *Why*, Jerry. Where—"

"Down at the mall. We saw him in handcuffs. Cop wouldn't talk to us. Was leading him somewheres—"

I looked at the others in the car.

"But why, for the love of God! What did he do?"

"Oh, but it wudn't nothin'."

"Jerry, it has to be something!"

"Well. Mr. Wangerin. Um, they said, I mean the store person said, accused him ... shopliftin'."

Thanne and I feel the frightful jangling of the *Beware* bells all up and down our bodies. This is it, isn't it? Our fears all coming true: white cops coming down on our black son!

Did he do it?

We call our friend in the department, a black officer named Gerald Summers, who immediately hangs up in order to find out as much as he can.

"An off-duty officer," Summers explains, "arrested Matthew for shoplifting. He's still holding him in his security room at the mall."

Summers gives us the room number.

"Listen," he says. "I just told the officer about you. He didn't know about Matt's parents, but he's heard of you. He's all nervous now because he has been and he still is calling, demanding that the precinct send a paddy wagon as soon as possible. You want to see Matthew there, you'd better hurry."

We find our son sitting in the small, hot, sweaty security office, a tall white officer sitting at a desk. The officer stands.

Matthew sees us, a stunned look in his eyes, marks of cuffs at the bones of his wrists. He doesn't arise.

"You were cuffed?" I ask.

Matthew whispers, "He just took them off."

I face the officer: "What? You let him sit here all this time with cuffs on? He's fourteen years old. What were you thinking?"

"Sir, understand my position. He tried to steal. He is a thief. This is what we do for all thieves."

"How do you know he tried to steal?"

"I know."

"You have the evidence?"

"I just know."

"Did you see him with—what was it, Matthew? What do they say you were trying to steal?"

"A record."

To the cop: "Did you see him with the record?"

"No sir. But the store manager did."

"Matthew. Did you try to steal that record?"

A brief pause. Slowly he shakes his head.

"What?" I cry. It must sound angry.

Softly, he says, "No."

"Okay," I return to the officer, "you have two versions of the same incident. Why do you accept one and not the other?"

"No, no, no sir. I am not accepting one and not the other. I'm doing my job. I'm holding the young man here until we can process him down at the station—"

"That's not what I heard!" I'm growing more and more heated. I am trembling, losing control of thoughts and beginning to spit my language. "I heard you've been calling to have him picked up and taken straight to jail."

"Please, sir … Wangerin, is it? Reverend Wangerin? People say good things about you downtown—"

"You didn't try to call *me!* Isn't that a part of your job, to inform the parents?"

"Not necessarily. It is not a regulation."

I snap shut. I glare at him. Thanne is standing slightly behind my side, quiet. What is she thinking? Matthew's sitting, his eyes on the ground, not looking at any of us. Not (oddly) rooting for me in this nerve-wracking exchange. What is he thinking? Did he do this? Could he have done it?

"Sir, you have discretion in matters like these!" I've lifted my voice, partly because I am not altogether sure if this is true. "It is within your choice" (take a breath, Walt) "*either* to arrest a fourteen year old boy *or* to call his parents." Take a breath! Take a breath! "And *certainly* you could have checked to see if he had a record—

"Matthew!" I know my voice has the whetted edge of the scold. "Did this man ask about us? Our names? Did he ask you how to get ahold of us?"

Silently, gloomily, Matthew shakes his head *No.*

The officer's lips are pulled tight, flashes of moist teeth peeking between them. His eyelids droop as if by leaden sinkers. The muscles at the backs of his jaw bunch, bunch.

Then Matthew follows his mute answer with the mumbling of several words.

"What?" I say. "I didn't hear you."

He directs his comment to the floor. With somewhat more articulation, Matthew speaks: "He said, 'You people.'"

You people. It's a prejudicial lumping of an entire class into a single opprobrious slur.

"You mean this officer here?"

Matthew nods.

The officer releases a hissing sound. It might be a sigh. It might be tension of his own. He seems to be reaching his limit.

"Speak up," I insist. "What exactly did he say? When did he say it?"

My son still cannot lift up head or face or vision: "When he came into the record store with the manager. The manager told me first, 'It ain't no thing. Wait here for me. I'm coming back. It ain't no thing.' But when they came back together, this man—soon as he saw me—he said, 'I don't know why you people think you can get away with this—'"

"For the love of God!" I square myself toward the Evansville police officer. "You know all about this *you people,* don't you? African Americans."

"Not what I meant," said the officer.

"Aw, what else could you mean?"

"Thieves. Robbers. Bad guys. I was talking about people who steal, why *they* think they can get away with—"

"You knew my son—on sight!—to be one of those *you people*, hey?"

"This much," the officer said, "I will do for you and no more. Reverend Wangerin, you can take the boy with you. You can drive him downtown to juvenile. Find out for yourself what a case officer will tell you there. But you gotta go right now. As soon as you leave me, I'm going to call juvenile myself. They will be expecting you."

Did he do it? I mean my son. Neither Thanne nor I can ask the question out loud, but we each know that the other is thinking the same.

Oh, my son, my son! All my efforts at discipline! Everything to persuade you to obey.... It is the *world* that will not love you.

We wait almost an hour in the juvenile department of law enforcement in Evansville.

Without warning a man in a slouch-suit appears before us, a folder in his hand. He nods wordlessly then turns into a small cubicle. It must have been an invitation to follow. His suit coat hangs like a polyester curtain at his butt. We enter. We sit. Briefly, not looking into our eyes, the man announces that this thing, Matthew Aaron Wangerin's arrest and indictment, must go to trial after all. No breaks. No choices. We can, his parents can, keep him in their custody. A word of advice: get a lawyer.

One of our friends is a lawyer. Actually, I am a close friend of his wife, since she and three others own a bookstore where I am often scheduled to sign my newly published books. But he has many children, he has sympathy for what the city can do to kids in general, to black kids in particular; so, although his legal work is corporate, not courtroom, he agrees to represent our son.

In a first consultation, he suggests that we have Matthew take a lie-detector examination.

"It cannot be used in court against him," the lawyer said. "But if he passes, I can use it somewhat in his favor."

Through every stage of this procedure my stomach grows more and more sensitive to physical bumps or sudden sounds. My stool turns watery. I startle easily. I am tormented; it seems I can read the rest of my son's life in the crystal of this miserable adventure. Sudden motion can shatter the crystal.

Did he do it?

We don't know. We do not know. And we are afraid that, if we asked him directly, he might say, "Yes," and then what? Practically, then he has no defense in court. And then what? Spiritually, he is halfway lost. Or else he might say, "No," and then we would be left with another desperate question: *Is he lying? Is he telling the truth?*

He doesn't exactly fail the lie detector test. But neither does he pass it. With genuine kindness, the man who tested Matthew explains to us (to Thanne and me alone) that Matthew was soft on several significant questions. The tester, therefore, cannot give him a clean sheet. Yet, for our sakes, he will not say absolutely that our son is lying.

In our state we cling (isn't this ironic?) to the *un*certainty of the matter.

And on the 18th day of February, 1986, the four of us go to court: Matthew, his parents and his lawyer.

Court is called to session.

The lawyer and the city's attorney begin with preliminary discussions which I cannot understand. Matthew is not sitting with us. He is up front, where other members of my congregation have sat for their own trials, men accused of deeds much more criminal than the effort to steal one record; but that difference means nothing to me; this difference does, that those others were kin to me only in spirit, but this child is my son, the core of my heart, an element of my own identity.

The city's attorney calls to the stand the arresting officer.

Once he is seated, but before questions can be put to him, our lawyer raises a question of procedure—something which seems not to comport with the rules or regulations of a proper trial.

The judge asks for a brief clarification from the city's attorney, who utters a sentence so short, I cannot catch it.

In the next instant, the judge is gaveling closure to the trial. It is, in fact (for reasons I never do comprehend), dismissed. Matthew is released, innocent. We all walk out into the chilly, spitting February weather. It is over.

Within four days I am sitting high up on the nose-bleed seats of the stadium where Michael Jordan is leading the Chicago Bulls to another victory. At one point Jordan is fouled so egregiously, he sits bent upon the game-court floor—his head hung low between his knees—for nearly six minutes in pain.

Matthew is not beside me. Already during the first five minutes of play he had raced down the aisle-steps closer and closer to the action, farther from me. My stomach suffers a thousand fears on his behalf. I cannot always see him so far down, so far away. He has Thanne's camera. He is pushing himself in front of those with courtside seats. Who knows whether the boy might get himself punched for such audacity. Who knows whether he might fall and I wouldn't know where to go to save him? Who knows whether he might be kidnapped. Or arrested. And I so far aloft would sit in my anxious ignorance until the end of the game, until the stadium had emptied altogether and there was no little fourteen-year-old boy nearby that I might look after him?

Who knows whether or not he actually tried to steal that record from the store in the mall? In all the years that have followed, even down to this one, 2007, twenty-one years later, neither his mother nor I have had stomach enough to ask him again.

But I think we should have. Early.

II.

There were for Matthew yet two shining moments, on a basketball court, the other standing on his own two feet before the people of our neighborhood.

Neither Thanne nor I could personally attend that January game wherein our son rose higher than a net, as high as bright divinity. It was played a fair distance away from Evansville, in a southern Indiana county quite as white as Bosse's Varsity team was black.

But we heard its story told with passionate clarity: first by Matthew at home that very night; then by a host of the team members, together with their parents and the fans who *had* attended. So intense were these performances, I might as well have been the shadow of my son throughout the event. Even now the drama plays before my mind's eye in color, with a breathless accuracy.

———

Our children might have gone to a private, Catholic high school, Memorial, a long walk from our house. Joseph chose Bosse High School. We lived in its district. The walk was a fourth of that longer walk to Memorial. And, though Evansville schools obeyed the courts, balancing their racial mixtures by bussing African Americans to schools in neighborhoods mostly white, Bosse was unique: its district lay half in the central city and half in quarters European. No bussing. Street friends were classmates. Street players were teammates.

Matthew was (as much as this was legal) recruited by the Memorial coaching staff.

But he knew the present players at Bosse, saw them strolling the regions where he watched and played, knew of several who were receiving visits from scouts sent from noble institutions: Duke. The Blue Devils.

Moreover, I saw his choice in his face, even before he thought he had made it:

We were sitting at supper one warm evening when the front doorbell rang. I got up and walked through the house. Even before I opened the door, through a side window, I saw him, our visitor: Coach Murrain of the winning Bosse Varsity Basketball program.

"Matthew. It's Coach Murrain. He wants to see you."

There: in the elemental stillness that overcame his body, in the stunned longing that had seized his eyes so that he saw nothing of the room around him, saw only the shining dream before him, in the unconscious O which his lips formed I saw his decision.

He whispered, "What should I do?"

I said, "Go on out there and talk with him."

My son became an acolyte filled with reverence and moving shoeless toward an icon.

In fact, far from anything numinous, Coach Murrain was short, balding, white, and a screamer. His teams often triumphed. His region ignited the stars before they came to him. But since Bosse was in those days a school to watch, it drew good players too by its reputation.

But that icon. If Bobby Knight wore red on his belly by the dye of his sweater, Murrain wore *his* red (oh, yes: the selfsame color!) in his face, his jowls, his eyes, and bright upon his balding head. This was the hue that suffused the small man's oatmeal flesh when he went to yelling. During a game, he yelled. Before and after and at the half, Murrain swelled like Vesuvius. He took his rages out on his players, by name.

To this day I do not understand—nor do I accept it—that a high school teacher of English cannot shout in a classroom; and if she dissed a student even mildly, she could suffer anything from a stern reprimand to the loss of her job, to a lawsuit.

But certain coaches can belittle boys who are still developing (body, character, mind, the sense of a self); coaches can argue the *benefit*—for the boys!—of such militaristic dismantling; coaches can get directly into their players' faces, screaming, cursing the soul of that particular youth, burdening him solely with the loss that has not put the whole team under the scorn of the school, yes, and even of the city!—and *not* themselves be reprimanded, sued, *fired!*

But so it was.

Little Murrain did what no student could do in the halls or on the fields of play.

And I watched the effect on Matthew

In the beginning of his high school career I dearly loved to see my son's genuine joy on the court. He was my emerging boy again, that kid who slithered down strawberry beds, who pumped his little black bike at high speeds around the house, laughing, loving the explosive activity for its feeling alone. Point guard, Matthew took the ball up-court like a shivering shot. That is, he lingered several seconds alone on his defensive half of the court, planning, assessing the opponent's setup; but once he crossed the division line he was a movie switched to fast motion, spurting, up to full speed, dodging, threading the "big boys" blocking the basket, disappearing into the melee, then suddenly fountaining out of the mob to finger-roll the ball over the rim and softly into the net.

He was what he had been: confident, a taker of terrible risks, a streaking confusion to his opponents.

And just as he went in with the skills of the Six Millions Dollars Man, so did he pass — though mostly with his right hand, and sometimes, to his failure, behind his back. He could dribble moving backward. He was a freshman. He made mistakes. But I thought he showed an exuberance that could fire a team, and a promise for his future years, would someone honor the talent and seek to direct it.

Surely, his manner of play caught the attentions of coaches (and other players). Murrain moved him from Junior Varsity to Varsity astonishingly early.

And then it was that Matthew's game suffered, it seemed to me; and I in the stands winced to watch the changes.

His sophomore and his junior years split him in two. I mean that when he played in our backyard or between the chain-netted hoops in the projects, he continued to dazzle onlookers. His risks paid off more often than they failed. He let his tongue hang out his mouth on particularly difficult moves. His vertical jump (such mighty pistons, his legs) continued to astonish me, and his speed while handling the ball stung my eyes.

But on Bosse's team, playing under Murrain's fiery stare, Matthew took longer and longer to cross midcourt, sometimes consuming seven, eight, nine — an eternity — of seconds. Then, once he *was* across, he'd pull up, dribbling to his left and his right, forcing the defense to come toward him, indeed, but also frowning, thrusting his lips forward in a funnel-like pucker; he showed signs of uncertainty: where would he pass the ball? — teammates yelling at him, yelling his name. For Bosse's Matthew had ceased taking risks. Not under the apoplectic Murrain, whose time-outs were times for screaming out his wrath. Once in a while he'd scream a player's name. And then my stomach imploded. Sympathetic, my suffering for my son. I think I was experiencing (hidden in the stands) what he was experiencing under spotlights both brilliant and red.

But he taught himself. I watched it and I knew.

In those days we had a VCR attached to our TV set. Matthew, still lying on the carpet in front of the set, would tape the Bulls, their every game.

Then he would return to the TV and replay a tape over and over again. Often he would reach up and stop the action in order to repeat a single move of Jordan's. His repetition of a remarkable shot might, for example, last twenty minutes: again, again, again. And while he watched the shot, I watched him — and saw that his muscles were active, twitching, tightening, loosening. What — ? Ahhh! I realized that he was actually performing that same move in his imagination, inviting his corpus into the action, flexing every part of him which would participate under lights, in the spacious air of an auditorium. Matthew was transferring Jordan's moves into his body, muscle, bone, mind and frame, so that ligament and tissue held the memory and not his brain alone.

That manner of practice bore the beautiful fruit I saw in the street. Sometimes, I confess, I recognized and delighted in such fruit on Bosse's courts; and then my heart leaped up; but at the same time my heart began to shake — for I understood what sort of bravery it took on Matthew's part to dart through that Murrain-bloody waterfall:

But of the tree of the knowledge of good and evil, thou shalt not eat of it; for in the day that thou eatest thereof, thou shalt surely die.

———

January 1989. Five or six of Bosse's basketball crew are with Matthew at our house. They've eaten a supper of frozen pizzas, and now they are in the basement. Matthew is cutting their hair in preparation for the game, which is to be played a longish bus-ride east and south of Evansville. Heritage Hills High School will be the home team. Bosse has made it a habit to look their best when sallying forth to best another team — and this team especially, since the county, the school and the fans who would fill the stands of the gymnasium have shown signs of racism. They bring images of watermelons to the game, slices of wooden and painted watermelon, knitted watermelon, porcelain watermelon. "Hungry?" they cried, jumping up from their benches.

Too, they brought hubcaps, the actual things, as a sign of Bosse's offtime hobby.

There is one white player regularly sent in for Bosse. That's all. The rest are African American. No one has to explain the signs to them. Not these, at least. But one would come to shut every African mouth and to suck the spit right out of them.

When Matthew and his friends troop up from the basement, I am able to see what Matthew's electric clippers has drawn in tight hair on the tip-top of his teammate's skulls:

Their names. Their nick-names. A cheerful challenge or two for Heritage Hills. Each player laughs at the other players. The joke is for them and on them.

They leave in a dying rouge twilight. The weather isn't snowy or rainy. It's humid, causing a chill that cuts right through the team's coats and clothing.

At the high school they board a yellow school bus of the Evansville School Corp. and strike toward the east. Matthew sits by a window on the left-hand side. Men's basso voices call out. They mock each other. They play a game which was brought from Africa by their ancestors, but they think it is their own game, as fresh as they are, played among black males in their private places.

Yo' mama held her nose and SNEEZED you out!

Yech yech yech yech.

Yeah, an' you? You jus' a fart gone hard!

Yech yech yech yech.

The game is one of insult. The best players are often skinny fellows or fat fellows, those who lack skills for sports, but whose mouths are a mile of blinding racetrack. They talk so fast, in metaphors so shocking and marvelous, that even strong men get intimidated. This is the pragmatic, nearly physical power of street poetry. The game has been called "Playin' the Dozens" or, an older name, "Signifyin'." That latter name goes as far back as slavery—but the practice has come forward in Rap and Hip-Hop; hence the license for a fast, dazzling derision in that art.

Matthew's friends, the ball players in the bus, call it "Scobbing." They are, you see, poets whose poetry is necessarily protective, more immediately useful than "Whose woods these are I think I know."

And if this version of the game can be traced back to Africa, it falls within the broader category of taunting, taunt-songs. These, too, were practical and protective, for this is what one ancient army would cry out to its ancient enemy army sometimes for a full morning before they engaged in battle. "Trash-talking" everywhere around the world! It has always been meant to reduce the confidence and stamina of a foe; the better the talker, the likelier the triumph.

But what is tossed back and forth in the school bus is not the sort of taunting this team intends to give its present foe, Heritage Hills' basketball squad.

No, Bosse will *show* their arrogance, their grit, pride, confidence.

For when they come out of the locker room, they will burst onto the court running, dribbling top speed, then race circles around the entire court, leaping for the hoops, leaping like antelopes without hesitation to slam-dunk ball after ball after ball: this at both ends of the court!

"It's how we take their space away from them," Matthew told me. "Make it our own."

The night is completely black. Clouds conceal the moon and stars. Farmland yields no light. The riders scarcely notice.

The driver slows the bus and begins to turn into the parking lot for Heritage Hills. There are high-standing lamp poles here; but they are all across a line of railroad tracks. By law, the bus driver must bring his vehicle to a complete stop before he finishes the turn. He does.

Matthew is casually looking out his window into the night. He thinks he sees motion directly below that window when the bus hisses its brakes slower and slower, stopping.

Suddenly a match-fire flares near the front tires.

Almost immediately the flare washes upward, swirling round a high post, sending Matthew's head back from the window. The bus is dead silent. The fire drives out left and right of the post, even as it tops the post, and Matthew recognizes the figure it makes. The driver makes his stop as short as he possibly can, then bumps the long bus over the railroad tracks.

It's a cross!

Why would someone set fire to a cross of Jesus?

A cross. Matthew's mouth goes flannel-dry. He can't swallow. By shootings in his stomach he knows that this is wicked. There is hatred here. And if this hatred laughs, it is not in joy, but in a malicious fascination with human pain, or in the satisfaction of a grinding hatred expressed.

They do not burst onto the court at Heritage Hills.

For the fans are in the stands. They hold up hubcaps. Slices of red, seeded, green-rind watermelons.

All in fun. Good, clean fun.

But Matthew, keeping his head lowered, even his eyelids adroop, sneaks glances up at the jubilant stands and wonders: *Who burned the cross of Jesus?*

He is subdued, as are the rest of Bosse's team.

Not Murrain. He screams them into the game. Right now his screaming feels not harsh and hurting, but good. A friend here. Yes, and a white friend.

Truth to tell, it is a desultory first half. Heritage Hills has not run away with the game. Even listless, Bosse is the better team. But its game is like a barrel rolling downhill, lolling, gathering some speed over the tussocks.

At halftime, Bosse sits on benches in the locker-room, knees spread apart, forearms fallen on their thighs and hands like dishrags hanging between. Their heads are down. Once in a while someone lifts a spade-wide hand and rubs the back on his neck. No one moves.

Except Coach Murrain. He's screaming. He tries mightily to shame them for playing a girls' game. Perhaps it *is* true that kindness was cut from the coach to *make* him a coach, that he lacks the attitude altogether, doesn't even know its language. For there seems in him to be no other method for igniting his players than to blame them, to scold them, to punish and to curse.

He may, during the half, offer stratagems devised to discomfit Heritage Hills, this present opponent according to their present style of play. But it's a fine question, whether the team pays him any heed or whether, *as* a team about to implement some new strategy on the court, they remember anything Murrain is saying.

What sticks brightest and hottest in their memories is this: short Murrain, leg-pumping back and forth, gesticulating, growing redder than the electric EXIT light. This pop-corning coach demeans his team when they are already so downcast, that his efforts to kindle their spirits is not different from kindling a second cross right here in the locker room, a flaming embrace before their bowed, clipper-lettered skulls. The shine is off their barber's humor.

The few Bosse fans who've driven here to encourage their sons and brothers and friends (the Copeland family among them) can hardly find voice enough to cheer the team which now returns to start the third period. Their heroes are walking. Their postures show them ashamed and afraid. They seem defeated already now, with a full half left to play.

Imagine how desperately the cheerleaders try to break the gloom, to revive and ennoble the men they support.

Approximately six minutes into the third period, Matthew does something spontaneous, thoughtless. Absolutely no one else is aware of the gesture, but Matthew notices its *consequence*. It's that consequence which alerts him to the gesture, and so he repeats it again and again, to marvelous effect.

His opposite on the Heritage Hills team floats upward to make a sweet, difficult three-point field goal. Matthew, over whom the player launched the successful shot, lowers his arms and trots past the other. In passing he pats his opponent's butt.

"Excellent," he says.

And the other player turns with a happy grin: "Hey, thanks."

That response—the grin and the thanks—sends a homely sense of camaraderie through Matthew's stomach. No, this fellow did not burn a cross this evening. In fact, how could *any* member of their basketball squad have burned the cross? They couldn't.

Matthew begins to pat bunches of butts, smiling, praising. Whether the other players become aware of his behavior, we don't know; nevertheless, it spreads. Bonhomie spreads. Friendship.

They are game-foes, indeed. But every player on the court obeys a single set of rules. This separates them *as a group, both teams together*, from everyone else in the gymnasium. Soon their attentions are all on the game. They begin to play hard together. Matthew grows more and more oblivious to the hatreds, the bull-baiting colors, the malice that surrounds them.

So, it seems, do the rest of his comrades, whichever school they attended in daylight.

A model, if you please. An icon of obedient behavior and *still* competitive passions requiring the utmost of either team. These rules are good rules. There can be no true victory without them. Here, O ye, the general populations! Here is a way to live, to strive, and all the while to exhibit a fine and moral spirit!

By the end of the game, Bosse has taken the lead and still is holding it. I would like to describe here a final finger-roll performed by my son, the ball balancing for one sarcastic moment on the rim of the hoop, till, slowly, it slips inside and through—*Hooray!* But that's imagination. I can't know what hand my son had in goals achieved.

While the teams form two lines and, like a slide rule, pass each other, slapping congratulations, this is commonly admitted: it's Bosse's statistical victory. And some people know that they are two groups of teenagers, black and white, who share the triumph of righteousness. It would be enough.

But here comes proof of the tensile strength of their virtue:

A white fan high in the stands has switched on a brazen bullhorn voice. Everyone looks up. He's overweight, sits as if he were a rotting apple collapsed and bottom-squashed on the bench, and he is not joking. He thunders down upon Bosse's team terms of bitter, racial insult.

Hearing this, seeing this, Coach Murrain, that furnace of a red-hot steel, explodes. His arms flapping beside him like flippers, he begins to charge up the emptying stands, screaming his own flaming oaths against the Heritage fan, who does not cease, but rises to the encounter. Warriors.

Without a word of discussion, both basketball teams are also racing up the stands, each with the same expressions on their faces. Bosse's "big men"—who usually play beneath the basket—form the head of a serpent ascending. They reach Murrain first. They grab him, his arms;

they pluck at his clothing. Their earnest pleadings slow the combustible coach. Their pleadings and one other thing.

Players for Heritage Hills—likewise rising in a snakelike line—have also reached their basso man, their bloody, abusive, Jabba fan. They too have taken hold, have seated him *THUMP!* into a fightless position, and have stalled a stupid brawl.

———

In the days that followed that ballgame, the sheriff of the county in which Heritage Hills High School advanced the education of its students pronounced the cross-burning to be nothing more than a harmless prank.

No, no, of course not. Though he knew the names of the three men who had pulled the prank, he was not going to press charges. Why should he? No one was hurt.

But we in the inner city scheduled an extraordinary meeting for the leaders—ministers, teachers, social workers, activists, city officials—and for the people at large, anyone interested in finding justice for the incident and for our sons and daughters (who, it seemed to us, had very much been hurt).

It was held in the fellowship hall of a black congregation. The room was packed—almost altogether with African Americans, though several white people stood out. City officials. Reporters (who had turned the event into an Important Story).

Pastors and leaders were seated on a small stage up front, myself among them. I don't recall which lawyers might have been present and spoken. I do know that we received certain legal advice which lifted our spirits and made the meeting meaningful.

Once it was declared open, there followed a loud disburdening of grievance and sadness and accusation. African Americans are by nature orators of dramatic force.

Someone asked whether hate crimes were, what? Federal crimes? Crimes against the State of Indiana? Surely (in other words) that dim-bulbed county sheriff was not the only lawman with jurisdiction. We would apply to the state's attorney and see what he said.

"But what happened?" someone demanded. "I mean, what *exactly* happened that night? We can't go on rumors only."

"Well, who was there? Who can tell us point by point?"

Together with Thanne and his mother, Dirkk Surles and Matthew were seated at the back of the fellowship hall.

"What about them?"

"Yes. What *about* you? Come on forward and tell us the story."

———

And now the second moment of Matthew's shining accomplishment. The second and, for years and years thereafter, the last. Skillful, moral, a soberly public glory before he left us for the university—and a slow deleterious descent into sorrows.

It was in a genuine humility my son stepped forward and took a place onstage. Stage right, its extremist corner. He kept shifting from foot to foot, casting his eyes down before him. But he described the event. He talked. Oh, my sweet Lord, *how* he talked. The African American mothers and grandmothers in whose eyes he was representative of all their children, nodded and dabbed their eyes and loved him. Fans who followed sports in Evansville; men with histories of physical prowess, some of them satisfied with fatherhood, some of them living ever in a faded glory, talked with him, encouraging his talk.

"*Thank* you! *Thank* you!" a woman cried out, lifting a statement of his and setting it afire.

Eyes were riveted upon my son, who knew not his persuasion, and gallantry, his exaltation: he was a knight for and of the people. He had the language and the courage. He did not mention his role in the turnaround. He seemed more sad than boastful. But the young man spoke well and clearly. He talked.

While I sat on the same stage, speechless with pride.

13
Of Revelations

Here is my servant, whom I uphold,
    my chosen in whom I delight.
I will put my Spirit upon him.
He will bring justice to the nations.
He will neither shout nor cry out
    nor make his voice brazen in the streets.
A bended reed he will not break,
    nor a smoldering wick put out.
He will not falter!
    He will not be discouraged....

Here, then, let me offer a handful of cautions to parents regarding their children:

———

What, I find myself now wondering, has ever been our ennobling act under the gaze of the heavenly Father? "Our," I say, referring to us as the whole human race; or, more compactly, "us" as a people chosen by God, a holy nation, a royal priesthood; or, finally, "us" as individuals, person, person, one and one and one. What, in other words, might *I* have accomplished in my lifetime to inspire in the recoiling heart of my Father/ Creator a quick twitch of pride?

I don't know.

Search as I might, I keep running up against my creatureliness.

Other things stump me too, of course. My unrighteousness seems to taint everything I put my hand to. And I am bred in guilt, was fed the gruel of guilt my childhood through. Guilt views even my best as riven with iniquity. Indeed: at the end of a day of perfect obedience, guilt will point to the smile of pride on my face and damn me as vainglorious. *Pride* coils beneath my pillow, the sin more subtle than the serpent in Eden.

But more than these several characteristics, it's my essential nature which blinds me to any pleasure the Lord might take in me, any pride he might feel for some act of mine. God is Creator. I am creature. We exist on planes categorically different one from the other. Without divine revelation, my ability to know my Creator is as unthinkable a thought as the thought that one of my fictional characters could rise up from the written page, see me, greet me (its author!) and shake my hand. I am not the blood son of the Heavenly Father! I may be his child by adoption; but I am not fashioned of his substance. I cannot of my own investigations pretend to experience what the heart of the Creator experiences on my behalf.

This observation leads me to the following suggestions regarding parenting.

———

I. Matthew is my son, too, by adoption.

But he is of my substance. We share the same plane of being. He is capable of knowing my heart, then, right?

If he does not know it now — or, more to the point, if he did not know how proud I was of him in January 1989, it is not the fault of cosmic reality. The fault is mine for not having told him. Or the fault is ours for having interrupted the communication granted unto families, or else for never having developed it in the first place.

As long as I do not tell him the blessings with which he blesses my soul, why, then I am the hidden Father refusing revelations, a deplorable God absconded. It is not enough to assume that Matthew knows my heart by the expressions on my face, or by a silence meant to be warm and tender, since a silence is a silence. For children especially need to be told. If we parents know that they won't obey except we tell them, then surely we must know that they mightn't trust our love or receive our praise — except we tell them!

We are not different in substance from our children; but we are different in age and education. Moreover, we've been appointed to lead them in all things, and "leading" begins by approaching them at their age, at their level, according to *their* manner of communication. As with the Heavenly Father, so with us: the burden of revelation is upon the parents.

That we, our children and ourselves, are of the same substance makes the communication infinitely easier than that with the Heavenly Father. It also makes new communications come to the child something like a buried memory: the kid had known it before, yes; but the affirmation establishes the news as true.

———

2. God the Father, whose being and whose right it is to remain unapproachable, unknowable, is better than that after all. He took Israel to himself. *Thus says the Lord: Israel is my first-born son, and I say to you, "Let my son go that he may serve me."* Then he revealed his power, his loyalty, his faithfulness by saving that son from the King of Egypt. Thereafter he revealed his tender mercy by returning again and again to covenant with an Israel returning so often to rebellion and treachery, chasing other gods.

This God, this Father, is a talking God!

"In many and various ways God spoke of old to our ancestors by the prophets; but in these last days he has spoken to us by a Son whom he appointed the heir of all things, through whom also he created the world." The Last and the First, you see. Omega and Alpha. This Son "reflects the glory of God and bears the very stamp of his nature, upholding the universe by his word of power."

Now, here *was* a son of the nature of the Father. Communication between the two of them was as intimate as between you and your laughter: "I'm happy!" and "I am satisfied."

And having a son, which he sent into the world to call the world back unto himself, this Father could and did communicate his pride in that child!

For Jesus was a black man scorned by a gymnasium full of fan/atics filled with hatred for him particularly, Christ, despised in his entirety! Jesus, his humanity ruined by their bogus accusations: "Thief! Crackhead! Gang-banger! We *know* you! Yes, and we know as a fact that you rape our sisters! And if we could beat the crime out of you, well, but you would go on dreaming it all the time!"

And, in fact, they *did* beat more than the crime out of Christ. There being no crime in him in the first place, they beat his lights out; they beat the life out of him; they beat him from breath to death.

But on the way the Heavenly Father uttered his pride for his son so majestically, that even the adopted children could hear it:

At his baptism: *This is my beloved Son with whom I am well pleased!* At his transfiguration, before three witnesses: *This is my Son, my Beloved, with whom I am well pleased. Listen to him!* And then again, six days before his crucifixion and death, when his heart was troubled by the terrible events immediately to come, Jesus asked, "What shall I say? 'Father, save me from this hour?' No! For this very purpose have I come to this hour. Father? Glorify thy name!"

Then a voice came from heaven, "I have glorified it, and I will glorify it again."

To which Jesus said: "This voice has come for your sake, not for mine." The pride of the Father for his Son is bugled across the world, to and for all the other children of the Father.

---

3. And we are *by* that "only-begotten Son" drawn into the love and the embrace of God as our own Father. By the Son we are ourselves made children of God: because "to all who received him [the Living Word, Jesus], who believed in his name, he gave power to become the children of God." And these (we) were born not of the womb of a woman, nor of the seed of a man, nor of their parental desire for descendants, *but of God*.

Therefore, I must now repair the first assertion of this chapter, that I cannot by my own understanding know the Father's heart, cannot perceive whether he has taken pride in some noble act of—well, of me or of others of his creatures.

In fact, he has "highly exalted" this Son who emptied himself, who took the form of a servant, who was born in human likeness and who humbled himself to death, even to death on the cross. Highly exalted? Why, God has "bestowed on him the name which is above every name, that at the name of Jesus every knee should bow, in heaven and on earth and under the earth, and every tongue confess that Jesus Christ is Lord, to the glory of God the Father."

If I seek a sign for the pride of the Father for some act of *human* nobility, I will—O my Christ, I *can't*—find it in my Brother, Jesus. And here, in the end, is a way to take a pure and sinless pride in the act myself, by calling it "His," my Lord's, but at the same time by calling myself "His" as well. And all that is his, therefore, is mine. Mine is his deed.

---

4. And now, by a pretty circle, do I understand the true nobility of my son's behavior in a gymnasium rocking with hostility. I know, now, the source of my pride, an everlasting joy despite the ephemerality of this one event in my son's career. I have in hand—I have objectively—the mute,

subjective standard by which my heart had measured my boy: Matthew was acting like Jesus! My son was behaving like God's Son! There was a divinity in the thing which even I did not recognize.

Ah, the Father continues his revelations after all. Only now he, by means of his Son's story, he is revealing unto us ... ourselves.

———

5. Please know the hope which is given parents and children in this circle of truths. As Matthew can act the part of Jesus both in ignorance and in purity, even as he withdraws into a kingdom of iniquities and loneliness, so will the Spirit of Jesus accompany him wherever he goes, however deep he may descend.

For no one has ever descended lower than our Savior on the cross.

14
1988 — 1989

And the king was much moved.
He went up to the chamber over the gate,
and wept.

I.

Once in the fall of 1987, while Thanne and I were discussing our family's finances (how would we, come the summer of 1988, cover Joseph's college expenses?) Matthew granted himself a giddy moment of boasting.

"Not for me," he said. "No one'll have to pay tuition for me. I'm the only one in the family who's gonna pay his own way. All four years. I'm getting an athletic scholarship. Ha!"

He wasn't exaggerating. He believed it completely.

I suffered the statement because it seemed to me that my son was falling for the grand, Satanic lie too many children believe, from which they must fall from disappointment into despair: *You can be anything you want to be! Do anything you want to do.*

This is the lie of the devil who promises limitlessness: *You will not die. For God knows that when you eat of it … you will be like God!* "Unlimited," daughter-child. "Infinite," proud son!

Among the most limited of people, the poor, the lie varies somewhat. It becomes the young man's conviction that his ticket out and into the sunshine of fame and fortune is his athletic ability. He dreams of the NBA. Against even obvious odds, he makes it his goal to play in the NFL. Unrealistic to the average kid. And damnable especially when they refuse to study, closing down *all* options except this one, the dragon's deceit: *You will be like God.*

"I'm getting an athletic scholarship. Watch me!" He lived already in the glow of the stadium, a truer, more visible reality than the classrooms at Bosse High School. "And not to just any old college. I'm goin' where Michael Jordan went!"

I'm terrified. I've watched the trajectory of that boast too often, with the same cruel consequence.

O Lord Jesus, save him from the land of Egypt and slavery and the domination of his own spirit!

II.

In the first term of his last year in high school, Matthew's mother gave that child to me. Thanne was at her wits' end. He became my sole responsibility.

For he never, never met his curfew. He came home at midnight—or later—every (every) night. When he was at home, the young man was a cipher among us, refusing to communicate, responding to our questions with a grunt or a shrug, disdaining his family when we ate supper together. I remembered how he used to delight in cleaning, measuring success by the simple straightness of his bedroom, by the shine on his floor and the perfect tuck of his bedclothes. In these latter years, however, he had come to disobey almost all our requests, hating to walk the dog (it embarrassed him so to be seen in public), begrudging the garbage.

He appreciated style. Style he would work at assiduously, ironing his own clothes, cutting his own hair, developing his own walk.

Matthew's obedience tended to honor the convictions of his friends. He took seriously the inner city's derision of good grades and the scorn it heaped upon those black students who made genuine efforts at academic success ("Playin' White").

Nor did certain faculty at Bosse help matters; for when he began to earn *C's* as a sophomore and a junior, his mother asked to meet the teachers who had assigned such letter grades to him.

The teachers said, "Don't worry, Mrs. Wangerin. He's performing quite well." Meaning: *up to his capacity.*

But Thanne knew (and Thanne declared) that Matthew was the brightest child in our family. His reading capacity, when he was in his first grades, had leaped to chapter books and beyond. Altogether on his own and by his own motivation, he had been reading Madeleine L'Engle when he was in the second and third grades!

"Our first son, Joseph, was your student last year. In your classes he earned *A's*; he earned straight *A's.* But Matthew is quicker, sharper, smarter than Joseph."

"Mrs. Wangerin, you're being overly concerned. Joseph is an excellent student. Matt's a good boy. He's doing good work."

Here is an observation already then published and statistically supported by sociologists; it reveals unconscious teacher-biases regarding gender and race. When many a Mrs. Magistra asks her class a question, she allows varying periods of time during which she allows her pupils to consider before (1) they actually answer the question correctly or (2) she moves on to another student. Note the variations, for the longer the time period the more she trusts a particular pupil to think through to the right answer. In grade school especially, but in high school still, Mrs. Magistra grants the longest period of wait-time to white girls. Somewhat more than *half* that time is what she offers to white boys and black girls. She scarcely waits for the black boy, especially once he's learned to screw up his eyes in a manner that says, *I'm thinking, but I don't really know.* It doesn't take black boys long to get the message. Their teachers' unexamined attitudes do shape the boys. How much easier it is to make a face and get off the hook, than truly to try. (Note: the one major shift which occurs in these attitudes is gender, not racial: near the end of high school, boys are expected to be smarter in the sciences and in mathematics, though since feminist victories, that shift is less and less observable.)

More and more Matthew took his self-image from his friends, from who they were as much as from what they said. They did not boss him. They represented freedom. Although they could rip on him in jokes or in jealousies, they granted Matthew an essentially positive sense of himself. Plus, they, too, were troubled by the household rules imposed by parents upon their righteous, more natural desires.

Even when he was grounded, when he seemed asleep at reasonable hours, our seventeen-year-old son was devising ways to sunder himself from us, our vision and our directions. He elaborated deception. For once the house sank into a sleeping quietude, Matthew was sneaking out his window, jumping to the ground, running the streets with his buddies throughout the night.

But people shot people at night.

And drugs peppered the air, needles scarring the arms of the best of our youth.

And dope put forth its distinctive dry-grass fumes.

As a senior, Matthew's grades were dropping at rates even more precipitous than before.

How did we know of his nightly desertions?

Well, early one morning, still in the grey of the first dawn, Mrs. Copeland's oldest son came knocking on our front door: "Is Jerry here?"

"No. Why?"

"Well, Jerry 'n' them went out last night an' never came back."

"Why do you ask us?"

"Milk [read: *Matt*]—he was with them. Thought they mighta slept over here."

How did we know?

In those days Thanne and I kept friendship with six or seven other parents, meeting regularly to discuss our children, our church, our music together. Any issue might come up. The things that most distressed us we could share with the others, discuss the matter freely, receive advice, laugh until the tears streamed down our cheeks. Most of the group were African American, which always consoled us by their comments concerning our black children: no, we were infinitely more alike than not. That parents and children might be black or white was of little consequence beside the fact that they were … parents and children.

One night the meeting took place in the living room of our house, 831 E. Chandler. There were windows in two walls of the room, several in front looked out into the front porch, and several narrower windows were on the side just opposite our fireplace. Below these three windows stood the sofa in which Matthew once had sat while I tried to make his flaming comic books resemble the fires of hell.

While the evening chattered brightly forward, we heard a loud *BUMP!* on the wall outside the house, just above the sofa.

In perfect unity, we turned to look—then burst into screams of laughter, laughing helplessly, wordlessly, until our sides ached. For leaning against that outside wall, visible through the windows, was Matthew's foresight, his plan for escape: a ladder, lit brightly by the lamps inside the living room. That night his deception was disclosed, and we parents howled with a gallows laughter. Matthew had a kink in his plan. He'd have to refine it.

And he did.

So, then: how did we know that these nighttime jail-breaks did not cease but continued in fashions of greater potential disasters?

Again, it was during that same senior high school year. I was hunched over the desk in my study, working. *Mmm-bmm, bmm.* Noises from above. I thought I heard a distant grumbling outside. On our roof? Not at all sure whether it was park-sounds or traffic-sounds, branch-sounds or the sighings of trees in a windy autumn night, I got up, put on a windbreaker, and wandered out into the backyard. At first I saw nothing untoward. But then I rounded the house and could see the roof of the front porch and suddenly spied an adult form there, *up* there: fixed; in silhouette; completely still. Adrenaline inflamed my nerves. I peered and peered trying to convince myself that the shadow was indeed human. What was happening, then? Well, breaking and entering, right? A B&E … in process!

I opened my mouth and, without a thought, uttered the stupidest line a tough guy could say in such a situation.

I said (I asked), "Can I help you?" — as if we were in a grocery store, and I the smiling stock-boy.

The figure moved. The slightest of gestures, but it was enough to show me the body of my son. Doubly infuriated — for his transgression, for my humiliation — I commanded him into his room: "Get inside, you [*Bliksit!*] — I'm coming up!"

I *raced* up. I snapped the lights on, bright enough to water the eyes. Matthew was just climbing into the bedroom through its dormer window. Joseph was awake, sitting in bed, watching, his eyes and cheekbones smeared with guilt. Matthew's bed was stuffed with pillows, a mockery, seeming to contain the body of a teenager, which teenager was now staring at me: *Caught!*

"Where were you?"

"Umm. Nowhere."

"Matthew! *Nowhere?*"

"Well, just going out."

In fact, as I learned, he was just coming in. He had *been* out.

What could I do? Grounding had lost all effect. Scolding was merely endured:

Matthew, what do you want?

-149-

I want to be free! I want my freedom!

What could I do?

Last year I thought I'd hit upon the most wonderful sort of disciplinary restraint. So elegant was it in all its parts that I actually beamed as I explained it to Matthew. It tickled me so much, I chuckled.

"For every night you miss your curfew," I said, "I will add a week to the day I let you get your drivers license. See? I'll delay your driving a week, another whole week. I won't have to get mad. I won't have to yell at you. I'll just write down this little note: 'Add a week.' " So cool was that comment, I chuckled. "And if you're late so many days that the weeks add up to months and the months to years, well, you'll have to come of age first! You'll be an adult in your own right before you're able to drive." Hee-hee.

Whether he actually came home at, or before, his curfew after that, I don't remember. If there was even a single evening when he obeyed our agreed-upon hour, I can't recall. Which causes me to believe that he never did. And to know that neither did this particular discipline work. Not once.

My son in jail. My son rejected, on the streets. My son! My son's self-centeredness justifying every cop's racist assessment of his value!

Already nervous officers had been forcing Matthew and his midnight friends out of their vehicles, official hands on the butts of their service revolvers, young African American hands on the roofs of the cop car. Matthew had already learned that blank-faced absence in the presence of the power of the enemy. *Don't contradict. Don't plead your case. Don't talk. Don't do anything, not anything at all, for it might be read as insubordination!*

And I had visited too many young black men held over in the county jail under false or silly charges, just because the cops (who did *not*, they swore, profile) didn't like a snotty attitude.

The world is a dangerous place.

No longer do we live on the river under flood—

By God, we are *in* it, borne along by the school system, the constabulary, the city administration, the general malaise of white racism, the godawful patronization of richer, whiter churches, the whopping lies of the inner-city streets, and dope and drugs and gambling and noise, and noise, *noises always*, boom boxes and shouting and (once or twice in daylight, more often in the darkness) the popping of .22 pistols, small arms, and glum stubbornness and arrests and remand-to-trial and sentencing and the *pride* of having served time!

What could I do to massage a necessary goodness into my son? In such goodness shall be his salvation—and I am not talking about heaven. I mean Egypt redivivus, and slavery, the loss of identity, the loss of principle possessions, the loss of purpose, the imposition of meaningless work, the abolition of one's present value together with one's hope for a future. Oh, my son! My son! If discipline doesn't work, what then? What shall I do? Drop discipline altogether? Grant you freedom? Allow you to do as you please?

But your pleasures have not redounded to your safety. Your pleasures have served and encouraged the more venal sides of yourself: this moment! this immediate desire! nothing mattering the "yet to come," nothing preparatory for a productive life. Your liberty wants license. Your license will lead you to licentiousness.

I do not despise you, O my darling child. I delight in you. It is not so much in your strength or in the legs of your vertical jump that I delight. I delight, rather, in your hope for the steadfast love of God, and your faith in my love, too.

I do not despise you, O my beautiful son. I hate restraining you—for once you ran so freely my own heart sailed the heavens with you. Once you sped around the paths of a tremendous snow pie, laughing like God's untamed nature. I hate restraining you as much as I hated the brace we put upon your feet in order to straighten them. You overcame that brace with joy. Can't you do the same this year, too?

I am wounded by his anger. I suffer everything *you* suffer. I am a black man. It is only by my love for you that I have come to recognize all the subconscious signs of racism, and the god-damnable power of it. I suffer with you our judgments and our disciplines.

But love simply *cannot* watch while the beloved systematically cripples himself. Love cannot *not* act.

What shall I do?

My son is my responsibility now. His mother has done most the work to raise him well, establishing the rules that truly did calm the child, curbing a wildness that scared even him. In the early years I was often gone, studying for long patches of time; thereafter I was ministering both day and night. She spent the love. She spent the imagination and the energy. Now, therefore, it is upon her that the greater crush of Matthew's repudiations have fallen.

Matthew is mine.

III.

Late autumn, near the end of the year of our Lord 1988, Thanne received a telephone call from one of Matthew's teachers, a woman of probity and watchful attentions.

"He's very late," she said. "At this point he was scheduled to have given me an outline for his term paper. Well, more than that, I should be reading portions of a first draft. Matthew hasn't handed these things in yet. Mrs. Wangerin, if he doesn't, he will fail my class."

Hers was an advanced English class. Matthew "hated" it, perhaps primarily because his mother had demanded he take it. She knew his capacities, and the value of improving his skills in literature, both his interpretive skills and his writing.

The teacher said, "This paper is meant to analyze a novel of his own choice."

Thanne said, "What has he already done for the paper?"

The teacher sighed. "Nothing. He hadn't even chosen a book until this morning."

Thanne was silent.

The teacher said, "Want to know how he chose the book?"

Thanne didn't say "No."

"He put the list flat on his desk. In sight of everyone he shut his eyes and stabbed the list with his forefinger. When he opened his eyes, he read the title his finger had hit: *The Invisible Man.*"

At which Thanne burst into laughter. So did the teacher.

Thanne said, "The hand and the finger of God! It's the truest book he could have chosen. He's making himself as invisible as possible these days."

Yes. Truly: Ralph Ellison's novel (1952) was an inspired opportunity. It follows the journey of a young, bright, innocent black man from his Southern comin' up, northward into Harlem. But this journey is as much spiritual and social as it is geographic. In Harlem the narrator joins the movement of black radicals and of common folk against white oppression. As time passes, however, the (unnamed) protagonist is more and more ignored not only by the whites but also by his black confederates. In the end (which was the beginning of the novel, since the anonymous narrator has been telling the story of his own past from his final situation) the man (representative of a host of minorities in America) has become genuinely invisible. He lives below the surface of the city, using power and water from other people's sources, unknown by the IRS, the FBI, or any other information-gathering agencies. He just ... lives. And he makes the best of a fearful isolation, only; just; barely; living.

And as Matthew was mine, this is what, finally, I determined to do: I would help him with this paper. No, not enough. I would drive him toward the completion of this paper. More: I would make it my goal to ride the youth like a mule, doggedly, kicking him forward to a high school graduation with middling to higher grades! And after that — on account of that — I would see him into a good university.

These things. These alone. My job, my whole purpose with and for my son. And then he shall be free. I will grant him the freedom he desires, to do with as he pleases.

But in order to assure these goals, I was willing myself to sacrifice every good thing that might have come my way from the love of my son.

I said as much to that Better Father in Heaven: "If, in order to grant my son this educational stair-step toward his success; if, to insure it, I must give up his love for me — O my Lord and my God, I will give it up forever."

I loved my son. That I could never give up, not ever. But I loved, too, the love of my son. I didn't ask honor or admiration. Just to be loved by him and therewith to experience now and again some expression of that love.

But I fully expected Matthew to hate me both then and thereafter. Oh, I set my teeth in order to prepare myself: he would, I knew, resent my "oppression"; for I would become, in effect, his jailer, the warden of his penitentiary, a constant bars-beating guard in his house of correction, his parole officer, all these officers in one.

In the face of his despising I would succeed. He would succeed. And then one of us would be free. As for the other: a love offered and unreceived is its own perpetual affliction. It is an amputation which never ceases bleeding.

So we went to work.

We read the book together. Actually, Matthew read it quickly, for he had the gift. We discussed it. I asked questions. I had taught at the University of Evansville from 1970 to 1974: I knew how to ask questions. Matthew would sometimes jump up from the chair in my study and run from the room. He would break for the out-of-doors, pulling up in the darkness of our backyard—sometimes weeping with frustration.

Then, in the dark, I would repeat the statutes as they presently existed: Study. Pass. Get good grades. Go to a good college. Then I will leave you to it—to yourself. Be mad at me. I am impervious. Be nasty. Hate me. I will accept your fierce wrath even until we both shall leave this earth. But Matthew: I will never not love you.

His teacher talked to us after she had read his completed term paper.

"I should give it an *A*. It is one of the best papers I've ever read. But because of his tardiness and his attitude, I can't give it better than a *B*."

There: *that's* the consequence of such behavior. A seeming injustice. An *A* paper gets reduced to a *B*. Evidence for my arguments. As far as he is concerned, equal evidence for his.

So went the rest of that year.

I did not coddle him.

His coach treated him even worse — and Murrain's approach was unjust indeed! Murrain refused to write him even the first letter of recommendation.

Matthew's hope for an athletic scholarship was dashed at university after university.

In fact, the University of South Dakota made an offer. But Matthew's opinions of that institution and of his own obvious prowess refused the offer. Surely, he could find better.

By the end, the best he could find was a non-scholarship offer from Florida Atlantic University. FAU in Boca Raton in Florida. The best their coach would do was to promise him the possibility of a scholarship by the end of the first season. Slim pickin's. To his chagrin, the only pickin's left.

He graduated. God kept his end of the bargain — and I began to serve mine. Matthew's grades and his SAT scores were good enough to get him accepted at any number of excellent institutions, and then he could surely have tried out as a walk-on. But the young man's mind was fixed. It would not be changed.

As soon as school was out and Matthew had his diploma, he began to lie around the house. Literally: lying on the carpet in the family room, dozing through the daylight.

Thanne said that he should get a job.

"Why?" he answered her. "It's my last summer for comfort. I won't get another. I plan to make the best of it."

Thanne said, "I've been reading about 'emancipation.' Do you know that we can 'emancipate' you?"

Matthew, blinking, asked, "What's 'emancipate' mean?"

Thanne: "We can release you from our parental power."

Matthew, considering with some spark of interest: "Welllll."

Thanne: "It's a legal thing. We announce in the newspapers, we get a writ, if we have to, that we are no longer responsible for our son. And then you are free."

"Well!"

"And so are we. So am I. No more I wash your clothes. No more I make lunches and suppers for you, don't even buy you food. No more give you a bed. A TV. A place at the table."

It was on that very same day in the summer of 1989 that Matthew went forth and got a job. To him and to all his friends, this was the basement of humility — to make a little money working under the golden arches. Mickey D's. But the food was free.

IV.

We drive him south, his mother and I.

We have a minivan now. It is filled with his possessions, anything he might need for college. He has been willing to discuss the finer items, his toilette, materials for study, with his mother. And she *is* an intelligent planner.

Matthew, in the seat behind ours, his basketball ever within his reach, mostly sleeps.

Somewhere near Atlanta we make an evening stop and stay at an inexpensive motel. It seems to us that Southern franchises are a little less kempt than their counterparts to the north.

In the morning, Matthew grooms himself with a mighty care. He comes out of the unaccommodating bathroom anointed, clean, a strutting male, splendid.

My heart has begun to break.

I am losing a son. I am diminished. One of my most important roles in life is perishing: to be a father. To have a child.

We drive south again during the day, conscious of an increasing heat and sunny mirages on the highway ahead.

We arrive in Boca Raton mid-afternoon. Find the university. Go directly to the dormitory designated for certain athletes who, in fact, are arriving ahead of the general student population.

The campus but whispers. It seems to me a cement wilderness. There is a counselor in the dorm. He shows us to Matthew's room. Gives Matthew the key. Leaves us. We do not see him again.

We help Matthew move his stuff up to the room. He really doesn't want us to help him arrange it, however, or to make his bed. But it's a mother's prerogative. Thanne does it while Matthew stands mute, gazing away from either one of us. His hair is cut very short. There is a small naked patch on the back of his crown, where surgery once removed the skin; the new skin lacked the properties for growing hair. Matthew thrusts out his lips in round contemplation. His winged eyebrows converge. But he doesn't say what he is thinking.

When we are done, we walk the echoing hall of the empty dorm. Outside our red van sits alone in a vast, concrete parking lot. Thanne and I hug Matthew. He hugs us with one arm. In the other arm, caught between his wrist and his hip, is his basketball.

Goodbye. Goodbye.

We begin to drive away. Slowly.

I look back. Matthew stands completely alone in this institutional wilderness. He and his basketball. I can't tell whether he is looking at us too.

I start to cry.

O my son Absalom, my son, my son Absalom. Would to God I had died for thee, O Absalom, my son, my son.

PART 3

15
1989 — 1991

When a people falls, don't they get up again?
If they go astray, don't they turn around?
Why then has this people fled from me
*   in a perpetual backsliding?*
They have held fast to deceit.
They have refused
*   to return.*

I.

I dreamed once that my son and I were walking on an endless lawn beneath a sky of a single hue, a solid blue. No clouds. A forbidding, impenetrable blue. And the lawn speechlessly green, reaching unobstructed to the round horizon. No trees. Not a stone. Neither rising nor falling to the pitch of the land. All on a level plane. Inhuman. It was a mown grass, soft beneath our feet, but laid like green latex ahead of us. Everything seemed a summer's day, temperate, windless, pleasant upon our faces, our feet, our motion.

It was a setting so impossibly perfect, I felt uneasy.

We were holding hands, Matthew and I. But he kept forcing his thumb between our two palms: a mild—no, a cheerful—effort to break free. Matthew was a child. Maybe four, maybe five years old, wide-eyed, voracious. I dreamed this dream while we still lived on Heerdink and two acres of land.

I held his little hand as tightly as I could, and fearfully, though I had no object for my fear.

Neither one of us spoke. Matthew's *action* shouted, causing the blue dome above us to vibrate sympathetically. He dragged at me. He pulled forward—though I could see nothing at all to draw him anywhere.

And then I noticed he was sweating. Perhaps his sweat was lubricant enough. Suddenly the child slipped my hold and dashed with a wild abandon ahead. He ran laughing, tossing his head the way a horse will whinny and stamp for the sheer physical pleasure of galloping.

Matthew! I cried, I think I cried. My throat had thickened as from too much crying. I was in a panic: *Matthew! Come back!*

The child had pink heels. When he ran, he kicked his heels as high as his waist. In my dream I saw those mother-of-pearl shells flash and fly away from me—while I could but move lumbering forward.

All at once he disappeared.

The green lawn and the blue sky closed together as neatly as a lid and its pot. There was nothing between them, neither a building nor my boy.

Matthew!

I shifted my heavy legs and ran as through water until I came to the place where my son had disappeared. Even before I had gotten there, I knew what I would find.

Here was a hole in the ground. Bottomless, black as a stovepipe, and wide enough to peer down into. To fall down into. My son had fallen down this hole.

Whether my dreaming self actually *saw* his body diminishing, falling still, or whether I merely knew it, I can't say. But now comes the most terrible part of the nightmare. I stood at the edge of that hole, fixed by a dilemma: should I run back for help? There was so little time! And he was growing smaller in the darkness. Or should I —

You see what a powerful effect this dream has had on me. At the age of sixty-three, I remember it still, in bright color and detail (though I must have dreamed it during my early thirties); and to tell it over again, as I do here, is to do more than remember my dread: it is to experience that dread, immediate, again.

Just at waking, when the dream still lingers in my mind, it seems that I'd chosen the second course of action. I did not run back for help, but jumped into the hole after my son. We both were falling, gasping, stomachs twisted by the precipitous drop.

And there the dream ends. In motion. But Matthew is so far ahead of me, each of us falls alone.

———

For my son, a passage from Wordsworth's Immortality Ode:

> *Thou little Child, yet glorious in the might*
> *Of heaven-born freedom on thy being's height,*
> *Why with such earnest pains dost thou provoke*
> *The years to bring the inevitable yoke,*
> *Thus blindly with thy blessedness at strife?*
> *Full soon thy Soul shall have her earthly freight,*
> *And custom lie upon thee with a weight,*
> *Heavy as frost, and deep almost as life! (ll. 125 – 32)*

II.

As far as I knew, Matthew's freshman year at FAU proceeded smoothly, not unlike the general adventures of most freshmen everywhere. He and his mother spoke on the telephone, though Thanne initiated most of the calls.

He came home at Christmastime with a set of first-term grades only slightly lower than they might have been. Chalk it up to adjustment, assignments and scholarship being different from what they were in high school. Professors leave you to your own devices and disciplines.

Matt spoke mostly of basketball. He was mildly concerned about Coach Loomery, who hadn't yet recognized Matthew's attributes, and upon whose good opinion rested Matthew's chances for an athletic scholarship at the end of the school year.

Joseph was in his second year at Valparaiso University (the institution where I myself have been teaching since 1991). Joe felt somewhat isolated, since the university was mostly white and middle class. His classmates would enjoy the stories he told about our neighborhood, his African American youth and childhood; but that was because Joseph is an excellent storyteller. They didn't actually *believe* him, that his tales were historically accurate. Unable to make himself understood, this milk-white undergraduate suffered the same unrecognized lonesomeness as the black student who is patronized by a "liberal" society.

Mary, in her junior year of high school, was enjoying herself tremendously. "Born to be a teenager!" she sang spontaneously. She dated. She was, sometimes, bruised. I stood near the doorway, once, while she received a phone call announcing her boyfriend's break-up. Hidden to her, but present nonetheless, I knew by her subdued tones that something was amiss. When she hung up, I went into the telephone room and took her into my arms. Her sorrows did not last overlong. Within weeks, the love for a boy forgotten, her love for the telephone flourished: before the second ring, however deeply the girl had been sleeping, she'd come floating from her bedroom, her pupils tiny dots, her hair mussed, singing sweetly, "I'llllll get it."

Talitha, a sophomore, was bound and determined to attempt every opportunity high school offered: volleyball, student clubs, languages. She began to learn Spanish. The child had, almost of her own accord, developed a need for order and strict discipline in her life. She kept her side of the bedroom neat, intelligently arranged — and looked with a wicked scorn upon Mary's perpetual mess. She slept according to an exacting schedule — and rose up in fury if she were awakened too soon. And she who had spent the first years of her life so passive as to seem damaged, now, by sheer force of will, began to achieve praiseworthy grades.

On Christmas Eve, this family exchanged presents with a pretty joy. All was well. All manner of thing was well.

———

At the end of that freshman year, Matthew came home under the shadow of a cruel gloom. Coach Loomery had not offered him the athletic scholarship after all. He had implied that there was still the chance that Matthew might "earn" it.

Matthew fed on such chances. Over time, by repetitive talking, he could give his possibilities a grounding and a structure. But the more they failed him, the denser the gloom surrounding him. Loomery's early promises having been betrayed, these latter blandishments seemed a calculated cruelty.

———

On the twenty-fourth of July, 1990, Thanne, the girls, and I left Evansville and spent nearly two weeks on the road, touring with some twenty members of the Sounds of Grace, our church's choir. Joseph and Matthew stayed at home. A rough idea of the extent of our travels: Philadelphia; Cambridge; Montreal; Ottawa; Toronto; Detroit; Columbus, Ohio.

On Monday the sixth of August we returned home .

At some point Thanne entered her tiny office on the second floor of our house and noticed the message light, flashing on her telephone. She punched "Play," and heard the voice of the Evansville City Police Department:

We have impounded your car. This was a boat of a vehicle, purchased second hand so that we might have two cars, the older of which our children used. A mighty old Buick LeSabre, massive and called "The Grey Ghost."

The telephone message continued: *But then we ran the trace and found that the registration is in your name. We have decided to release it to you. You can come to—*

Why "impounded"? Where had it been? Parked in a no-parking zone?

We retrieved the Buick, the car alone, no information.

I tried to play my stereo system and discovered that one whole set of speakers had been blown out. Literally. When I removed the front screen, small bits of grey paper fluttered out.

Within several days of our return, Mrs. Copeland talked with Thanne. She too had received a telephone call the weekend before our return, also from the police station, but not from an officer. And so it was that we pieced together the mystery.

Matthew, riding with one of his more felonious friends, had been caught stealing hubcaps.

The friend had escaped. Matthew, too, tried to dash into the midnight darkness, but this was a K−9 unit. Dogs. The officers let loose a mighty beast, which in a flash was upon our son, knocking him down, fixing its teeth in Matthew's thigh.

He was apprehended, placed under arrest.

He was also wounded. So they transported him first to the hospital where the deep punctures in his flesh were cleaned and dressed. Then he was borne downtown for booking and imprisonment.

At his first chance, he telephoned Jerry's mother, Mrs. Copeland.

Could she please—would she come downtown to bail him out?

"No. You deserve what you're getting."

Good old Mrs. Copeland! Matthew had more mothers at our church and in our neighborhood than he could stand.

"Matthew," we asked him, armed with indisputable information, "why did you do it? Why steal hubcaps?"

Hubcaps, jumping into the pit of scorn which racists had dug for every young black man! *Hubcaps!* Giving them proofs for their idiot opinions!

We said, "What sort of money did you think you could get, selling them?"

"Wasn't going to sell them."

"Well, *you* don't need them. Why, Matthew? Why did you take them?"

"Because ... I wanted them."

His answer. His only answer, sufficient for himself—a sorry revelation for his parents. The mere wanting was enough. It justified thievery. It drove him to take terrible risks, or perhaps it blinded him to the risks.

*When a people falls, don't they get up again? If they go astray, don't they turn around? Why then has this people fled away in a **perpetual** backsliding? They have held fast to deceit. They have refused to return.*

In time we received a bill from the hospital. Of course: who else would pay for the washing of the wounds of our nineteen-year-old son?

And Thanne felt it an ethical requirement that Matthew inform his coach of his record.

How often in those days, having scolded Matthew for missing another curfew; how often didn't I wake Thanne in order to moan my misery and weep for the guilt of howling at him and hurting him again? Even in the midst of my fatherhood, feeling my way forward, my faults came close to killing my spirit. I did him wrong. But I knew not what else I *should* do.

Likewise, in these wiser days Thanne would never demand that Matthew confess to Coach Loomery everything.

In those days, though, she did.

And in conjunction with such a difficult task, we thought it right to drive down to Boca Raton, there to visit our son and to meet this Loomery.

I disliked the man on sight. Perhaps I was predisposed to a quick disapproval. But when we stood in the doorway of his huge gymnasium, the man slapped my back as if he and I were of the same stripe, while Matthew was something else, a creature of a different category.

Loomery winked and poked fun at Matthew: "Yes, yes, a tiny Michael Jordan, we call him." To Matthew: "Gotta get that hallucination outa you, right? Right?"

Loomery was losing his whiff of hair; was only a little taller than Matthew, shorter than me; told me, buddy-buddy, that his background, too, was Lutheran, although he wasn't as church-going as he knew he ought to be.

No; he never swore in my presence. Neither did his language ascend past the blockish nouns of a *Hardy Boys* novel. My son, especially because he had bet all his merit and all his future upon basketball, was in this man's hands. Loomery, whether he knew it or not (though I believe this is precisely what he wanted to achieve) had the heart of my son in his hands. He could make him or break him.

And by all the evidence I could see, by his transparent patronizing of Matthew while that poor player had to stand by nodding and smiling as if the coach were a humorous fellow of wisdom and truth, Loomery was breaking Matthew even now, before my very eyes.

What could I do? When I told my son of my suspicions, he didn't argue with me. He may even have accepted what I had to say. On the other hand, he was convinced that my opinions were uninformed. If his father knew little of the game itself, how could the man know anything about its locker-room politics, or about the sweat lodge of a coach's office? And this was his ticket, after all. This was the only route Matthew could see for himself.

During his freshman year Thanne and I had met Leonard on the telephone. This was another ball player, a Jamaican with endless compassion, Matthew's friend. In certain respects, Matthew's guardian.

During his sophomore year it was sometimes Leonard who called us to ask how he might help Matthew. He was worried. He was at a loss.

And then he would put Matthew on the telephone. We heard our son bawling, sobbing so deeply he could scarcely form words.

"Matthew, Matthew, what's the matter?"

All his torments would spill out of him. He wasn't being played. He was beaten down by Loomery. He couldn't study. His grades were a disgrace.

He was (he did not say it) drunk.

We were loath then to call him on it. Since neither he nor Leonard touched upon the subject, or even the possibility, it seemed we would be spying once more on him, assuming the worst.

But he was drinking. And he was drunk.

———

The following summer brought home a different son. He had gotten a job from one of the members of our congregation, Herman Thomas Jr., who had begun his own business. Matthew became an assistant, a gopher, an all-around helper. They liked each other, these two men. Their relationship was mutually friendly.

As for Matthew himself, his physical and mental condition, he seemed reduced to something as thick and moist and slow as a slug. He came home late, after we had all gone to bed. In the morning he woke so grogged that he would but half dress, then lie down on a floor somewhere, any floor, no matter, and fall back into a stupefied sleep.

I recall trying to rouse him in order to get him to work on time. He was lying midway between the family room and the foyer—the spot I occupied while Mary suffered her telephone break-up. I took my son's arm. I shook him hard. He seemed oblivious of any sort of intrusion at all.

Drugs? Alcohol? I didn't know. Truly, I didn't. I assumed it. I accused him of it. He didn't answer. What it is, is: I didn't want to know. For how rocky the road then? What would he have to do then?

This was the summer of 1991. Mary had graduated from high school and would be attending Butler University in Indianapolis come August. She had looked at Valparaiso (to befriend her brother Joseph?) and one or two other places. But almost the moment she walked onto Butler's campus the twenty-seventh of June, with her customary cheer she had found her home for the next four years.

"Born to be in college!"

This was also the summer when Thanne and I were traveling north to Valparaiso ourselves. I had in 1990 received a communication from this university: "If you designed a fully-endowed chair here, at this institution, according to your interests and your talents, what would that chair look like?"

Oh! So far as I know even today, there is no finer academic offer than that. Design my own chair? The way I like it? I spent time writing to friends of mine who were writers-in-residence at other state universities. I talked to poets and playwrights, several the chairs of their creative writing departments, both undergraduate and graduate. I began to build a dream. And now we were at serious negotiations. I was flying.

Long before this summer was done, I had accepted. We would have to sell our wonderful house on Chandler Avenue. Thanne could not accompany me until the end of the fall term, because Talitha had that term alone to finish. In the spring she would study in Costa Rica. Thanne had to stay in Evansville with her. When we had driven her up to Valpo to view the city, our daughter had literally shivered: "Too *white!*" she had announced.

It was in mid-August when I moved some of my stuff north, into an office and a single bedroom, rented. The rest would have to come when Thanne and I moved all of our possessions to our new digs.

We put 831 Chandler on the market. It sold with surprising speed. We closed on the twenty-first of August, hooray! But suddenly Thanne and Talitha were scrambling: directing the movers to pack our stuff (books, furniture, linens, clothing, etc.) in two separate batches. One would have to wait in storage until our real move took place after Christmas; the other was to be delivered that week, across town to the apartment they had thunder-rushed to find and to lease for themselves. There they would spend the next five months of their lives.

There: on the fourth floor of a downtown apartment building, two bedrooms, a half kitchen whose counter opened into a dinette area. Claustrophobic. It lacked doorways direct to grass and fences and a liberated breath of fresh air. Cement caused leg splints. To find good earth beneath her feet and the scent of living blossoms abroad, Thanne had to extend herself: taking long flights of stairs down echoing wells, or taking the tight enclosure of an elevator poorly ventilated. Thanne has always loved to wander outside on a whim, to kneel in the soils of flowerbeds bordering the front of her house....

We were very busy when the three older children prepared to leave Evansville for their various institutions of higher learning. We made the greatest fuss over Mary, since this would be her first year apart. Joseph and I could drive together to Valparaiso when I went, but his packing presented an unusual problem: within days of our arrival north, I would drive him to O'Hare where he would board a plane and fly to Germany, Ruetlingen, where he was scheduled to study until Christmas. Personally, I was up to my elbows organizing and planning the classes I'd begin teaching, August the twenty-eighth.

More than the rest of us, Matthew had to make his own plans, travel his own way deep into Florida. He was entering his junior year, his head already bent beneath a heavy load. He'd ended the last term with wretched grades. He was returning with a probationary status.

Leonard would be near. O God, bless Leonard.

III.

It must have been late October or early November when Matthew appeared at the fourth-story apartment which Thanne and Talitha shared.

He was done.

Whether or not he'd made his intentions known to the authorities at FAU didn't matter much to him. You have to work to get into a place. He understood that. The place had something to give you for that work. But why should he have to work to get out of it?

He'd quit. He hated FAU and Florida too.

Thanne was pragmatic. "If you don't drop your classes officially, or if you don't arrange for incompletes to be finished later, they will all become *F's.* And leaving without a formal severance, well: one day you're going to want your transcripts, Matthew, as official records of your grades—as proofs of the number of college courses you've already completed—"

Matthew wouldn't talk about it.

Oh, he would not stop picking the scabs, compulsively repeating the stories of every one of the grievances he had suffered in his basketball career. It was a refrain of failure; but the tune was *Not My Fault.* It had been done to him. But the humiliation of coming back to Evansville like so many others which his friends had laughed at, what none of them would ever be; coming back to the city of his previous glory, of a strutting certitude and of his public boasting: this reduced the young man to soot, a dusty shadow prepared to be puffed to nothingness. My son's comforting countenance now was perpetually pinched, lips rounded and pushed forward *(Don't nobody talk to me!),* cheeks drawn, eyes small and red, his face ashen.

Regarding the deepest experiences at FAU, the telling ones; more to the point, regarding what final events caused him to abandon everything, his education, his nascent reputation, Matthew said nothing.

He was here. He was in despair. Ah, my Lord: despair silences even the mind.

Within two days he had fallen into old habits, sleeping on the carpet all day long in front of a mindlessly yakking television set. Expecting food, yet finding dinner with his mother and sister distasteful. Foraging the pantry and the refrigerator, cooking ramen noodles for himself. Frozen pizza. Gone like sunset, wandering the streets at night.

Thanne would stumble over his zonked body through the daytime. This intensified disappointment within her. She strove to make him aware of her schedule, fixed, unchangeable. Soon there'd come the day when she would take Talitha to the airport, and the youngest child would fly off to Costa Rica. And the day when the lease on this apartment would end. And then the day when all of the furniture, boxed, would be packed into a moving van and driven away, leaving the rooms hollow and echoing.

"No, Matthew. You can't stay after we've left the place. It's not your apartment. We haven't the money. You got to plan for the move; for your future. No school? Well, you'll need a job."

While I was visiting my handful of family over the Thanksgiving holiday, we watched a movie on the VCR: *The Silence of the Lambs.* Riveting, this horror. Human-sized, hence my permission to let it approach me — but at the same time sized to the universe: an unapologetic, unlimited empyrean of human malice. Hannibal Lector represents something worse than a social pathology. He is the image of a rational man, a man of courtesy, showing neither anger nor vengeance nor any cause for perverse behaviors. (Later films plumbing psychological causes diminished the horror of the man.) Lector, at the same time, is a man who lacks absolutely a conscience or even the least inclination toward sympathy.

Then why am I rooting for him?

Why do I hope that his cunning might find liberty in the end?

Why do I begin compulsively to imagine for God's enemy even the softest pulse or decency?

On the other hand, Matthew slowly withdrew himself from the movie. He managed to watch its first act. He saw Lector muzzled in an elegant leather-and-metal fright mask. But his eyes grew heavy. They closed. And Matthew fell asleep.

16
1979

Come.
Let us reason together,
* says the Lord.*
Though your sins be as scarlet,
* they shall be as white as snow.*
Though they be red like crimson,
* they shall be as wool.*

I.

I beg patience, good reader. Just now I have an observation which requires that I tell you an earlier story first.

When he was eight, shortly after we'd moved to the large house in Evansville, Matthew ran away from home.

This is the cause-effect sequence as best as I can remember it. There was a bleak, reasonable logic to every successive step—each stage clearly built upon the previous stage—so that I can understand why the boy should have run away.

I've already written about the prayer we prayed at night. Perhaps I haven't mentioned how frequently little Matt would, in the middle of that prayer, hop out of bed to do things not wrong but mightily inconvenient.

"'Jesus Savior / wash away / all that has been wrong today / Help me—' Matthew!"—my interruption—"What are you doing?"

Well, he might have slipped from the sheets to sit on the floor, suddenly emptying a cardboard box of five hundred football cards.

"Sorting my cards. Terry Bradshaw—"

"No, you're not." Through my teeth: "We're praying. It's time to go to sleep. Get in bed. Fold your hands. Now: 'Jesus Savior / wash away / all that has been wrong today. Help me / every day to be—' Matthew! What are you doing?"

He might be trotting from the room.

"Goin' to brush my teef."

Well, yes, yes, tooth-brushing was my rule, after all. And his mother's. And the boy was obeying a rule. How could I countermand rules when he, of his own accord, chose cheerfully to obey them?

When he returned, broad-grinning, white-toothed, content with himself and hopping into bed, we made white-knuckled prayer folds of our hands and again marched to Jesus as into a battering sea: "'Jesus Savior wash away—' *Matthew! Where are you going!*"

To the bafroom. To the bafroom. To the bafroom, Daddy. "Forgot to pee."

When he bounced back into his bed; when he folded his hands so sweetly, a child innocent of sin, unconscious of the violence of his interruptions of devotion to God!—he noticed a certain fire in my countenance.

"Aren't we gonna pray?"

"Tomorrow! We've worn the prayer out tonight."

"You going to hug me?"

"Tomorrow," I snapped, and left.

Tomorrow.

Breakfast, then:

Thanne called the children, all four of them, to wash their hands and come to eat. Three of them responded. One of them didn't budge; was reading the sports page on the living room floor.

I was no longer a patient man. "Matthew," I said. "Didn't you hear your mother?"

"Yes," he said. "I heard her."

"What did she say?"

"She said, 'Wash your hands.'"

"And why haven't you washed your hands?"

Without looking up, and with perfect rationality, the boy lifted two fingers and said, "Because she didn't ask me two times."

All my rhetorical skills, honed by years of preaching, flashed in the living room, slammed the walls — damned a child for a no-account, and withered his soul to nothing. In round terms I condemned my son.

In the language of Moses and the prophets, I sinned against my son.

That afternoon he ran away.

Clarence Fields, his and Joseph's Cub Scout Leader, telephoned from church: "Isn't Matt coming today?"

"He should have come with Joseph, right after school."

"That's an hour ago. Wait a minute."

Clarence covered the phone and murmured through the flesh of his hand. His voice lifted into a question.

I heard the tones of Joseph's voice.

Clarence to me: "Joe says he doesn't know where Matt is either. But he says his brother ran away from home."

Joseph took to phone. Quietly he spoke to me. "He said he wasn't worth nothing." Joseph's voice trembled.

And my heart hammered. I had to gulp the air to breathe it.

The Cub Scouts deployed, some running, others leaping into Mr.

Fields' car, good-deeding it through the city, crying, "Matthew!" out the windows.

For my own part, I didn't know what to do. There was a flood in me that threatened to drown my soul — and I could have been glad to die, or to weep. Lord, how I have mishandled my son, my son, my busy, exuberant, vulnerable son!

I went out the front door. I wandered into Bayard Park and began to cross it toward the southeast, through the trees.

Guilt is a very real pain, thick in the chest, sharp in the gut, and almost intolerable. The guilty man will hunch and cup his belly in order to hold the pain. But a broken posture does not ease it: there is no one to blame but himself.

Then I saw him. Matthew, dragging his small self across Powell and into the park, coming home!

I took a place beside him and began to walk at his speed. I didn't touch him. I hadn't the right.

"You ran away," I said, to be talking, to invite his talking in return.

"Yes."

"But you came home," I said.

"I saw a man," he said. "I thought he was going to kidnap me. I was afraid. So I came home."

Ah, Matthew! The home that I made for you is only the lesser of two fears: a place to hide in, not to live in.

I had no more words to say, wretch of a father. We walked the rest of the way in silence. When we entered 831 E. Chandler, he went to his room, and I to my study, where I sat in my chair and could not move. The chair was at angles to the open door. I did not rise to close the door. This is not the only time I suffered a treacherous guilt with regard to my son. I sat grieving for the past and the future together. A harsh white sunlight streamed through the window and whacked the side of my head. Headache.

I think it was half an hour later when Matthew passed my door on his way to the stereo with a record. He glanced in, passed on.

In less than a moment he returned and stood in the doorway, looking at me.

"You okay?" he said.

"No."

"You sick, Dad?"

"No. Yes."

He kept gazing at me. I dropped my eyes. Without a sound, neither sobbing nor sighing, I cried. Quiet tears.

"Ohhh," said Matthew softly. "I get it."

He came into my study and put his hand on my knee. "I love you," he said. He popped a brief grin. Then he left.

Sometime later his act of forgiveness rose for me to the level of divinity. I found myself thinking: *That child had no right to forgive me so.* I meant, *Where did he get such knowing? Such spiritual maturity? The power to make me his son, and to make his son free?*

Except God be in him.

II.

Cause and effect.

Even to this day, April 24, 2007, and to this writing, I confess my responsibility for Matthew's suffering during his coming-up years. No, I am not so foolish as to take upon me the entire cause of the thing. I'm aware that there were other factors. The stinging scent of his infant urine and the acidity of his small-boy sweat might have been signs of some sort of chemical imbalance — signs which, in a later day, doctors are better prepared to diagnose and to pursue.

Some thirty-five years ago, though, our doctors' diagnoses and remedies consisted of a number of uncertain procedures. Since he couldn't control his bladder on his own, the doctor prescribed Tofranil during his first, the second, and the third grades of his education. But the drug also had the effect of calming him—or, as Thanne remembers, "flattening" his expressions and gestures. This was troublesome. She took him off the drug by his fourth grade, nine years old.

The doctors confirmed Thanne's recognition that sugar, sugar products, artificial colors, all sent Matthew through the roof. She cleansed the house of them. She used honey instead—but now believes that this was as stimulating as the sugar.

We both noticed how jazzed our kids got after a Saturday morning's routine of TV cartoons. Matthew *became* the thing he watched. He was any of a number of superheroes, swooped in to save (read, "assault") his sisters. So Thanne nixed cartoons.

She discussed with several physicians Matt's hyperactivity. One gave her the advice she found most reasonable: "As long as you don't feel like taking his head off," the doctor said, "I don't recommend drugs for the child," such as Ritalin. "They can interfere with his natural development."

Thanne observed, too, what would keep him attentive and properly active in school. At the start of every year during his elementary experience, she approached his teacher with these words: "Matthew will be either your worst student or your best." Then she made two suggestions: (1) Keep good order, classes changing always at the same time, so that he can properly adjust his moods, activities and anticipations. (2) More importantly, keep him busy. Not make-work! It has to be difficult, a genuine challenge for him.

During his fourth grade, Mrs. Johnson heeded and praised the advice, for she set Matthew to reading the encyclopedia and writing papers of various topics. He delighted in the challenge.

On the other hand, I let my impatience ride him hard as a mule.

While still a crib-baby, he would (as I've already noted) cry and cry. Revise that: he would *shriek* both evening and night, unable to sleep. At first I walked him, enclosing his entire little corpus within my broad hands, my winglike arms and the cradle-board of my chest. As close as his mother's womb. I sang and offered him a slow bounce in rhythm with my low-throated song.

It worked. I've told you this already. And this: once I lay him down again, he shot straight into that caustic, angry wailing again.

This next I haven't told you. On certain nights of utter frustration, I would cover his mouth and nose on the exhalation, subduing the sound, somewhat baffling the force of his expulsion—but then open his airways completely when he sought to draw breath again.

That act troubles me still. Could it, at so early an age, have inculcated a sense of instability? The provider as untrustworthy? And he must fight for his very breath?

Before I was a pastor, when we worshipped at Redeemer, I hated, I despised the eyes of the congregants, turning in judgment upon my son, or else offering indulgent, lying smiles at the kid who kept on crying. I would gather poor Matthew tightly in my arms and rise to escape this phalanx of the faithful. Could Matthew even then sense the rages in his daddy?

O my son, what did I do to you at the very foundations of your personhood?

Having never myself received praise from my parents, I made a point of praising my children. And I strove to set my praise upon truly praise-worthy characteristics and achievements. In his eighth grade, Matthew's ability to run track put him at the very head of his class, the champion of his school and then of the region. Hooray! Countless the records he broke. Hooray, you bounding antelope!

On the other hand, I kept trying to instill in his soul a genuine humility, promising that this was the ideal of human relationships and that would repay him with genuine friendship. Not humiliation! Not his abject mortification did I seek. Rather, a proper sense of the value of the Other. This seemed to me a necessary lesson more especially because Matthew's broad exuberance seemed always to *ignore* the Other. He seemed to lack empathy for his brother and sisters. He made so much of a triumph that an opponent could indeed feel humiliated—though Matthew intended no such thing.

So I sought to ease that natural sense of superiority in him, together with his crowing boast.

I know he believes that such parenting weakened his spine. Even his confidence. I know he has felt burdened by it. And now I could not argue this feeling—though it's still a mystery to me whether my training was the single cause of that behavioral limitation.

When people began to use him to their own ends, Matthew would give in. "Matthew," so said his father, "don't think of yourself first! Think of others!" But in basketball he suffered an internal compulsion to elevate other players—teammates as well as opponents—over himself, even at his own expense. (Though he hated this "weakness" on his part.)

As I've noted before: when the point guard ought to have been aggressive, forceful, he fell back in quietness.

Matthew, no. Matthew, who do you think you are? Don't you care what other people feel?

Until came the day when I caught him squashing his brother's chest, wrapping his arms around Joseph's chest, and I tore them apart.

"Matthew, doesn't it *bother* you, what your brother suffers? Look. How do you like it when someone does it to you?"

III.

Do you remember, Matthew, when we drove the Toyota pickup to the city dump, you and Joseph and me? The bed was filled with metal trash, roof-trash, the cracked, despoiled sides of the chicken coop, now torn down?

I found a narrow prominence of solid, dry soil, pulled on the emergency brake, got out and asked your help. You and Joseph slung down the pieces to me, so that I could pitch them over the edge and into a gorge of garbage.

I believe that you were nine and eight at the time.

The division of labor worked well for a while. Two boys wrangled that heavier machinery together. I wrestled alone, paying full attention to my job.

Then you screamed, "Dad!"

I turned. Joseph stood transfixed in the truck bed. You were in the cab. Somehow you had released the emergency brake. The Toyota was rolling toward the edge of the gorge.

I lost my heart to terror.

IV.

And then this: How often was I gone the delicate years, while you were being shaped. Thanne has described to me what anxiety you suffered at my absence. Anything that disrupted the order and the fullness of our family disturbed you deeply.

Ah, Matthew!

I spent the entire autumn of 1973 at Miami University in Oxford, Ohio, studying toward my Ph.D.

I spent the summer and then the autumn of 1975 in St. Louis, completing the seminary requirements for Masters of Divinity.

You were two for my first abandonment.

You were four for the second.

And then, following 1984, came my constant departures to travel through the U.S. and even abroad which left the children without a father.

I am sorry, my son. I beg your forgiveness.

I was growing smart in matters of my own, while you grew skilled and canny in matters I neglected, leaving them unto you. And you were kind; you did not scorn my evident stumbling when the topic of our talk was yours and not mine.

What are the causes and what are the effects? Can they be traced truly from the parent's early behaviors (causes?) to the behaviors of the child now grown older? Effects?

Well, and precisely because there cannot be precision in such an investigation, it turns into the sad labor of finding fault and suffering guilt.

For which reason I return ever and again to the divine hope made manifest in that brief moment when the run-away came home in 1979. You did the thing you could not have done by your natural self. You mercied me, Matthew. Little boy, you granted me the grace of God, the oils of healing—and I was healed indeed. What was the source, then, if not you? Whence the blessed power to re-create your father as pure again?

Why, that was the Spirit of Jesus. A sign that the Christ was present between us.

Consider the changing of water into wine. (John 2) Consider especially this verse:

*Jesus did this, the first of his **signs**, in Cana of Galilee, and revealed his glory; and his disciples believed in him.*

First those poor fellows saw a consequence that could have had no "logical" cause: wine does not and cannot come from water, all in a trice, from nothing but the water itself. There must have been another ingredient.

It is a sign for something else.

As they look around they discover the Something Else, the most unscientific cause of an observable result: Jesus, who proves himself thereby the divinity, the Creator, the lover and reviver of people.

In you, Matthew, Jesus.

Jesus then, Jesus now, and Jesus all the time between.

Here, my dear son, was the source of my hope even through the most ruinous periods of our drama: not that we will find all the iniquitous (and natural) causes; but rather that we will rest on the One who transfigures, water into wine, sickness into health, the woeful abuses of fatherhood and disappointments of sonship into a relationship as pure as is the Holy Father's with the Beloved Son.

17
1992 — 1994

My people are bent on turning away from me

I.

Here is the brave vigor of our youngest daughter's will.

Talitha came to us sucking her thumb with a dreadful concentration, pressing that thumb so steadily against the roof of her mouth that what had been a natural aberration turned into a serious problem. So high had the bony palate been raised that it crowded her sinuses and interfered with her breathing for years and years. Once the second set of her teeth had grown fully in, it was clear that they could not find their proper occlusion. It was difficult for her to close her lips. Eating — even keeping liquids in her mouth — was difficult. My butterscotch daughter! Her dark eyes, her long-lashed eyes and the broad wisdom of her forehead: her lower face was somewhat distorted by the thrust of the front, upper teeth.

When she was in high school, therefore, first our dentist suggested we have Talitha examined by a maxillary physician, who prescribed correctional surgery.

"This will be a difficult procedure," he warned us. He looked at Talitha. "A long one too." The doctor described the procedure both to Talitha and to her parents. We three agreed.

And so it was that they broke Talitha's upper jaw, cut the parts to form a tighter angle, resectioned the palate, closed the bone together again, then wired the entire jaw shut. It would take nearly two months for the sundered, shaved, refitted bone to heal to strength again. Talitha could not chew. She took her food as liquids through straws. Her speech came through gritted teeth, as though the bars of a jailhouse window. She was fiercely restricted even in the common, habitual behaviors of daily life.

But Talitha played clarinet in the high school band.

And over the Christmas holidays that year, the high school band was scheduled to tour southward into (I believe) Florida.

And our daughter was absolutely determined to make that tour!

No, the wires would not have been removed by then. Yes, to play the reed instrument was worse than uncomfortable; it caused pain.

But (by heaven and the will of this woman!) Talitha would be on that bus. She'd pack and carry the necessary liquids with her. She could — she would — take care of herself, no burden to anyone else.

This puissance of our daughter's will. Willfulness. Resolve. Resolution. Or, as it sometimes seemed to me: stiff-necked mulishness.

Of course, the woman went.

She went, in fact, with, on the one hand, no sense of triumph, nor with, on the other hand, any hint of self pity. It was the thing to do. She did it. 'Nuff said.

Such was the same tough willfulness that drove Talitha to complete her high school education a full half-year earlier than her classmates. And, as I've mentioned before, she meant to spend what would have been her senior spring semester in Costa Rica, practicing her Spanish, attending classes in that country, traveling broadly, providing her own protection, her own itineraries, her own companionship, her own forthrightness, her own fearlessness, her own woman. *Punkt!*

Shortly after Christmas, 1991, Talitha went.

After she left the United States, Thanne and I finished packing our belongings in order to move ourselves permanently to Valparaiso.

It was a hard day. What would we do with the things of the son who, like the hibernating bear, still slept on the carpets of that apartment?

Matthew. Slack-faced. Watching us working.

Well, we packed his possessions too, but in boxes; and we carried these downstairs for him. It was as much as we could do.

Thanne's departure had not been without warning. We intended no surprise. Often and often his mother had urged him to consider transferring to another school, to write letters, begin the process — and then make choices. There were two colleges in Evansville; in fact, I had taught at one of them when first we had arrived there, 1970. My recommendation and his own name, Wangerin, could help his being accepted.

"Or else, Matt ... find a job."

Often. Often.

Nevertheless, Matthew felt as if he were being blindsided after all. He stood, watching, inert with surprise.

*You can't **mean** it, can you? You never really meant it before. You were ... you hadn't told me **two** times.*

Matthew remained behind, alone in Evansville.

II.

I know little — and I can recall even less — of our son's experience during the next year and a half. There are at least two reasons for the lacunae.

First: those years were cruel to us all, Matthew, me, Thanne. Joseph. Living in the white fires of the strikings of flint and iron, of our son and ourselves; caught between the millstones of guilt and discipline, our guilt, his guilt, our duties as parents to him, moreover, to the refinings of his *best* self; living as much in remorse as in judgment, our capacity for the storage of memory did itself become a ragged thing. Even now, when we turn our minds back to 1992, 1993, the times seem chopped, ripped, skewed, scattered.

Second: in chagrin, in his rage and grief at our unexpected treacheries, Matthew determined to clean cut us off, as hard as the Hebrew *Herem.* No calling, no writing, no communication whatsoever. Pay-back and punishment: we would be as dead to him as he had been to us.

So we didn't hear about his life. Not from him. And, whether he ever could know it or not, his chastisement worked. We suffered his silence. *The loss of a son, is it now?* There was no telephone number. There was no address. There was no knowing his circumstances at all.

Remember, O Lord, my sacrifice and our covenant! I will give up his love for me — so long as you will see to his success in this world. A crippled, limited father will stand back, that you, his Father of Power and Mercy, might step forward. Do! Do cover my son Matthew with your right hand! Care for the child, so far away from me.

Even so, I know my sins. They are ever before me. I must confess that there were days when I felt the relief of his absence, the lightening of my heaviness.

Upon her return from Costa Rica, Talitha applied to and was accepted by Spelman College, traditionally an institution for African American women. No scholarship at Spelman. Not yet, at any rate. That school chose to help those students who, by their sophomore and junior years, had proven themselves. Talitha had actually received an offer of a full-ride scholarship from a Midwestern state school. She refused it for Spelman, believing this to be her own decision. Well, if she thought for a minute that her mother had been praying for this outcome precisely, she'd never have accepted a place at Spelman. Our youngest daughter tends to be contrarious with most of her mother's suggestions. But on this they (secretly) agreed: at Spelman college in Atlanta, Georgia, the black woman was elevated, empowered, and honored.

Simultaneously, Mary entered her sophomore year at Butler, blissful, unhurried, unworried!

Because he had spent his previous semester — January through May — studying in Germany, Joseph lingered at Valparaiso for an extra semester living near us. Three of our children were in college, the youngest and the eldest at the extremes, the beginning and the end. In August Talitha had begun. In December I found myself preaching in the vast Chapel at Valparaiso on the morning of our eldest child's graduation.

They moved. They developed. These three were traveling well along. Thanne and I enjoyed the empty nest and in it our newfound intimacy, the revival of a marriage.

No, that's not altogether true. Thanne and I were aggrieved by empty nest, but for the lack of one, the one who had taken the wings of the morning and flown to the uttermost parts of the sea.

How does that one do?

This is a true and trustworthy saying: a mother is never happier than her saddest child.

But, fly however far he might (skimming the waters like a tern, like Icarus finding his wings grow thick in sea-foam, whipped by the winds of storm, sinking down to drowning) bits of information did sift back to us. We had (still have) the benefit of many friends in Evansville.

Thereby did we hear that even the most affectionate and merciful of Matthew's friends' mothers was growing increasingly distressed by his behaviors. She would never have spoken directly to us with accusations. She loved us all. Our sorrow would have caused her to sorrow. She had taken Matthew in. Spoke softly to him. Had given him shelter and food. But in time Mrs. Copeland could no longer permit his lifestyle to trouble her household. She sighed and asked him to leave. Find somewhere else to stay. Because Matthew had been going out of her house at any time, day or night, without locking the outside doors. Worse, because late at night he'd bring unsavory fellows into her house, characters crosswise with the cops, felons with guns and street reputations as pushers.

Matthew was out. Soon Matthew was in again.

This time it was the mother of another friend, an explicit woman neither affectionate nor inclined to like us. Matthew had been with her only days when she telephoned Thanne. She wanted to speak to us directly.

"I'm finished with him. Your son has stayed at my house long enough. I don't have the money to feed his foraging. Come and get him."

Thanne answered, "No."

"Then send me the fare. I'll put him on a bus for Valparaiso."

Thanne said, "No."

"What? You're abandoning your son?"

Under these circumstances Thanne could scarcely explain our decision, which was to allow him to touch bottom in order to *experience* the harsh consequence of bad decisions and worse behaviors. As long as we supported him, he'd stay fixed in a teenager's self-centered expectations; disobedient to and disdainful of his parents; foolish regarding his own future and destructive of his present life; but, being fed and clothed and therewith contented, he'd continue to lack motivation; he would continue incapable of learning or planning or succeeding at the most basic skills of living.

All that Thanne could say to this unappeasable woman was: "Abandon? I suppose it looks that way. But how else is he going to learn adulthood?"

"Well, then," she spluttered, incredulous: "Then what am *I* supposed to do with him? He's yours! He's not *my* responsibility!"

Thanne breathed deeply. How often would this single, difficult decision have to be remade, re-decided, questioned and grasped and remade over and over again?

Accepting the blot on her reputation, she said, "Kick him out. Don't feed him. He ought to get a job."

Censure smoked through the telephone. How wicked, these white parents! Selfish! Hincty! Turning their black son out on the streets like trash in a basket! What else can the lad become but criminal?

No, but we had met the rich physician who really did turn back his adopted daughter. This was the man who could consider the child "damaged goods." Yes. It happens. But it is not what we are doing!

During those years, Thanne's spirit was crushed. If she had not loved her son, she could have gone like that physician untouched by blame both false *or* true. Love kept her tied to the child afflicted. Love made us suffer what he suffered. Love ties our hopes for our own lives, ties even our health to *his* decisions, for which we can only wait, praying.

Thanne prayed by means of the Psalms. All of them, 1 to 150. One a day. Reshaping each psalm to embrace her son, as in her own bosom, or like the flaming chariot which embraced that other Elijah, rising on the whirlwind of her motherlove to God the Father.

During our last year in Evansville, an African American woman had told Thanne face to face that Matthew's problems all stemmed from his having been adopted into a white household. The woman was forthright, not angry; making what she considered a cool, inside analysis.

"Matthew's confused about his identity. Really, he should have been in a black family."

This particular woman was, in fact, a friend of mine. A paralegal who had worked with legal aid lawyers until Reagan pulled the plug on such federal spending. The lawyers left. She herself *became* the office, exhausting herself with advice for the poor regarding landlords, insurance frauds, section eight, social security, the scandalous insolence of the police. We, weary with well doing, worked together against racism in the city. We admired one another. Perhaps she never would have uttered so sharp, so dismissive an analysis to me. But she felt she was bound (always!) to tell the truth. Truth hurts. Never mind. And though Thanne never once gave credence to that judgment, though it was clearly an easier surmise than a harder truth, Thanne was wounded nonetheless. My friend did not know what she was talking about. Yet she got away with such ungrounded accusations because she was herself black.

This is how Thanne and I approached that same issue: what if Matthew had not been adopted at all? What if he had spent his formative years in an orphanage, where the imposition of inflexible laws is necessary, despite its crippling of single children? How would he have coped then?

Few black families were adopting in the '70s. It was only in the 1980s that activist African Americans began to raise the matter of white/black adoption to the level of a social ill, another sort of racism. White arrogance. Some went so far as to claim that white adoption was a form of cultural genocide. Again, how would our son, acting out, requiring genuine (but personal) challenges to his body and his intellect, showing behaviors not unlike Attention Deficit Disorder—how would he have coped in a series of foster homes?

Or what if Matthew had been adopted into a (white) family who had *not*, by the grace of God, moved into a black neighborhood? Thanne had taken her bachelor's degree in exceptional education. She had been trained to recognize deviance in children, and she knew how to respond. There was no doubt that Matthew needed a consistent love and an ordered household.

That he was our child, then; that Matthew had been raised in this home, our home—raised too by scores of black aunties and uncles at Grace and in the central city—seemed to us evidence of the hand of God. It was a divine thing.

And the wonder is that our faith shall have been vindicated by the end of this narrative—

But we are not yet at the end.

We have a rough road to go before we can get there.

I'm sorry.

III.

I believe it was in the spring of 1993 that Matthew found time and the quiet to sit and write a long letter, which then he posted to us.

I cannot in my imagination see the room, the table, the light of his writing. I doubt that anyone else was with him in the room—unless it is the library. I can, however, see my son, bent, writing with his left hand, his lips pinched.

Two pages of school-ruled three-holed paper. His small, half-printed handwriting cramming every white space side to side between the blue lines. His pen's tip pressed hard upon the paper, almost an etching of his mind. I see how the joint above the nail of his forefinger buckles.

When we took the letter out of its envelope and tried to smooth its sheets of paper on the kitchen counter, we found them so impressed by Matthew's printing, they kept rolling up.

It came to us with a confession, an abbreviated chronology, and an appeal. He described the terrifically difficult times of his life those last eighteen months. Almost as bad as anything else was the shame he felt at having returned in ignominy to Evansville, where he heaped greater and greater shame upon himself by making a public thing of his failures.

He confessed his desire to punish us by his silence. Reading those lines, remembering them again and again thereafter, caused me to cry. My sadness for him. For the isolation his little effort to salvage pride had forced upon him. Yet at the same time I wept tears of an odd gladness: for, I realized, to the extent that Matthew believed he could hurt us by the removal of himself, to that same extent, he must have believed in our love for him.

The effect of the letter was to reopen communication.

Yes. Though we said it in our souls with deeper feeling than we said it aloud to him, Matthew would get another chance.

Should we rejoice at the prospect?

Dare we?

And hadn't that archetypical father leaped down from his roof and flown in joy to his returning prodigal? Hadn't he interrupted his son's abject confession with his own best robe? With the ring of family and fellowship, with sandals for his finest guest, and a public party to shout it out the city-wide: *Hey! My kid is back! He was dead; but here and home he is again—and alive!*

But the prodigal's parable ends with that party. What happened afterward? How vulnerable ought our love to render us?

Once can be an aberration. But twice predicts a pattern.

When Mary returned to Butler University in August 1993, Matthew went with her. Our son, her brother, began to attend classes. Opportunity number two.

Yes. Of course we would pay his tuition, his bed and board. But please, we begged, get a job to help us help you. Several of his FAU classes had been accepted in transfer; many had not, both because the grades could not qualify and because they'd been courses peculiar to Matthew's program at FAU. If he played ball, it would be a walk-on at Butler. But he registered like any other student.

And, strength to his new beginning, Matthew had a steadfast, affectionate, unjudging yet undeceivable companion in his sister Mary.

They talked often.

None of Matthew's siblings ever held it against him that greater portions of our resources, Thanne's and mine and the family's, were expended on him than on the others. When he was young, he nearly consumed our attentions. Likewise, high school. Likewise, college and thereafter. But Joseph's love for Matthew was never shaken, not since that first salutary kiss which the bumble-bee boy popped onto his brown brother's cheek.

Talitha always maintained a particular camaraderie for the other adoptee in the family. She felt, in fact, that she knew all about being black, all about being adopted, all about the mistakes of white, adopting parents. Therefore she would get on Matthew's nerves, telling him what to do, how to act, what was wrong with his situation, how to make it better. But she *did* talk with him. Nor did she blame *him* as much as she did the exigencies of their common up-bringing. She was his sister. She intended to be his mentor too.

And Mary?

Unflappable.

Once while she was a junior in high school, I overheard my daughter take a late telephone call.

"Hello?"

Bright her voice; ever bright; ever expecting some sort of good news, some sort of friend.

There followed a pause.

"Hello?"

Her greeting hadn't been sung this time. A genuine question: *Is somebody there?*

But neither was this second greeting answered, as I discovered when Mary continued in her sweetest, eye-battingest, most chatterful mode:

"Oh, I know. Now I get it. You want me to *hear* you, but you don't want to talk in my ear. You *could* whisper."

She waited. Then:

"Poor man. Be happy. Be glad. I *do* hear you — your breathing, I mean. Good strong breathing. I'm gonna guess you don't have a lung problem. Is that right? Different kinda problem, right? Let's see. *Lonely!* You're lonely. Poor little man. Well, we could have a conversation. You don't have to talk. I'm good at — "

Long pause.

"Hmmmm."

She turned to hang up, and saw me standing by.

Mary grinned and shrugged and dropped the receiver in place. Then, half-dancing from the room:

"Poor little man didn't want to talk. His loss."

Unflappable, this Mary.

In August 1993, then, she *and* Matthew drove south to attend the same school, she a junior, he, considering which classes transferred, somewhere in his freshman year, perhaps now in its second quarter.

I can't explain how it is that individuals come to love each other: the causes are mysterious and deeper than my intelligence. Or how does that love become an indestructible thing?—a rich, inexhaustible vein of kindness, mercy and forgiveness? Yet I have witnessed such a love. I know it to be true. I must believe, therefore, that so sweet a fountain flows from the side of the Savior, for all the rest of creation is too limited to pour forth so motherly a water.

In this manner does Mary love Matthew.

While she was in her junior year at Butler, she continued to keep him company. The young man still was sporting upon the treacherous shore, though this shore was no longer of the infinite seas; it bore the crashing waves of world-wide judgment and absolute renunciation. His sister Mary befriended him. Her life presented a remarkable structure nearby. She became a fine model of stability—even if she could not be *his* stability or a structure of his own, within him and surrounding him.

Perhaps it was already during his first semester at Butler—certainly by his second semester, spring 1994—that Matthew was missing classes again.

And before the end of the school year, when it became clear to the authorities that Matthew had ceased studying at all, he was run out of the dormitory. He found lodgings with schoolmates, in whose rooms he had stayed until the end of the semester when no one could stay in the dorms at all.

And then Mary left Indianapolis to spend her summer at home. The lonely time thereafter broke the spine of Matthew's resolve.

He had become a sucker for the pre-approved credit cards with which the yellow teeth of financial wolves bit—into the wooly brains of the college undergraduate. Our son got them, then maxed them out. He also took out student loans, certain chunks of which bought more than an education.

Matthew ran himself into debt.

When Mary began her senior year in August, Matthew found support again. He sought her goodness, as much as she could grant him, as much as his debilitating shame would allow. He drank of the liquid of her love. He ate of her breadlike steadfastness. And she, talking, encouraging, making supper, hatching plans and solutions, loved him.

18
1994—1996

The sword rages against their cities!
It destroys the bars of their gates!
It puts an end to all their plannings —

I.

In December 1994, several weeks before his siblings, Matthew came home initiating his holidays a whole month early.

He brought with him everything he owned. All his possessions in paper bags. There was no place in Indianapolis where to store them. Perhaps this was his sole reason for schlepping the stuff to Valparaiso. He told us so.

But no report of his success at study followed.

Always after a long absence it was good to see him. He wore a crooked smile and approached me at a sideways gait, the way a horse trots forward, its head cast aside.

In those days we were learning to hug. Actually, Matthew was teaching me.

But in two days he was sleeping the daylight hours away in front of the television. He would rise and eat and watch TV the dark hours through.

Before the rest of the kids came home, I took my son on a winter's walk. For the first ten minutes I restricted my observations to the season and the weather. The woods were snowless, the shagbark hickories, those tall spears, shivering. The ground was soft. Autumn had been violently windy. We stepped over new-fallen trees.

"You can't stay here, Matthew," I said.

Neither of us broke stride. His jacket was fashionable and altogether useless against the cold. He had stuffed his hands in the pockets. He said nothing.

"You're twenty-three. You must, you must make a life for yourself."

His lips pushed out, round as a kiss. Puffy eyelids, squinting under the colorless sun. His eyebrows had dropped like a window shade.

Matthew's skin tends to take a dusty white patina in freezing weather. His ears and his neck were unprotected.

"This"—I forced myself still to talk—"this is the only way I know how to help you anymore."

Two months earlier in this same stretch of woods I'd caught sight of a doe some distance through the trees. She was lying on her side, her head raised.

I crept toward the doe. Great-necked, somnolent, her ears did not so much as twitch.

I snapped twigs. The sound didn't startle her.

Then I noticed that her head was in fact leaning against the bold of a white oak, thrown back at an impossible angle. No. No amount of sound would rouse her.

I walked around her bier of leaves and sticks, then came up straight and stared.

Flowing from her abdomen was something like an ivory falls. Moist, twinkling with motion, it seemed the slow sluice of a thickened rice-meal pouring from the deer's gut to the ground.

Of course it was nothing so splendid or so nourishing.

It was a great congregation of maggots, such a myriad of white maggots that they seemed a single mass, glacial and flowing.

Now as Matthew and I passed that same place, I saw the deer's bones torn from their skeletal structure, the pelt shrinking upon its shoulders.

"See that?" I asked Matthew, preparing to describe the previous stage of the doe's dying.

He kicked at a canon bone, cracked open the marrow, then stepped over the whole and kept walking.

I said, "Between now and the twenty-first of January we have more than six weeks of days. Matt, you've got to find a job. Any job, I don't care. Before the twenty-first—there's no help for it—you've got to start earning your own money, then mom and I will help you find an apartment, help you with furnishing it, too. Because January the twenty-first is your deadline, son. After that you cannot stay in our house."

I think I saw him nodding. His red eyes looked like gun barrels in a blind. He stepped up his speed. He did not speak.

"Wait, Matt," I said. "Stop a minute."

He did. But he kept his face turned away from me.

I said, "Well, and I think you know the alternative."

O God, help me!—this was so hard.

"If you don't have a job by then, you and I and all your stuff will drive back down to Indianapolis. I'll let you out wherever you want. Because after the twenty-first. Well. You can't stay in our house."

And so the weeks began to pass.

Still while we three were together alone, Thanne and I raised the topic of alcohol with Matthew. Surprisingly, he quite easily confessed his dependence on it.

Thanne, then, found a counselor willing to work with Matthew regarding his dependency. He spoke well of her. She gave him a number of mental devices for avoiding booze at least for controlling it. He believed they could work. My heart was lifted. If he could do this thing, surely he could do the other too.

But he still hadn't tried.

I offered to use my contacts and my influence about town. That suggestion he refused on the face of it. What he would do, he would do on his own.

But he didn't do anything.

Customarily we purchase and decorate our Christmas tree close to the Nativity itself, keeping the tree up all through the season until the twelfth night, the Epiphany. Ours is not a celebration defined by retail economics, but rather by ecclesiastic tradition and a focus on the Christ-child *come.*

So Matthew helped string the tree lights. Fellowship!

On Christmas Eve after church, when the lights were low and pine sap scented the room and cider warmed our cups and our stomachs, we exchanged gifts among ourselves, one child distributing all her presents at a time. This too has been our custom.

Talitha gave us stuff from Spelman. Joseph's pocket was shallow; he gave us each one of his works of art. Mary bought inexpensive gifts suited to each recipient. Matthew at his turn suddenly jumped up and rushed from the room.

When he came back, he was grinning, spitting a little laughter between his teeth.

"Heh, heh," he said. "Heh, heh. This is for next time." He had begun to pronounce the word *tohm.*

He was handing around small cuts of paper, each folded in half. Unfolding them we found the message: *I O U one present. MW.*

My heart sank for the sake of my son. How poorly he must have felt that Christmas Eve.

And the New Year came. And the other children returned to their lives in Atlanta and Indianapolis and (Joseph) Minneapolis. And Matthew lingered, lying in front of the TV, rising only to keep his appointments with the psychologist, but never yet to seek a job.

For two days it snowed. The woods lost all distinction.

I did not want to overbear my son.

"January twenty-one." *January twenty-one.*

On Sunday, the fifteenth, I preached in the Chapel of the Resurrection, Valparaiso University. The lesson was the wedding at Cana and the changing of water into wine. I wanted to tell the story of Matthew's forgiving me when he was four. Just as the wine had no right to be in the six stone jars, except that God were there, changing the water — even so forgiveness had no right to be in my son, except that Jesus were there changing sorrow into love.

But how could Matthew receive such a story except as an unsubtle lesson?

And did the scriptural demand my own forgiving him at the last hour? Relieve him of the January 21 head-chop deadline?

No, but I *have* forgiven him, over and over! Forgiveness can surely be granted, yet not at the same time be received when the sinner is unrepentant. It means nothing if nothing changes. It requires an Assyrian defeat. And then again a Nebuchadnezzar. It requires a genuine awakening, a self-examination, a recognition of one's own persistence in decisions and behaviors that kill the soul so dead a million maggots may flow forth. It requires repentance.

On Monday, January the sixteenth, the campus celebrated Martin Luther King day.

On the nineteenth, with my heart in my mouth, I flew north to give a lecture in Minneapolis.

By Saturday I was home again.

And Matthew had not yet even begun to seek a job.

II.

In all my life, this was the most difficult task I've ever been forced to do.

Without a word, Matthew climbs into the car with me. He would have gone into the back seat and slept, but I ask—I order—him to sit in the front. I don't know whether Thanne is watching as we drive out onto Division Road, turning right and turning right again on Indiana State Route 2.

I ask Matthew a question. Speech alone causes a seismic whack in my chest. Surely it affects my voice.

I say, "We're going to Indianapolis. Where do you want me to drop you off?"

He slouches down in the seat. He pulls a ball cap over his forehead and eyes. He doesn't answer.

We do not talk.

I suffer something like a tightening vine around my bowels. My face stings. It must show red. This is my son. Here is my son beside me. We are going up the mountain in Moriah where I must place him on stick on an altar, there to offer him as a whole burnt offering.

Christ!—let there be a ram in the thickets!

We are humming south on Interstate 65. Cruise control. My foot is not steady.

The trip will take no more than two hours down and two hours back for me. It's miserably cold and overcast. The sky is not blue. The fields are not green. They're patched with blown snow. We pass the Lebanon exit. The Zionsville exit is next.

I don't glance at Matthew. There is no labored breathing. I think, with a deeper shuddering, that he must be awake, sentient beside me, thinking, thinking—and very far away. What can my son be thinking?

I want to believe he's finally coming to understand that he can't come home again. Not as he was. Not as he is. And if he will not discover and honor the hard laws of adulthood in the general order of things, whether social or spiritual, physical, economical, governmental or divine—well, well: he is discovering them in me. His father.

"Matthew," I say. I pause. My mouth clicks for stickiness. I didn't bring something to drink. His name on my tongue is a paste. *O God, how I hate this!*

We're closing in on I-465, the beltway around the city.

"Where do you want me to drop you off?"

If you will not listen, says the Lord to Judah, stiff in its sinning:

> *If you will not listen,*
> > *my soul will weep in secret for your pride;*
> > *my eyes will weep bitterly and run down with tears.*
>
> *But I will scatter you like chaff*
> > *driven by wind into the desert!*
> *This is your lot,*
> > *the portion I have measured out for you,*
> *says the Lord,*
> > *because you have forgotten me and trusted in lies.*

Matthew stirs beside me. He removes the cap from his eyes. He blinks and peers through the windshield. There is traffic all around us, most of it whipping by.

"Um," he says. He shrugs. He has not given me his countenance. "Where I used to stay."

"What do you mean? Where is that?"

"Butler."

"Not with your sister, Matthew! You must not become her burden."

"What do you think I am?" he snaps, looking at me. His eyes are bloodshot.

I don't know. I set my sight ahead, watching for the 38th Street exit which will take us to the university.

Sullenly, "I have some friends. I got some friends there. They'll take me."

He doesn't say more.

Within twenty minutes I've turned and am driving north again, the vehicle vastly empty. And I am crying. I blind myself with tears. And I am shaken by sobs so huge I must pull to the side of the highway and shut off the engine and cover my face with my hands and press my knuckles against the rim of the steering wheel.

It is me, now. I have lost my heart.

I am dead.

My Joy is gone. Grief is upon me. My heart is sick. For the hurt of my poor people am I hurt. I mourn, and dismay had taken hold of me.

Is there no balm in Gilead?

III.

Some years ago Christians exchanged countless copies of a greeting card entitled: *Footprints in the Sand.* The picture showed two sets of walking prints suddenly becoming one set only. The legend written for this picture often took the form of a brief dialogue.

The recipient of the car, gazing at the loss of a set of feet, says sadly, "You told me you'd always be with me. But look. In my time of trouble your footprints vanished. I traveled all alone."

To which the Lord responds: "No. I never left you. In your time of trouble, friend, I picked you up and carried you."

Thus the mystery is solved by the Lord's support, his personal attention to the recipient, and his strength. We are to envision ourselves as the lamb the shepherd carries on his shoulders home again.

But I have lived at the side of the sea. I have walked its sandy-ragged beaches, leaving prints behind me; and I know by its night-storms raging, by the foaming, torn-weed turbulence in the morning—yes, and I know by the quieter tempests I've suffered both as a son and as a father—that footprints may as well be obliterated by crashing waves and by trouble.

The loss of a set cannot always be sentimentalized as the comfort the shepherd has given the sheep. Experience refuses platitudinous revisions of our histories. We were isolated! We were lonely. We were strangers, foreigners, wanderers in a trackless wilderness.

When we learned that we were clean cut off and could not find home again, in that day we were lost. And then we were dying indeed.

Then we were Matthew in Indianapolis without plans or purpose.

And we were one parent in an empty vehicle, sobbing.

This, too, is the plot of our lives.

Suck it up!

It is, perhaps, the longest stretch of the journey.

———

Again, from Wordsworth's Immortality Ode:

> —But there's a Tree, of many, one,
> A single Field which I have looked upon,
> Both of them speak of something that is gone:
> The Pansy at my feet
> Doth the same tale repeat:
> Wither is fled the visionary gleam?
> Where is it now, the glory and the dream? (ll. 51 – 57)

IV.

And then it was that Matthew lost his last and his best support.

In the spring of 1995, his sister Mary ("born to be a teacher!") graduated from Butler University. We helped her, Thanne and I, to pack everything. We moved her north to Valparaiso, but only for a visit, lasting no more than a month. After that she took six weeks' training in order to prepare to serve the church as a teacher overseas.

On the fourth of August, a Friday, Thanne and I drove Mary into Chicago. We parked in an O'Hare long-term parking lot, then waited with her until her flight was ready for boarding: three forty-five in the afternoon.

Finally Thanne and I watched Mary take her place in line. Cheerful almost to the point of skipping, smiling, wearing sunglasses as big as windshields, shorts, bare knees, slopping along in flip-flops, looking for all the world like the prototypical tourist — our brave young daughter boarded an intercontinental jet and zoomed off for Cameroon, Africa. There is one sort of gone; and then there is another sort; and they are not alike. Our hearts went with Mary, surely. But so did our glad anticipations. Like her brother, she was taking the wings of the morning to dwell in foreign nations; but she carried our hearts with her, and she would keep contact, and she would grow the more mature, enriching our parenthood as well.

Even so did Matthew lose his best, last support.

In Boca Raton Matthew had developed friendships he still maintains, Leonard's favor in particular. In Evansville, he could crash with old friends. In Indianapolis he had had Mary.

For the first time, Matthew was completely on his own. The Invisible Man to every element of society. The Other. A stranger — even as he must have felt in that silent ride beside me, south to Indianapolis.

Again, Matthew lapsed into silence. This time I could not be convinced that it was for punishing us. This time I believed it was a state of being. If we, his parents, had gone south in search of our son, we would never have found him. This is the truth. Matthew had gotten himself so lost this time there were neither pebbles nor crumbs to lead him back to his soul again. Even he did not know where to find himself. Every sort of communication had been cut off. Every relationship had putrefied. Every kindness he'd accorded to people pretending friendship had been repaid by thievery — till all his little pile of personal stuff was gone.

And with it, himself.

These things I knew, though I was far away and blind.

V.

Drop me from a window with no alternative of turning, and the end of the fall will be sudden, certain, and hard. We could measure the time and the length of it, because at the end is an ending. *Punkt.*

But grant me this alternative of turning....

Do this:

Before you drop me, bind me in braces attached to a bungee; attach the other end of the bungee cord to something stationary near the window. Keep the cord short enough that my heaviest stretch won't reach the ground.

Now, then, drop me down.

The end of that fall—which is itself not an ending but a turning—is no longer as dramatic as a splat. In fact, it becomes harder and harder to measure since the fall begins to slow, slows by degrees which themselves grow tighter and tighter—until there must finally come on infinitesimal, scarcely measurable instant when the cord that had been stretching starts to contract.

There must have been a stopping, of course, in order to make a turning. But the stop itself is so brief as to be quicker than a stroke of the bee's wing.

This is meant as an analogy.

When the human spirit leaps into a wretched descent from the Father, since the distance is so great, the drop at first seems easy. There is all around me, above and below me, so generous a breadth of wish and dream, fulfillment and possibility. I can be whatever I want to be, do whatever I want to do. I am as free as an eagle spiraling vastly downward.

The farther the fall into darkness and isolation, however, the more dramatic becomes the experience. The speed can take my breath away. And perhaps there is a period of exhilaration. But soon set in a breathless desperation. Hurtling faster and faster downward, I can't think straight. All help, all my resources, have withdrawn. Wingless, flightless, I am on my own. Precipitously, the ground swells, the rocks expand, the ending grins and spreads its arms and rushes up to break not only the fall, but the faller too.

That's a story with a memorable climax.

My son's is another story altogether. The love of God has never let him go.

If his fall had ended in stark death, I would write it in a grand hand. That ending would need extremities of image and action, an organ chord, something monumental.

But the end of his fall is a *turning* after all.

We call it *metanoia*: "conversion."

And such moments in the life of the spirit (despite St. Paul's dramatics) are often as quiet as a mother's breath.

Elijah the prophet, running from a series of dramatics — his defeat and slaughter of Jezebel's priests, Jezebel's threat to slaughter him in return — has gone a long day's journey into the wilderness. He has lain down under a broom tree, has begged God to let him die, and then has fallen into the sleep of despair.

What, then, turns the prophet's soul around?

What changes his purposes from death to life again?

No, not some white-hot extravaganza.

First Kings 19:5–8: *An angel touched him and said to him, "Get up and eat." He looked and there at his head was a cake baked on hot stones, and a jar of water. He ate and drank, and lay down again.*

The angel of the Lord came a second time, touched him, and said, "Get up and eat, otherwise the journey will be too much for you."

He got up, and ate, and drank; then he went in the strength of that food forty days and forty nights to Horeb, the mount of God.

These are the gestures — so common, so plain, so small as to be scarcely noticeable — by which the spirit is turned around. The soul's conversion, O child of God, by three simplicities: a word, a touch, a meal of bread and water. And the prophet arises. Forty days and forty nights is a fullness of time. Elijah makes it through.

In this way, Matthew turned around.

Neither Thanne nor I was there to see its modest beginning.

Nor do I think Matthew himself noticed the infinitesimal moment.

Just this, as Jesus observed in the Prodigal's parable: *and the young man came to himself.* And lo: he was dwelling among the swine, friendless, penniless, hopeless.

And lo: our son was dwelling in the most wretched sections of south Indianapolis, sleeping among a filthy roomful of nameless, rootless men. And something happened.

That room might just as well have been in an abandoned apartment building: foul, greasy, broken, loathsome. And the neighborhood outside was not better. The weeds were ruinous, the concrete downright dangerous, addicts, head-bangers, robbers, alcoholics, men half-mad and murderous, packing weapons of every sort.

And something happened.

This rough setting is not drawn from my imagination. I am describing what Thanne and I have with our own eyes seen. After that tender, nascent turning had begun in him—before anyone could truly identify it, let alone build a trust on it—Matthew directed me as I drove through south Indianapolis and that crashed neighborhood. He sat in the back seat. I forced myself to go slowly, aghast at the danger of this place. What if the car stalled? I'd rather know a direct way out and take it.

VI.

And then it was one year after Matthew and I had driven in silence down to Indy and to Butler: *I got some friends here*—

Thanne and I had found our way to our son again.

It was later January 1996. We'd driven down to help him move into an apartment he intended to share with a friend.

Matthew was working in a restaurant downtown. Tips, change, free meals—and a small wage. The fact that he could eat well once a day was what enticed him to apply at restaurants in the first place. He worked at several places, one of them an Outback eatery. Steaks. Another a more gracious restaurant in the mall downtown.

These things he had initiated on his own.

I fell all over myself praising his progress.

He had added certain things, now, to his stuff. A bar and wheel-weights. Outside his new apartment, shifting stuff from the truck, one of the twenty-five pounders slipped from my hands. It dinged once on the gunwale, then hit on the big toe of my right foot, causing such a sudden, impossible pain that I hopped around in an astonished laughter: *It can't be! How can I be **thinking** under such pain?*

It broke the toe.

And then Matthew and Thanne were sitting on the edge of his bed, discussing alcoholism, making plans for—and organizing the finances of—his future.

We three spent an afternoon in the downtown mall. I bought two pairs of shoes. Matthew, genuinely smiling, encouraged me to spend more money than my thriftiness—my penny-pinchingness (what was it? so tight I could make Abe Lincoln squeal?)—would justify.

"Style," said the all-knowing son, since his father lacked the least thread of it. "Style is worth the money, Dad."

We talked about the fact that Talitha was getting ready to graduate in four months.

Later that day Matthew suddenly returned to that topic. He said, "Can I go with you?"

"Where?"

"Down to Atlanta. For Talitha's graduation."

"Of course!"

And so *that* plan was fixed. And I was tickled to be making plans at all. It bespoke a future. Together.

Before we left Indianapolis for the trip back home, Matthew asked whether Thanne and I would drive to the south side of the city, into a neighborhood which began to frighten me on sight. Hurricane fences torn asunder, allowing full-grown men to scramble through; hiding places and routes of escape at night: from the police, from one another; grit and crumbled pavement; a blanched, angry weed-bunch wherever we could set foot. Men hanging out, smoking dope. Evil sleeping low on the air, flipping its tail like a yellow cat.

Matthew said: "This is where I used to live."

———

No: you mustn't for a minute assume that after such a weekend all was well between us. Take it, rather, as a sign for hungry hope. Feed upon it! Frame it. Set it as a photograph among the keepsakes on a living room shelf. But do not relent because of it.

There is so much work before us yet.

And we find our ways by touching the path no farther ahead than a mere three feet. We parents find our paths by tapping white canes as blind folk do.

The miracle is almost never in something's suddenness. It rather arrives in the soundness of the thing, softly, in the smallest degree. And in this: that a transformation proves itself to last longer than a rainstorm in the desert. By the passing of many days, by long and longer months the change *becomes* a miracle inasmuch as it is durable and repeatable, a rising, reputable thing, a new reputation among the public which can finally earn the trust of that public. By its becoming ingrained and a spontaneous pattern does the change emerge a miracle. Drawn upward by a cord of love.

This change is not a change of clothes. It is rebirth.

19

1996 — 1997

How can I give you up, O Ephraim?
How can I hand you over to be stoned?
My heart recoils within me;
my compassion grows warm and tender

I.

While she was yet in high school, Talitha stood watching an Oprah Winfrey show. Thanne had called her into the family room, thinking the girl might be interested. Oprah was bringing together, live, on screen, certain birth-mothers and the children they had long ago given up for adoption. Huggings and tears, the pressings of faces into necks and shoulders. This, their first meeting since the girlhood of one and the infancy of the other, produced deep sobs of joy.

As Thanne recalls it, Talitha watched several such reunions, saying nothing. Suddenly her daughter turned from the TV and slipped into a nearby bathroom, whence, Thanne thought, came sounds of sniffling.

They had a conversation, mother and daughter: perhaps Talitha would like to find her birth parents some day. But perhaps she ought to wait until she's eighteen. Because ... well, what if her return brought up secrets which might ruin her birth-mother's private life? Or what if that mother rejected her? But when she is eighteen, her mother (hum: her *adoptive* mother) will help Talitha every which way she can.

And so it came to pass that, once the younger was eighteen, Talitha and Thanne began their sleuthing. They knew where she was born, both the state and the town. We all drove through it once when driving Talitha home from Spelman: very white. Conservative. The two women began to check records in whatever place they could imagine: hospitals, town hall, schools.

As though it were divine, a significant key to the identity of her birth-mother was vouchsafed to Talitha and Ruthanne. It gave them both her name, Mary, and the name of her father. What a leap in their investigations! But it did not unlock Mary's present location, phone number, address. In order to gather that information, one of the women would have to telephone an unknown man.

How much to be gained! How much to be lost upon this call.

"You do it," Talitha said. "I can't."

Talitha was back in Atlanta at Spelman. Two spies hunkered down, co-conspirator's breathing down the necks of folks who did not know how near the huntswomen were.

Thanne would call. She agreed. She prepared herself by praying trembling prayers. She refused to lie. On the other hand, if she spoke the *whole* truth it might cause fear in a father's heart. He might hang up and the link lost forever.

She dialed.

A woman answered.

Thanne asked for Mary W's father by name.

When he came on the line, Thanne spoke into the darkness: "My daughter and your daughter knew each other a long time ago. But they've lost contact. Could you give me Mary's address? And her telephone number?"

There was a long pause. Perhaps Thanne heard a woman's voice in the background.

The man said, "Wait."

Finally, through a slow fog of hesitation, the rough-sounding father of Mary W gave Thanne her address. And his daughter's phone number. He hung up without a question.

In the months to come, we would learn that a woman *had* spoken in the background; that she had had a sense of the importance of this particular call; and had persuaded the man to tell the truth.

Immediately Thanne called Talitha.

"She lives in Dallas, Texas!" Thanne announced, panting.

Then she, too, hung up. She stayed right by the phone. At that very same moment, Talitha was dialing the number in Dallas. My wife and my daughter were blessedly intimate that afternoon, a perfect unity of hearts and goals. The adoptive mother dwelt in the terrible joy of her daughter, as the younger one sought to talk with another mother completely.

The phone rang.

Thanne snatched it up.

Ah — and then a mother almost weeps for her daughter's disappointment. They spoke softly a while, and then went each about her own business. The number in Dallas had been disconnected. They'd come to a dead end.

Where one father fails, the Father Infinite succeeds. Here, again, I recognize the love of the Creator for each one of his children, and I take my fatherhood from such gestures as this:

Shortly thereafter Talitha traveled to Evansville on a mini vacation. She visited a number of her old friends there, among them a family that lived near 831 E. Chandler.

On the tea table Talitha noticed a high school yearbook, its title clearly visible. The book came from the high school in the town of her birth. Its dates placed the *year*book at about the time her birth-mother might have been attending there.

"Did you," Talitha asked the parents, "go to that high school?"

The father said, "Yes."

Wow! After so many years of knowing each other, it was only now she learned this fact about the man.

Talitha: "Did you know someone named Mary W?"

"By name. She was several classes behind me."

"Then maybe you don't know where she is today."

"No. You know. So many years—"

Well, it had been an impossibly long shot.

"No, wait!" the man bethought himself: "They had a reunion last year, and I know who might have a list of the names and addresses—"

A week later the man kept his promise.

And late that night Talitha called home screaming through the earpiece: "I have it! I have it! I got Mary W's telephone number in Dallas. Different one. She must have moved—"

Step by step they were closing in on the flesh and blood woman. Jungle vines and the steaming jungle leaves were just about to part.

Thanne introduced a note of caution.

"It's late. Don't call her tonight. We both know how much you hate to be awoken. Call her in the morning."

How long can the child wait to meet the she who's been invisible all her life? I myself, countless times, had sat at a table across from my adopted daughter, squinting my eyes in an effort to visualize the parents behind her features. They must have bequeathed her the shape of her face, the swoop of her nose-bone, the luxuriant eyelashes, the etched eyebrows. I squinted, I blurred my vision, I tried to find the ghosts in back of her; and I lost the sight. I, too, could scarcely wait to meet the woman—

Early in her morning in Atlanta, Georgia, Talitha could wait no longer. She dialed the number. She heard the pulse of the ringing in Dallas, Texas. Then the connection was made.

A woman's yawning voice: "Hello? Hello? What!"

Talitha tells me she had framed two questions to be asked, and then a statement to follow the answers to her questions. Like Thanne, she planned the thing:

"Is this," Talitha asked, "Mary W?"

"Yes." A lingering assent. An uncertain tone.

"Did you have a baby girl on January the ninth, 1974?"

A breathing pause. Finally, now acutely alert, the woman answered: "Yes. I did."

Talitha's statement, formally spoken: "I have reason to believe that I am the baby that you had."

There stretched now a silence between Dallas and Atlanta too long, too weighty to be pleasant. Talitha kept the receiver to her ear. She did not hang up. She listened. What if she were again losing the link? Maybe this telephone call was like a stick in a hornets' nest. Talitha offered her birth-mother a means of release:

"I can call back later," she said.

But the invisible Mary W did finally choose to speak: "I always knew that you would call," she said. Though not quite wistful, the voice bore the worn varnish of an old truth. Then it turned sharp.

"I just didn't think you'd WAKE ME UP!"

II.

As we drove south to Atlanta, Thanne and I discussed the experience about to embrace us. Matthew seemed to sleep in the back seat.

Talitha had kept us abreast of her deepening discoveries of the blood families she now had. Carter M, her birth-father, was African American. Mary W, was white.

Thanne and I had traveled with Talitha to her birthplace in order to meet the man that Thanne had talked with, Mary W's father, his other daughters and the wife of his remarriage, following his divorce from the woman who was blood grandmother to Talitha. In fact, the man met her with a small, prepared speech.

"You are one of us. You can come here whenever you wish."

Evidently there had been some serious trouble in that town when his daughter came home from military service impregnated by a black man, *the* black man who had begun to hang around his house. Early, around Talitha's birth, he had cried the black man off his daughter and out his town.

You are one of us, a member of this family. I believe that his speech was the self-conscious erasure of that.

Except for one of his sons who lived not terribly far from Valparaiso, this man and his family were the only ones Thanne and I had actually seen before our trek south for Talitha's graduation. It was there we would see the rest of her forebears: her birth-father, his sisters and his mother Trula, Mary W herself.

Matthew shifted in the back seat. I glanced in the rear view mirror. Could he be disconcerted by our talk? By the prospect of meeting these people?

Carter and Mary, who had not seen each other at all since shortly after their daughter's birth, had gotten in contact with one another over the reappearing of the child. Carter traveled from the east, Mary from the west, to meet up in Atlanta where Talitha was.

And Talitha's birth-grandmother, Trula, had telephoned Thanne straightway after having talked by phone to Talitha herself.

"She called me 'grandma!'" the elderly woman had wept with joy, even to this stranger, the other mother named Thanne. "The baby called me 'grandma.'"

"What's the matter, Matthew?" I asked from the driver's seat.

He shrugged and rounded his mouth.

"I would never do this."

"What do you mean? Find *your* birth parents?"

"Never."

"Why?"

"Don't know. On account of what it could do to the family."

"Well, you don't have to," I said by way of comforting him.

He was quiet a while. Then: "I wish Talitha'ud leave things alone. She didn't have to push so far."

"Because of what it could do to the family?"

He closed his mouth and rounded his lips again. He didn't want, I gathered, to speak his feelings right out loud. Perhaps he couldn't. Perhaps he lacked the language for defining them.

But he nodded. I saw it in the mirror.

At that moment Thanne recalled how anxious the child Matthew would get when I spent days away from home. It seemed he desired his family always to be whole. Structured. Protective. So it occurred to Thanne just now that this could be his sticking point at his sister's knowing better than anyone else. He was afraid of what her heedless, headstrong charge might do to the family. Rip it apart? She had too many parents among whom to choose, allowing these two, we two with him in the car, possibly to be left dangling and bewildered.

But he had brought clean clothes with him.

And he initiated another topic, something more congenial to his present state of mind: *If his little sister could, why mightn't he . . . ?*

"Talitha told me about Morris Brown," he said.

This was another traditionally black college among the black colleges of Atlanta, Georgia: Spelman, Morehouse, Clark Atlanta University — but Morris Brown distinguished itself by accepting African Americans who had had difficulty at other universities.

Matthew said, "While we're there I want to check it out. See if I can't start college again. Academics," he said quietly. "Not basketball."

———

Actually, we all ran into one another in the parking lot outside the church in which Spelman's baccalaureate service was scheduled to take place.

Under a blinding sun, upon the shimmering concrete, women's high heels clack-clattering, we came together: Carter, his mother Trula, his sisters and their spouses, some nieces and nephews; Mary W and her own son by another marriage; Walt and Thanne and Matthew.

Trula was immediately a comforting woman. She approached Matthew as she did the rest of us, with a tight clasp, a genuine embrace. She was not tall, but lean enough to make her seem tall; a woman the color of walnut shells, a clean and melancholy face.

Matthew did not deny her the hug. Spontaneously he patted her shoulder then stepped back nodding and smiling a humble, charming, pinched-mouthed smile. He kept his eyes on Trula's, acknowledgement of her kindness and kindness in return.

We entered the crowded church. We climbed stairs and all found seats high and in the back, near the ceiling of the great nave of the African American congregation. In Thanne and me — nurtured so many years in a black parish, finding our children likewise parented by a black neighborhood — sitting in the midst of several thousand black faces produces a dear sense of community. (Even in airports we find ourselves unconsciously drawn to the loud laughter of African Americans.)

You are home, our hearts are thus consoled. *These are your people. Here is the blessing of the Heavenly Father. Be at peace.*

We craned our necks and squinted, trying to find Talitha down below.

The president of Spelman preached a potent sermon, praising her graduating daughters and repeating admonitions for their lives to come. It was from the muscles of her stomach that she drove her words mightily forth. I glanced over at Matthew. He wasn't sleeping. He was listening to the grandeur of this woman's spine and spirit. Oh, I was so jammed with gratitude. He had come. Matthew was witnessing the glory of black accomplishment.

Did he know? Had we told him that his sister had searched the web and found an annual scholarship for her graduate studies? That the size of the scholarship (offered by industry to African American women) would cover her expenses for every year she worked toward her Ph.D. in mathematics? She had applied and had been accepted at the University of Connecticut. U Con.

We sang fiery hymns, we thousands, lifting our women unto the attentions of God their Father.

And then we dispersed in order to meet again at Stone Mountain, there to share a picnic lunch before Talitha's graduation.

The more adventuresome of our party thought they'd like to climb Stone Mountain itself — a solid granite mass rising 800 feet into the Georgian air; grey, smooth, the figures of the Confederate best carved into the sides of the rock: Robert E. Lee, Stonewall Jackson, Jefferson Davis. Other members wandered off hoping to find a train to the top. Some folks went to purchase trinkets.

Trula and I stayed behind, sitting on opposite sides of a picnic table. Matthew, though removed to the very end of my bench, stayed with us too, never speaking, leaning his head on the palm of his hand, listening.

"Cassindra Marie," I intoned the name in a lazy manner. It was the name given our daughter at her birth. It was the name whereby Trula had known her all the years of her life until Mary W told Carter and Carter told his mother: "They named her Talitha Michal."

I looked at Trula, whose face and hair were dappled by the high leaves overhead, shot through with a May-time sunshine.

"How did it feel," I asked, "when you found out that Mary had given the child up for adoption?"

Neither Trula nor Carter nor any of her immediate family knew of Mary W's choice until the deed was done. I thought it must have been a jolt — especially now that I knew the generous heart of the woman before me.

But she said, "We gave the baby up to God. Never, though. We never did stop praying for her." Praying the name "Cassindra Marie."

Matthew, are you listening? Can you comprehend such love, lacking its object? And such a faith?

I considered what might have been a difficult subject, then ventured into it.

"Trula, when we went to court for an official decision regarding the adoption, we were told that there was no father in the picture. So he wouldn't have signed his permission, releasing his daughter to us. Carter wasn't consulted. Only Mary W had signed the papers. But you prayed for the baby. Did you know the circumstances?"

She folded her long, knuckled fingers together on the wood of the table. "We knew," she said.

"But then, why didn't Carter say something? There were a number of months between the time we brought her home and the time of the court's ruling. He could have stopped the process. *You* could have."

This is how quietly we three were sitting: the squirrels playing on the ground nearby began to snatch crumbs from under our table, scurrying around our ankles.

Trula said, "We didn't want to make trouble."

"Ah. Mr. E.," I said.

She may have nodded agreement.

Thanne and I knew what sort of trouble *he* would have caused in those days, his daughter great with a half-bred child. Therefore I could imagine what trouble Trula referred to, Mr. E's as well as her own. And Carter's.

"Wasn't that silence difficult for you? I'll bet you considered bringing the baby into your own home."

In fact, I now recalled that, one year after the adoption, Talitha's paternal grandmother had written the adoption agency, asking whether she might have a picture of the child. She wrote that she knew what the infant looked like, but not the yearling. The agency laid the issue before us. Our decision. Thanne and I refused. We feared we might be raising hopes which could never be fulfilled — or which we *hoped* would never be fulfilled, for that might mean the invasion of our home and the loss of a daughter.

But here was that grandmother, Trula, in front of me. Had we in those days known her heart (had we known how vastly accommodating is the black community for every wandering child) we might have been more forthcoming. In effect, we blinded Trula to her grandbaby until that baby came to visit her from Spelman College, grown.

"Wasn't that silence hard on you?"

"Oh, honey, yes. Very hard." She looked at me. She looked at our other adopted child, slouched at the corner of the table. She said, "But we got by on prayer. We prayed for her every day. We celebrated her birthdays, you know, year after year. And we took comfort in God's eyes—he watching over her wherever she was and however she was."

I gazed at her. As much as we received the benefit of a daughter now graduating, her sights set so marvelously high, so much had Trula missed all the years of Talitha's—of Cassindra Marie's—life. Such a loss. Or, rather, such an offering to God.

I said, "I'm sorry, Trula."

She said, "Oh, honey, it's no need for sorrows. The girl was ever in the hands of our Father who art in heaven, hallowed be his name."

Evidently, that Father's hands were faithful; and this woman's faith in the Father, as well as in her praying, granted her the conviction of her granddaughter's protection.

I said this in my mind: *Her granddaughter,* and the depth of the loss came clear to me.

"In the Father's hands," I said. "And that was enough for you."

Walnut brown, aged, a lank lady in a cotton dress, Stone Mountain a grey curtain behind her, Trula leaned and stretched her arm across the table. But she did not take my hand. She took Matthew's while looking me steadily in my eyes.

"Yes," she said. "And I have the proof before me now. He sent the baby to your house. It was you, y'all, that gave my child such Godly good care."

Matthew did not deny her this offering either, her dry brown hand to hold his moister one.

III.

In the fall of 1996, Matthew had begun his further studies at Morris Brown College. In August he had a car for driving himself south. Likewise, then, he had a car for driving his own self north and home for the Christmas Holidays. The young man tended then, as he tends still today, to take his long trips all in a single gulp. So he left Atlanta early in the morning and pushed hard all the way through Tennessee, Kentucky, and Indiana home by the dark of night—where all but Mary Wangerin were there to greet him.

He came into the house blowing huge and husky bellows-full of air. His eyes were wide. "You won't believe it," he said. "You won't believe it."

He took his coat off and shed his wet shoes. But he couldn't sit down or else control his hissing energies.

"Ah'm driving up sixty-five—"

Matthew has begun to pronounce his hard "I's" like soft "Ah's," though not always; it depended upon whether his mood and tone were casual or not. *Sixty-five* refers to the Interstate Highway which he took from Nashville, all the way north through Indianapolis, turning off at Indiana 2 east of Lowell.

He is so overwrought by the story he's about to tell that we all gather to watch him pace and hear the tale told.

"Near Lafayette," he said, "mah tires started to let go the road, you know? Black ice, Ah think. Ah tried to slow down. Just tappin' the brakes—know what Ah mean? No more'n that—"

We decided that the event took place just north of the exit for Rensselaer. In the twilight. Long cones of snow caught in his headlights. This vehicle was heavy, enormous, a great, speeding pile of automobile, my son's personal "style." With a gentle affability, the car began to remove itself from Matthew's control. The steering wheel was as ineffective as a rubber hose. Both his brakes and his accelerator went mute. The boat began to drift, its rear end sliding left, the front end glaring toward the shoulder of the road and then the snowy fields to the east.

Having made a full balletic rotation at seventy miles an hour, facing forward again, the whole car slid sideways into the roadside ditch, through the ditch, up with a tremendous bump and over the next embankment, the exploded snow blinding his windshield, *all* his windows, his right side clipping the metal fence-stakes—finally the vehicle came to an absolutely silent halt.

The kind wind blew the snow away. Matthew hadn't breathed throughout the whole *pas d'action.* He drew in a shivering bit of air. His entire body prickled. If there was a thought in his brain, it had clotted. He couldn't find it. The engine had shut off on its own. These two things alone were pressed against his ears and his flesh: that the engine had died. But he was alive.

The rest was instinct.

He shifted the gear into *park*. He turned the key in the ignition. The engine purred to life again. He shifted into the lowest gear and touched the accelerator. The tires gripped. Slowly, gathering momentum on the field-side of the ditch, he drove forward. Farther. A little faster. He could not see how much of this snowy strip he had left. So he chanced a crossing. The car turned into the ditch, tipped radically left, causing the driver to gasp; but he kept his foot on the pedal, angling through the ditch, by momentum up the other side, slowing, then gaining traction again just when the motion of the car, on coming up the highway-side of the ditch, had fallen nearly to nothing.

So I tell Matthew's story. The gist is right, though I may have lost details in his own headlong rush to disburden himself of his mortality and terror.

He sat then.

He shook his head.

He said, "Ah think ... I'm thinkin' it was God."

Talitha shot up her neck. Shake the girl and advice'll fall from her mouth: "It's a sign, Matt! Never ignore a sign!"

He looked at his sister blankly. He spoke to the room, "The car didn't wreck," he said. "Not even a headlight out. Ah think it was God. He ..." Matthew closed his mouth. He opened it again: "saved my life."

That Christmas Eve he went to church with the rest of us. At the appropriate moment, we all arose and trooped to the table for Holy Communion. I took my place beside Matthew, praying that this gesture of his was authentic, not a mere deference to our standards, Thanne's and mine.

During her early years at Spelman, Talitha had tested several religions. How deeply each, I don't really know. But there was a period of time when she met with a group of Catholics in order to study the Bible. Perhaps she attended Mass as well. More seriously, after the Catholics she began to move among the Muslims with a more focused intensity. The level of her entrance into the Islamic religion can be calculated by this: that, though she went to church with us when she was at home, Talitha ceased to partake of the Lord's last supper.

Curiously to me, our daughter was at the same time reading, arguing and assimilated "Womanism," the black counterpart to Feminism. Talitha rejected the arrogance of the white female assumption that both races had suffered the same patriarchal dominance. *All oppressions look and feel alike!* No: Black had suffered as well the racism of these same white feminists! Thus the paradox of Talitha Wangerin: while she was emerging as a black woman, and proud of the status, she was considering a religion which "protected" its women; and even if this (male) protection came of a genuine love, nevertheless it reduced the female's freedoms. It narrowed severely the sphere of her life.

Which of these would finally wrest the heart of our daughter?

One Sunday, without a word of explanation, Talitha rose with us from the church pew and walked forward to the table of grace. There the body, there the blood, there a return in perfect silence, and therewithal, a sign. And though this was her only sign, it was enough. She was back among the Christians.

I tell you of Talitha's care regarding sacred things to explain my hopes for Matthew when he, too, received holy communion with the family on Christmas Eve, 1996:

For I prayed fervently on his behalf, that like his sister he would *not* do what he did not believe in. That he, too, was among the Christians.

But what could I know for sure?

I think it was God. He saved my life.

What did that mean? What did such a proclamation reveal about Matthew's stance before his almightier Father?

I don't think he was attending church in Atlanta. And though I, his pastor more than twelve years ago, had trained him in the faith for his confirmation examination; and though I myself had heard him recite the meaning of the second article of the Apostle's Creed: *I believe that Jesus Christ, true God, begotten of the Father from eternity, and also true man, born of the Virgin Mary, is my lord!*—yet I could not calculate how much he had delivered his soul to the words.

Thanne prays. She prays during that period when all the rest of the congregation is ushered forward for their crumb and their sip. She bows her head in the pew beside me and is, in some measure, transported on a sacred wing. She becomes an earth mother appealing to the sky Father on behalf of the offspring which they (and I) do share. She begs heaven to keep all her children in its care and, when we shall have died, to bring us safely there together.

I have no doubt regarding Thanne's faith and the puissance of her praying. I do not doubt the Father to whom she makes her supplications. Why, then, did I in those days find myself night-frowning for the sake of my son.

This, too, the parent must in love sustain: the not knowing. Allowing the adulthood of the child by letting him alone, no longer peppering him with questions, granting both space and time to *be* his own person who labors at self-discovery, while his parents stand back and wait. In a blind unknowing to wait for the thing that may never come: conclusions of the child/adult's wanderings, after which a clean revealing of his mind.

I think it was God. He saved my life.

Can I believe the full theology behind his comment? In spite of its frequency and its banality, the cliché which unthinking people use to explain why some crisis did not kill them, could Matthew mean it after all? And though this phrase mimics another just as knee-jerky: *God must have some purpose for me yet,* can I believe in the deeper implications? Even banalities can testify to a faith in God.

Oh, Heavenly Father! You transform a slim beginning into a sturdy conviction. Even so, remember my son. Stay with my son. By your breath bring him to birth, a new creation.

> *Can a woman forget her suckling child,*
> > *that she should not have compassion*
> > *on the son of her womb?*
> *Yea, they may forget.*
> *But I will not forget thee.*
> *Behold, I have graven thee on the palms of my hands.*
> *Thy walls are ever before me.*

20
1998 — 1999

I am God and not a man,
the Holy One in your midst
who will not come in wrath.

When I roar
my children will
come trembling like birds from Egypt,
like doves from the land of Assyria,
and I will take them home again,
says the Lord.

I.

Saturday, the sixteenth of May, 1998.

I'm wearing my wheat-white alb, a cincture and a stole, preparing to lead the liturgy and to preach for a wedding.

Sitting near me, on a folding chair, at a table in the fellowship hall of the church, is Ray Washington, dark skinned, handsomely black. He is nervous and exalted at once.

"I can't get over it," he says again and again, shaking his head. "So many friends! So many of my friends have come to my wedding."

In what I hope is a soothing voice, I ask about his nerves.

He smiles. He gazes at the wall.

"I'm fine."

But his fingers are playing a fast tattoo on the table.

His best man comes in, a man I haven't known till last night's wedding rehearsal. He indicates that it's time to step toward the front of the sanctuary.

We all walk there. We stand waiting behind a closed door. Stuffy. Faint sweat smells.

The organ music begins the piece I've been waiting for. My signal. I shake Ray's hand. I tell him how proud I am of him, then I go alone through the door. I walk out into the chancel of the church. I cross the carpet and take my place before the altar, facing the congregation, a sweet mixture of black and white.

I am delighted to see how many folks have come north from Evansville to celebrate with our daughter. Old friends, good friends.

The processional begins.

And here comes Talitha, my daughter triumphant. As she passes forward, she acknowledges her birth-mother, Mary W. Oh, lovely Talitha! She chose a dress both simple and luxuriant and (best of all, to her way of thinking) inexpensive. Up the aisle by a lingering step, come to be married by me to the handsome Ray Washington who now stands close before me. Behind me, on the altar, is a handmade clay goblet which I shall use as an illustration of marriage and which, then, I shall give the couple as my gift.

During the reception later, Ray and a number of his fraternity brothers sing a formal song to his new bride. Ceremony and then a hooting break into laughter.

It is finished.

On the very next day, Sunday the seventeenth, people gather again, but this time in our living room. These are the same friends from Evansville, African American. Now friends of our daughter Mary dominate, as well as the friends and family of *her* husband, John Sauger. This time I am not robed, but I've dressed in a black shirt and clerical collar. I have one more glad, official duty to perform: the baptism of our first grandchild, infant Noah Sauger.

There is a flaming maple tree in the field behind our house, one I purchased and planted three days ago, naming it the "Noah" tree.

Just before the ceremony begins, Talitha and Ray come in. Oh, what a happy day! Everyone is here. We sing. Joseph's girlfriend, Catherine Preus, plays the piano. At the baptizing itself, while I flood Noah's head with a drowning water, his mother, our daughter, Mary Sauger weeps with joy. John drops a few tears of his own. So does Joseph's Catherine on the piano bench.

Then we take up the wide bowl of baptismal water. I carry it out the screen door into the backyard. All the people follow. Thanne holds her grandson, the babe in her arms.

It is around the skinny red maple we stop and draw ourselves into a tight circle. I ask Thanne to stand with Noah in the tree's shadow. I speak an invocation and pray. I then discuss three trees and a fourth.

— The Tree of the Knowledge of Good and Evil, of which we all have eaten, making us rebels against our God — who sent us from the garden before we could eat, too, of the Tree of Life.

— The tree on which our Savior died for our sake — for the sake of Noah Sauger, fat, kicking fellow in his grandmother's arms.

— The Tree of Life again, which we shall see again at the end of this age: *on either side of the river, bearing twelve manner of fruits; and the leaves of the tree are for the healing of the nations.*

"Noah has drowned," I say. "He has died to the first tree by the strength of the second tree, the benefit of which tree became his own in the flood of his baptism. And he shall surely find the third tree hereafter and eat of its eternal fruit."

I poured the water at the roots of a fourth tree, the maple, which is meant to embody the story of all three trees, and which symbolizes Noah's life in Jesus.

And when the people turn back toward the house, the Evansville contingent begins to sing. We all join in: "Blessed assurance! Jesus is mine. Oh, what a foretaste of glory divine …"

I follow behind the recessional, heartily weeping. Both in the marriage yesterday and in the baptism today, we have embraced a number of beginnings again. Moreover, in this baptism, which reminds us of our own baptisms, we've held death in the left hand and the beginning of life in the right. Stretch our arms, stretch them ever so wide, this is the full span of our reach: from an Alpha to an Omega, from birth to life to the first, worst, of all our dyings, and then to life again.

———

And then Matthew.

Actually: Joseph and Catherine, once more enriching this year, 1998.

They chose to marry in Minneapolis on September the sixth. Catherine's father is also an ordained minister; therefore we shared the leadership of this wedding ceremony. I got to preach. We both got to share the chancel as a dancer interpreted a hymn sung grandly by Catherine's cousin, Mary Preus:

"My life goes on in endless song … How can I keep from singing?"

Watching the soaring dance and listening to the music and gazing on the remarkable couple before me, my heart ached as though of hemlock I had drunk: Joseph, bretfull of experiences harsh and jolly and holy, gentler than he knew, tougher than known as yet, surviving on art and on humor; Catherine, as blonde and strong and fresh with health as the Norwegian snow cliffs, filled with laughter and the carnelian emotions that brightened the value of any scene, until we all are made to feel the same: Gloriana! Sense and a hankering fancy, prudence and impulse in the both of them. My heart ached, I say, but not for envy of their happy lot, rather for being too happy in their happiness.

This provided the context for Matthew's emergence.

He was Joseph's best man.

As such, it became his duty to raise a toast to the newly wed couple, his brother and his sister-in-law.

Though he stood on no dais or elevation, he made himself visible to all the flush-faced, craning wedding guests by shifting from one foot to the other, seeming thereby to be stepping up a step and down a step, presenting a solemn brown countenance, for what he had to say was serious, serious.

He took his time.

He began by describing his fear, his immediate aversion to this girl ... friend of his older brother Joseph. On account of: Matthew could see how much they liked each other. Might-be, loved each other. She was an interloper, a smiling woman of devious plans. Matthew loved his brother more than she could ever love him. And what if liking turned to wedding? Why, Matthew would have felt that his strong and structured family were being torn apart.

All the hall was silent. Matthew was so solemn.

And then his parents (us) gave him, Matthew, the gift of airline tickets to Minneapolis to visit Joseph. My son took my winter coat.

Catherine kept smiling at him. Hmph! She asked him questions. She listened to his answers. She made him feel good. Hmph! See how devious a woman can be? She may smile and smile and still be a villain.

One afternoon they got up a game of boot hockey. A bunch of friends appeared. And Catherine (smiling, smiling) took the stick as if it were a weapon. Oh, what a catamount was she! A cougar of cuffs and true competition! She gave no quarter to anyone. The game became fierce — but never invidious. It was a game, remained a game, did not progress to war.

Matthew was exultant. He let himself play as hard as he could. I know. I have the evidence. He tore out the zipper of my winter coat.

Up and down; stepping up and down, the solemn Matthew turned his audience into a roiling zoo for laughter. He put me in mind of that senior high school game at the cross-burning, which also had developed into an intense contest, but not into the malicious battle the racists had sought.

In spite of himself, Matthew grimly continued, he started to like Catherine, in whose game there was nothing devious; all of her, her entire self, was open and tough and equal in spirit to his own game. Like her? Came to love her. Approved her for his brother.

No, that family had not just been shattered. It had received another sister.

At the end of his speech he rounded his lips, lifted his insouciant eyebrows, and black-strolled back to his seat.

What a debut! I had never known what an excellent story-teller Matthew was. In fact, both of our sons by nature knew how to bewitch an audience and, like some wizard, to lead the people both hither and thither.

II.

On the sixteenth of January 1998, and at his invitation, I met with Doug Haugen, the director of the Lutheran Men in Mission. He was already beginning to think about an LMM convention to be held in the summer of 1999, a year and a half hence. We met in his office, situated in the headquarters of the Evangelical Lutheran Church in America. I was in those days the host of the church's radio outreach, called "Lutheran Vespers." I taped its programs in the same building; so it was easy to ascend from the floor where I worked to the floor of his office.

He wondered whether the "Lutheran Vespers" personality might take part in that convention. Would I be willing. I considered how one could serve the other, my speaking for LMM, and for me, the men of LMM discovering Lutheran Vespers.

Yes, I would be willing.

But, Doug said, the LMM board would need to meet me first in order to approve his, Haugen's, selection. So, then: would I be willing to meet with his board and give some sort of presentation during the semi-annual meeting? It would be in this same building.

Of course I would.

Nearly a year later, at two in the afternoon on the tenth of December, 1998, I did.

I arose stood to speak to the LMM Board of Directors, all of whom sat around a semi-circle of tables. I told them a story, and I received a blessed friendship in return. No finer approval than that.

In consequence, Doug Haugen asked me to give the keynote address at the convention, now scheduled to take place in Breckenridge, Colorado, the thirteenth through the fifteenth of August, 1999.

I think it was within two months that Doug telephoned me in Valparaiso:

"Listen," he said, "you know that the theme of the whole convention will focus on the generations. Father, son, you know? Grandfather, grandson, all the generations of male family relationships. How faith impacts them. So we're inviting all the members of LMM to bring *their* sons or fathers or grandsons or grandfathers.

"So, I got this idea: why don't you bring your sons along with you? And, you know, if they're willing, they might play a part in the keynote. Speak with you to the men. What do you think?"

"Well," I was thinking out loud, into the telephone, "I believe it *is* a good idea. But I can't speak for my sons. Tell you what, Doug: give me a week or two to ask them what *they* think, and then I'll get back in touch with you. Okay?"

After Matthew had begun his second semester at Morris Brown, spring 1997, there had followed another period of silence. We knew that he had once again dropped out of college. That summer and fall he dropped out of sight as well. For the third time, his old patterns were repeating themselves. He tells us of nights when he was forced to sleep in his car. Homeless. Of encounters with the cops, dancing the ancient dance with them (be not cheeky or get cuffed, get hauled down to the precinct offices; permit them to search your car with no more evidence than that you are black and young and male—and your car is nice).

But slowly, slowly one more time, Matthew began to pull himself up (as they say) by his own bootstraps. (The image is, of course, impossible, except a person knows how to fly; except the angels of the Father come down to lift a person into flight.) Matthew sought jobs again in restaurants. He scanned the "Help Wanted" sections. In the end he was given a position in a fast-food franchise—where he worked himself up from a line worker, slapping sandwiches together, to night management, to the self-fulfilling position as general manager of his own restaurant.

By that *annum mirabilis*, 1998—surely before May that year—we were in communication again. Matthew had his own apartment, where Thanne and I had visited him; his own DJ equipment; a huge collection of records; the biggest TV a person could buy; a YMCA where he worked out—a life! Matthew had a life.

So I called him and Joseph both.

What did they think of this idea: getting up on a stage with me and addressing an auditorium full of men, all ages.

To my happiness, to my astonishment, neither son hesitated. I truly don't know what they imagined then; but they both said Yes. Of course. Why not?

Thanne would come with us. Catherine would come, too. And Thanne took pleasure in planning visits such as to her sister in Kalispell, Montana, and our relatives in Denver. The church-wide assembly of the Evangelical Lutheran Church in America was scheduled to follow on the talk of the LMM convention. I would spend official time there while Thanne and the other two visited.

Oh, what happy anticipation, several weeks in Colorado!

And yet, what a shivering set of nerves unmanned me. I didn't know how my sons would do. I would have no real chance to save them if they needed it, certainly not after they actually started their speeches.

We planned, therefore, all to meet in Minneapolis on Monday the tenth. Joseph and Matthew and I would seclude ourselves from Thanne and Catherine all day Wednesday. We would use that day for planning. Each of us would indicate what he was preparing to say during his time in front of the lights. And the sequence of the evening—who first, how to accomplish transitions—had to be established.

Thus was our plan. And we fulfilled it in the end.

But the day took on a glory I could never have anticipated, not in all my years of faith and expectation.

We closed ourselves inside something like a sun parlor, a porch/living room windowed on three sides of it. But there were leafy trees outside that cut the sunlight. Or else the room projected to the north. Somehow I recall the space as dimly lit, causing the three of us a kind of bedbug intimacy.

I went first. I said I thought I'd tell of the time when Matthew stole comic books. If he didn't mind, I would include everything. Three times he kept stealing. Three times I disciplined him—all the way to …

Matthew indicated that he didn't mind.

So I began to recount our common experience, pacing up and down the little room.

When I got to that part, the third punishment, the spanking of my second son, I started swallowing. My voice swooped up a level, surprising me. And I broke into tears. I smiled, I tried to keep speaking, but couldn't. I had to sit down. I wept. I couldn't stop sobbing for all my sins these past twenty-eight years. For the suffering we, all three of us, had endured.

Yes, but there had always also been this thing which brought us back, each to the other again. Look at us! O my sons! I can see in your faces how love has bound us so indestructibly together. Tender, tensile strength. One family. The men of this family.

So I found myself crying the tears of an ineffable joy.

Joseph and Matthew recognized the change. They grinned. Their eyes glinted with moisture. They joined me in this sweet, mysterious relief, in the wholeness and the happiness that follows.

I stood. We put our arms around each other, and there was nothing to deny us the kindness. No chasm. No cruelty. No anger, or guilt, or shame. No misery. Neither distances nor silences to isolate us each from each—

"I love you, Dad."

What? What did he say?

Softly but distinctly, within the humidity of his breathing, the word had been murmured in my ear, *I love you, Dad*, and I was granted fatherhood all over again.

Ah, Matthew, my son, my son—here it is! This is the sacred thing. After long years of underserving, the unexpected thing: our reconciliation after all. Isn't it wonderful? (I feel whisker-stubble against my cheek.) Nothing divides us any more.

How I love you, the warm embracing of your arms. My old fears are defeated. I am flooded with the love of you. I don't want to open the doors of this small solarium. I want to stay in this place forever, nothing changing till I die.

Then Joseph took the pacing floor and told the story he planned to tell on Friday. We laughed. We laughed till we coughed.

And Matthew told his story, which was for me a healing revelation, an insight into my son's spirit, the spirit hidden from me when he sat in my study, slouched and frowning, and I sought better and better ways to scold him. Matthew granted me the thing that would have consoled me through the last twelve years but which, coming now, became my crown and my glory.

Before the afternoon was finished, we had worked out the parts and the transitions of our presentation. We'd have three chairs on stage. I would begin with an introduction, then give the stage to Joseph. When he was done, I'd take the stage myself to recount the disciplinary experience which I shared with my son Matthew, both of us being changed thereby: *No, but because Daddy cried. I quit because he cried.* Next I'd give the audience that same son for the telling of *his* tale. When Matthew was done, I planned to conclude the evening with some final comments. What these were going to be, I didn't yet know. Well, and if I *had* known, I would have had to pitch them out. They could not have applied any more, so divine would that evening become.

III.

> *The living! The living!*
> *he shall praise thee*
> *as I do this day.*
> *The father to the children:*
> *he shall make known thy truth.*

We pace and pace behind a curtain hung to hide the space behind the right side of the stage. We listen to the swell of male voices out in the auditorium. Fixed within the curtain is an enormous screen upon which the projector here above us is displaying a series of pictures. There's another such screen behind the other side of the stage. But we can't see it. Entertainment runs on the screens while the male generations stroll around and find their seats.

Soon we see, but reversed, the logo of the Lutheran Men in Mission which the projector has frozen above us. A music arises, signaling Doug Haugen's approach to the podium and shrinking *my* guts, if not the guts of my sons, into sausage links. I have a terrific urge to go to the bathroom. Matthew wears his lips pooched out, his eyebrows low: the black man's nonchalance. Joseph's cheeks are pinked by — I'm sure of it — his tension. None of us looks at the others.

"Walt Wangerin, and his sons, Joe and Matt."

Electrifying words.

But we walk out onstage seeming filled with confidence and grateful for the welcome. Men are applauding. I think it's more their mutual camaraderie, their happiness to be together, than it is for praise of us. But their happiness grants us several minutes' genuine credit. If we spend the credit well, they will have come for us after all.

Joseph and Matthew sit.

I walk to the microphone and slide it out of its cradle.

"Fatherhood," I say among other things, "is a duty given to us by God for the sake of our sons — who are His sons, too. As God is a Father who continues to struggle with his children's free will and the foolishness of their decisions, so are we. You can see, then, that fatherhood does not ask a buddy-hood of us. Nor does it offer us the reward of buddy-hood. Sons are not so much buddies as they are unlearned pups to be raised and trained by men older and wiser than they are — however the teenager might dispute that adjective: 'wise.'

"On the other hand, God is *our* father too. He uses our sons to witness to us of him and of his (our Father's) ways. They may not know it, our sons; yet their very innocence ought to keep us from sinning against them. It can reveal both grace and mercy to an earthly father. In which case, it is the son who is father of the man, and the source of wisdom after all — to those who have eyes to see it."

There are other things I say to get us started: a little pinch, a little praise for everyone. And then, by way of presenting Joseph, I speak our theme: "If we can, the three of us up here, we mean to lead by our own experiences, our faults, our sillinesses, yes; but also the power of God's mercy among us."

I hand the microphone to Joseph. He takes it. I sit. He walks slowly to the lip of the stage, head down as if in thought, pulling at his magnificent chin. The auditorium watches and waits.

Oh, look! I can see Thanne and Catherine, sitting far back on our right-hand side, by the side aisle too, under the lower ceiling and its lights, a brightness among the bulls!

Without a smile to give himself away, my son begins a story which, like a cobra, rises up to bite me, breaking the auditorium, shattering these men into fits of laughter.

He recalls our life in the inner city. He describes how often the young folk would gather in front of the library across the street from our house: loud hip-hop music, drinking, shouting, dancing, gambling, smoking dope. He speaks of my resentment for these late-night revelries—how I said that they would lead to fights and carnage, putting our family at risk.

With fair accuracy, Joseph explains my strategies. If we could get the few, the early junk-heads to move away the very first nights in spring, while they were still (like the queen bee) seeking where to spend their summer nights, we'd be free of them the summerlong.

My strategy, Joseph says, was to install two flood lights above the windows of our—his parents'—bedroom, the switch right there in the bedroom too.

"Pow!" Joseph suddenly explodes the word. "Two a.m.! Dad would hit them with his lights, and they would jump. Sometimes it worked."

Eyes of the audience, shifting from my serious son to me. Where is this going? What does son number one have in mind?

Now he narrows his scope to a single night in the middle of the summer. His descriptions are sharp, marvelous. They make me nervous all over again, even as I was that summer's night (oh, yes, I remember it!).

"Pow. But the floodlights didn't work. Nobody looked up. Nobody drove away.

"So at half past two dad came into my room. 'Joseph,' he whispered. 'Joseph, you awake?'

"I was.

" 'I want to borrow your flash. Not the camera, just the flash.'

"I got up and got the flash for him. It had its own battery, flashed just by pressing the button.

"I followed him downstairs and into the front porch. He was dressed for sleep, in his underpants and nothing else. He crept into the porch. I stood in the doorway to the foyer.

"He said, 'If they think I'm taking pictures of their faces they might leave—'

"Dad flashed. He flashed and flashed the camera light, jumping around the porch so it always seemed as if the camera were in a different position.

"Now the partying people *did* look at the house, directly at the porch."

Joseph dips his head and pulls at his mouth and chin. A long face of woe—but his eyes peep up at the crowd and they are twinkling.

"Of course they looked, but not because dad's strategy was working. No, every flash flashed back at him, reflected from the windows. What the street people were seeing was a white man in underpants, jumping around on his porch in strobelike lights.

"It wasn't me alone that was laughing then …"

The audience is howling. Oh, how they roar as I get up, seeing me (I'm sure of it) in briefs, knob-kneed and white as the screen on which my head was swollen, huge.

Thinking of the story to come (Matthew and me and the comic books), and striving to settle these raucous men (*O Joseph, what you have left for me!*) into a mood ready to receive a genuinely sober story, I take the mike and say something like this:

"Not buddy-hood, right?" Pointing at Joseph: "That story does not make that man my buddy!"

And then more seriously:

"Often it is the father who must teach his son the laws, ever before those laws shall blame him and shame him and cut him off from society. It is the father who must invoke the laws of God for the sake of one's son, communicating them by causing the lawless to suffer their consequences. For without knowing in his bones the Heavenly Father's commandments, a maturing son cannot know that Father's mercy. This is our sacrifice, my brothers, fathers like me: that we may have to give up the love our little boys once had for us; we may have to give it up for good, because the law-bringer is feared; he can be despised; but will not then be given the complete trust and sweet affection which he, the father, desires from his son. He may have to suffer the Moses-role in his son's life, nevermore to experience the glad adoration which the Virgin-Mary-role still receives from the church today. And so we do, don't we? We sacrifice the love of our son in order to prepare him for the world; and if we prepare him rightly, then someone else will get the glory of teaching him the Gospel. See? If we did not suffer the death of Jesus on Friday night, we would not truly rejoice in his resurrection come Sunday morning. So someone humbles the son that someone else might bring him back to life again."

A difficult doctrine. So far this evening, I have been the more boring of the speakers here on this stage. On the other hand, the more studious are nodding, as if my words were the real grist and preachment, all stories being entertainment.

Well, then next I entertain them. I lift the generations as if they were a child in the crook of my arm. Fathers and sons arrayed before me in the dark experience both sides of my tale, Matthew's persistent stealing of comic books and my persistent effort to train him up in the way that he should go—to train the man behind me, my Matthew sitting there. I do not choose to list all the other ways by which I became Torah to him. But they all, *all* those ways, bear hard upon my heart even now, in the telling of this particular experience. I grow sad all over again.

Why had I not learned about the blessedness of the tears of love right then? How could I have missed the Heavenly Father's most persuasive revelation in Hosea, chapter eleven: *How can I give you up? My heart recoils within me; my compassion grows warm and tender*: these, the tears of the Lord God Himself.

I introduce my son Matthew to the quiet crowd.

Just as I had arisen within the atmosphere of Joseph's superior scorn—and the peppering laughter of his audience—so now Matthew arises in the atmosphere of my judgments, my stages of training, his own transforming of the law into mercy.

He takes the microphone. Neither Joseph nor I nor Matthew will bind himself to a mike-stand. We all roam about. And now I get to see Matthew's feet while he tells a story, stepping up, stepping down.

And once again, he is my son. For each of them has received an inbred talent to tell an enchanting tale.

Matthew sets the scene. He was a teenager. We were living in an inner-city neighborhood. I was a white pastor among African Americans. Yes, he had his driver's license.

On a particular Saturday night he asked for permission to drive our car for the evening. It was a little white Reliant in which the family had taken continental trips, a sturdy vehicle.

His parents gave him the keys.

He drove to a friend's house, a good fellow, respectful to everyone including his, Matthew's, parents.

Soon he gave the keys to that friend who, since he was responsible for her that evening, drove with his young cousin at shotgun.

Matthew — up a step, down a step — makes sure to note that his friend never thought about seat belts.

So this friend, in Matthew's family's Reliant, drove up on Lincoln.

Up on Lincoln: this is a phrase referring not only to the Avenue named "Lincoln" which passed through the inner city close by the projects, but also to the activities that occurred there after dark: gambling, headlights bright in the eyes, cars crowding the avenue, boom-boxes and car radios causing the very air to tremble, dancing and dope and alcohol and periodical ram-fights, hollering, the testing of reputations.

"You know what Ah'm talkin' 'bout."

So his friend drove on Lincoln Avenue. Actually, it was jerk-driving, waiting behind vehicles, then shooting into any open space, then hitting the brakes: a jerky sort of driving.

Two, maybe three car-lengths opened up in front of the Reliant.

Matthew's friend accelerated. He shot into an intersection—just as a cream Cadillac, coming out a side-street, filled that same intersection.

The friend found Matthew.

Matthew walked and ran home.

He found his father (as always) in his study.

Matthew knew his face was filled with pain and fear.

As soon as he saw his dad, he said, "My life is over."

"What? Why?"

Then he, Matthew, told his dad a piece of the problem.

"There's been an accident on Lincoln. The Reliant. It won't go."

At which his father surprised him. Shocked him. (This is Matthew's story!)

He said, "Let's go."

Together they returned to Lincoln Avenue.

Matthew never thought that his dad would venture into the lions' den. But the white man never hesitated. More surprisingly, some of the toughest black men up on Lincoln *knew* his father, greeted him and joined him as he approached the dead Reliant, offered to help.

How did his dad …?

And then the whole truth began to come out. People had witnessed the accident. It didn't bother them to give information to this white man, though they would have withheld anything and everything from the cops.

The truth: Matthew's friend had been the driver. He had gotten up to speeding. Look at the side of the cream Cadillac, bashed in. Fortunately, not the driver's door, but the backseat door.

And look at the windshield of the Reliant: there was a round bubble pressed into the glass, which had been punched outward without breaking. This was made by the head of the little girl-cousin who had had no seat-belt on to restrain her. Matthew's friend had already taken the child to the hospital.

(Truly, I think to myself, remembering: they were not bad boys.)

And then Matthew felt an admiration for his father, because he handled it. And he took responsibility for the accident, though he declared that Matthew's friend would have to help with the payments.

He exchanged insurance information with the owner of the Cadillac — who was not inclined toward anger! The Reliant was towed away. Remarkably, the mess was cleaned up within the hour.

How brave the man, as handy on Lincoln as he was in his own house — with Matthew. And this time handiness meant no punishment! How could that be?

I have bowed my head. I've dipped my tender expression into shadows. I wish I had known. But I know it now as the crown of my fatherhood; and I know what my final remarks this evening must be: my son had good feelings for me! — even while I was berating him for destroying his curfew night after night; while he was slouching so deeply in my reclining chair that his chin was on his chest; while I was the hard force driving him into good grades. And "What do you want?" I would beg him in those days. And "To be free" he would answer, making sour faces under frowns unmentionable for blame and dissension.

And here was freedom after all. And it wasn't he alone set free. Why, it was his father too. And his brother, after years of such love that Joseph had suffered on behalf of, and for the sake of, Matthew.

Freedom.

The finest kind of emancipation.

Then Matthew can't help it. Freedom allows him, too, like Joseph, to poke fun at his father, though his sort of joke is the more indirect since he tells it from the point-of-view of a little boy, awestruck at (but how could a little boy know it?) the big man's stupidity.

"There is a storm coming," Matthew says. He has set the scene. The family is living on Heerdink Lane. The house has a half basement, dug after the house was built, surrounded with concrete.

"There is a storm coming. Tornadoes predicted. Mom has taken us all, all the children, into the basement. Ah'm scared, know what Ah'm sayin'?"

Murmurs from the audience, his men, every male under his control, knowing exactly what he means.

"But dad stays outside! He's picking plums. He's high in a plum tree, pickin' plums. 'What a man!' I think to myself. 'What a hero! The Hulk unafraid!'

"And then mom makes me admire my dad even more. She says, 'How stupid is that man! If the wind doesn't get him, the lightning will.'"

So Matthew has accomplished what Joseph did before him, caught their father in the glare light of mockery.

I rise, laughing myself, at myself, because I can see Thanne under the side lights, nodding with her arms folded across her breast. *You know it's true.*

And, filled with joyful emotions, I speak the final words. They were just made true, publicly before this spread of men, but privately in our secret, familial hearts, my sons and mine.

"Yes," I say softly. "Yes, we make the sacrifice, my brothers, fathers with me. Before the eternal, ever-present, all-powerful Father in heaven we exchange the love of our sons for our sons' success in the world. I mean: for love *of* them we give up their love of *us.*

"But then comes the miracle. It *is* a miracle, because it cannot be but by that Heavenly Father, whose son has taken the place of every one of our children here on earth, transfiguring them, an act of pure grace.

"And then we are astonished by the miracle—for if it had been expected, neither our sacrifice nor this reversal itself could have the power to transfigure us too.

"The miracle: our sons are given back to us after all. Though the offering was accepted; though we, like the Heavenly Father, had suffered the loss of our sons, yet they are resurrected.

"My sons. They have come to love me again. When I am least deserving. This is impossible. I cannot find the cause that makes such an effect.

"It comes from God.

"They will love you again, too. When that love cannot have come from them! When its only source is the Father.

"In *their* love, my brothers, is God's love, wrapped up in bows as any gift might be."

I lift my voice. It is the preacher's voice. I raise my two hands high.

"The Lord bless us and keep us.

"The Lord make his face to shine upon us, and be gracious unto us.

"The Lord lift his countenance upon us—and give us peace."

Making a huge sign of the cross, something afire to lighten the hearts of every man and every woman filling the vast auditorium, I cry: "And let the people say ..."

They say, "Amen."

Louder: "And let the people say ..."

They shout: "Amen."

And louder still: "Let *all* the people rise and say ..."

To which every father in all the world roars his convictions, a thundersome: "AMEN! AMEN!"

Let it be so.

Walter Wangerin Jr.

Interlude: Wife and Mother

Interlude: Wife and Mother

As Walt's wife and Matthew's mother, I was both participant in and observer of the events in this book. As in any intersecting lives, these events can be and often are perceived differently. Both Walt and Matt experienced joy, pain, frustration, fear, and sometimes near hopelessness. As Matt descended from pure exuberance and joy in his early years to sullenness and anger during his adolescence and finally to separation from his family, the love between father and son remained a constant.

As an adult, Matthew observed on three separate occasions insights that are apparent in this book. I remember them because they are not unlike our own activities and attitudes toward our Heavenly Father at various stages of our lives. I summarize them here in a few sentences:

1. If you hadn't been my parents, I would probably have ended up in jail.
2. There's nothing more that you could have done to help me avoid the difficult years than what you have already done. I was going to do what I was going to do.
3. I always knew you loved me and that you would receive me if I chose to return to you.

When Walt asked Matt and Joe to participate with him in the men's conference on the generations of grandfathers, fathers, and sons, he knew that both of his sons were more than capable of contributing to the conversation about how faith is passed down from generation to generation. More than that, he knew that this could be a turning point for Matt and that it would be a way for this father and son to deepen their reconnection. I watched as Matt eloquently told his well-developed stories with impeccable timing and good humor, and I knew that something in him was being transformed not only in this event, but in the preparations leading up to it.

Years later, when Walt wrote the first draft of this book, he used some of the experiences between him and Matt to bring his message to life. At some point in the writing, he felt that since so much of the book involved events in Matt's life perhaps Matt should have the opportunity to tell *his* side of the story. The two of them talked and Matt agreed to contribute to the book. They discussed the theme of the book and what the trajectory should be, but they didn't talk about what specific events should be included or how they should be interpreted. Each would tell his own story in his own way. Walt's only specific suggestion to Matt was to make a sign to tape on the wall above his computer: *Father and Son: Finding Freedom.* If Matt felt he was getting off track or wandering too far afield, he could simply look up to be reminded of the theme of the book.

During the next months, the two of them worked apart from each other, without discussing what each was including in his account. Each worked in his own place at his own pace and in his own words and style. In the end, they discovered that they had written about some common events, but from different perspectives. As you read on, you'll notice discrepancies in the memories of events. Neither Walt's account nor Matt's account is inaccurate, and both are true. In the end, this is a love story between God the Father and his children as it is revealed in this father and his son.

Thanne Wangerin

Book II: Son

PART 1

Two eyes open. An early morning sunlight phases through glass panes. Sluggishness. Dry mouth. Hangover. The two eyes survey. Poor recall. Last night. Nothing. A skyline of smoked glass on a table. Numbed by liquid. Unwashed clothes. A plane ticket.

I turn over in my bed and try to put pieces together. I know I am supposed to do something. The clues to my mystery are scattered throughout my small two-bedroom apartment, lying just beyond my mattress. I barrel-roll to the edge and try to put a leg over the side, but it is heavy, as if made of lead, so I roll back to the middle of my bed, where I left a warmth.

I look at my ceiling. In one corner I see a small spider working in silence. I look at the other corners. Each is as white as the other. Something has been in one of those corners, though. I can feel it.

Urgency overcomes me and I ride its wave, and throw myself out of my bed. I veer straight to the bathroom and look in the mirror. My eyes have a soft red glow of overindulgence. My stomach protrudes. A foulness from a breath flares my nostrils. I turn away from the mirror quickly, partly in disgust.

"Who would want to know about me?" I ask myself.

I walk into the kitchen and turn on the light. I open the door of the refrigerator. There are partially eaten burritos scattered around the insides. I reach for a soda bottle, whose contents no longer pressurized, has lost its snap. I take the cap off and drink. I awaken more. I finish the soda and toss the bottle into an overflowing garbage can. I move to the countertop and look at a letter. I remember opening it months before. The contents of it make me uncomfortable and nervous, but potentially triumphant.

Dad is inviting me to join him and my brother Joseph in Colorado to speak to a group of Christian men about legacies. The weekend during which we are to speak is devoted to fathers and sons and their lives and relationships.

"I'll do it," I tell Dad. I do not know, though, how I will do it.

Dad knows me. He knows things about me that I myself do not know. He was there from nearly my beginning and has been there in some capacity ever since. He knows of many of my highs and lows, my life moving like a volatile stock. He knows of my passion and drive. He knows of my attention to detail and problem solving. He also knows of my melancholy and self-destructiveness. He knows when things are jagged in my life when I say they are smooth. He knows me.

Dad and I have spoken of what my value could be to others. Some people do what they ought to do. Others do not. For those that do not, there are reasons. Maybe some are born with an extra bone in their foreheads, causing their resistance to "the way," closing their minds off from enlightenment, teaching and good decisions. Or maybe those particular persons need to hear a voice of experience. Maybe some people, those who live a life of hardship and adversity, need to hear from one who also walks the same as they, only to finally have emerged from a thicket of frustration, which discourages their lives. Problems always exist, but one can learn to attack them, as compared to compounding them by their own hand.

If there were an expert giving financial advice, many of those listening would receive the information as being correct solely because the person talking is considered an expert. The words rolling off their tongue remain unquestioned. There are others though, that will ask questions.

"How do you know?" they will ask. "Are you rich?"

If the answer is no, the expert will have lost the ears of those listeners. Dad insists that my value is with those who ask "that" question. He knows I was "that" person. I am both an expert and rich with "that" experience. How would I do it?

I begin to think about my life. Is there proof of Dad's legacy in my life? I look at my life as a slow-cooking stew. Have I placed the proper ingredients into this stew? Have I put the wrong ones in the pot? Or have I put in the right ones, but in improper proportions? I roll back my time to the beginning, in search of the answers. How would I do it?

1
Early Years

On my first day as a Wangerin, I meet my new brother and life partner, Joe. We grow up and grow close together, each day tightening our bond. My bones stretch and I learn to walk. Each morning, I look for Joe—my better half—usually still sleeping. I need someone to accompany me in my early life adventure. We play in the sandbox and chase insects in the yard. We investigate nature like miniature scientists. We decorate ourselves with food during meals. Little hands work fervently, cleaning our rooms, working adroitly, as we arrange stuffed animals and tuck in bedspreads, anticipating Dad's inspections. Many afternoons are spent drawing, painting, building and coloring. I often look over Joe's shoulder to see how his drawing progresses. The characters in his drawings always seem to have more dimensions than my stick figures. His lines are straighter than mine. I return to my paper, trying to improve on my artistry. As much as I try, my lines do not straighten and my colors do not blend like my brother's. I feel emotions and senses budding in my brain. I feel proud, proud that my brother is good. There is also an emerging competitive spirit and a realization that some people do things better than others.

On an afternoon when sun rays shine through the trees and warm our small bodies, Joe and I dash around the yard on Heerdink lane. We design games with rules of our liking. I am under the influence of heroes, having become obsessed with the Six Million Dollar Man and the Incredible Hulk. I leap and bound, imitating the sounds and actions of both. I am a crusader, as is Joe, though not as obsessed as I. We search for tree branches and rocks, anything which can become weapons that can be used to battle the darkness. I find one and rip it from the ground. I have a three-foot wooden tomato stake, which in my imagination, could be either a spear or a lightning bolt, whichever I choose. I want to show my brother my discovery and my new might. In a display of power and potency, I show Joe my new weapon, not by thrusting it over my head as do heroes on the cover of a comic book, but instead by hurling it at him. The tomato stake moves in a small arc, traveling slowly through the light breeze of summer, and cracks Joe in the back of his head.

I stand motionless, not knowing what to do. I see the stake connect with his head, but do not feel it. Joe's hand moves to the place of contact. His face turns from the pink of activity to a red of pain and suffering. His eyes squint and tears fall down his face. I am sad.

Mom moves Joe's hair away from his injury with bobby pins. His scalp is wet with blood. My stomach is plagued with nausea and my head becomes light. I apologize to my brother in my mind. I think to myself why I did what I did. Did I want to hurt someone whom I loved so much? My shame disperses as, after a short time, Joe looks at me and smiles in forgiveness.

2
Mom and Dad

Many mornings, while living on Heerdink Lane, after filling my stomach with scrambled eggs and orange juice and then peeling myself away from cartoons, I pass through the kitchen and porch, on my way to the backyard. Mom finishes the dishes. Her efficiency is astounding as everything has a place and a meaning. Her motion is a science. She uses a spatula to clean food remnants off of plates. She places leftovers in Tupperware. Potato peels and egg shells become compost. After the process, dish towels are folded neatly over the faucet. There is no waste in anything she does. Though she finishes, she is not finished, not looking to sit down and relax. She progresses to the next matter, as the list in her mind and on her tablet are checked off step by step. I observe briefly, then tell her I am going out to play, which is to her liking, as I will burn off energy outside instead of inside.

"Click, click … click, click, click, ping!" Dad types on an old typewriter. It is his passion. I walk down two steps and into the porch. His books ascend to the ceiling on shelves of metal. He pauses, breaking away from a theme. "Hi, Matt," he pats me on the shoulder, making me smile, as I rush past, a pinball, shot into the yard.

The battery which electrifies my bouncing body extracts its power from sugar. My cells are greedy for its sweet joules and place orders which I must pack and ship to them. Mom combats my cravings, designing her cupboards to distance me from the drug. But I am a scavenger and have evolving tools of guile which I use to fulfill my need. Sometimes when Dad is away and Mom is showering, I inch to the kitchen, silent as a cat burglar, and quiet my appetite. I make sugar sandwiches and drink syrup from the bottle. When a dessert sleeps under the cover of a cloth, I lift it and shave off piece after piece, like a surgeon carves away at a small mole, not noticing that ten shaves equals a gaping hole. As I bounce off the walls, day in and out, I pull my sisters and brother into the melee, and we have the time of our lives.

Mom and Dad are in constant movement, owners of the perpetual energy of children. They plan and then execute. They work separately and as a team. They have love, bound by faith. They are both teachers *and* doers. I learn from them, consciously and subconsciously.

Sometimes I watch Mom and Dad and notice how they do the same thing differently. Take driving. Riding with Mom is often excruciating and nearly unbearable. I often look over at the speedometer and roll my eyes as the needle matches the speed limit to an exactness I cannot endure. I squirm under my seatbelt, seeing everything we pass clearly as there is no blur. Mom's hands grip the steering wheel as the diagram in the driver's manual shows, and she checks her mirrors and blind spots again and again. Predictably, we arrive safely.

Riding with Dad is packed with action, and on my part, a touch of fear. Joe and I climb into the cab of Dad's lime green Toyota truck and fasten our seatbelts, which are never tight enough. Dad gets in and slams his door. We are going to the junkyard with our trash. Dad starts up the engine. Joe moves his left knee to the right, as the gear shifter, which comes from the floor, is put into reverse. I clutch the side of the seat, for I know what is to come. Dad becomes someone else. He puts the gear into first and crushes the gas pedal. Joe and I are pushed back in our seats. We giggle. I clutch my seat harder. An enemy driver accosts us, or so Dad leads us believe, and he makes his countermove, as his brow furls and his teeth grit. We swerve in front of the fool challenging us. We approach a red light and Dad smashes his brake, throwing us forward, then slamming us back to the seat. We giggle more. We finally turn into the junkyard, nearly on two wheels, before skidding to a stop in the gravel. Dad jumps out, on to the next step of our mission. Joe and I unstrap our seatbelts, our hearts still racing. We throw our bags on the mountain of garbage. We climb back into the truck and I clutch the side of my seat.

3
Dad the Pastor

Dad paces when he prepares sermons. I take great interest in his transformation from the beginning of the weekend to Sunday morning, when he preaches. On Friday nights, he "lowers the boom" on us during games of monopoly. No matter what strategy our tiny brains devise, he somehow manages to own hotels on Boardwalk and Park Place and then vacuums our pockets inside out, sends us to bankruptcy and then to bed. On Saturdays Dad paces for hours, sometimes sipping coffee and listening to soft classical music as he prepares spoken Manna. Many times while he is at church working, I explore his office. I open his communion case, examining the wafers and wine. I hold the cords from his robe, absorbing religion from the cotton, admiring the crosses and tassels, as if discovering a hidden lair. My eyes pass over the unending columns of books as I attempt to comprehend the knowledge he chews and swallowed.

Sunday mornings, as I remove crust from my eyes, a door slams. Immediately, I rise and look out the window and see Dad long-step through the baseball field towards Grace Lutheran. As my weary body enters the church, Dad greets me, as if he hasn't seen me in years. A hug and a scratch on the noggin from Dad uplift my spirit, momentarily taking my mind off the doughnuts sitting in the church basement.

After a roulette of readers share the Gospel, Dad takes his place in the pulpit. Sometimes he brings out props, mostly a chalkboard, diagramming the day's lesson. His message, most of the time weaved in a story, connects to a central theme. I look around the church and see people nod, acknowledging the truth in the words booming from Dad's mouth. His words are powerful and wise, caring and nurturing, for those whose ears and hearts are open.

Early on I recognize that being the son of a pastor makes one different. As soon as one becomes aware of who your father is, people scrutinize your methods. If you act exemplary, of course, you are the son of the pastor. If your choices are deviant, you are a P.K., which stands for "pastor's kid," a term meaning poor behavior can be excused because your father (or mother) is a pastor. Your dissection and critique by others becomes increasingly complex when different elements combine, as with interracial adoption, brown skin and hyperactivity. For me, though, in my youth, in my being, in my obliviousness of these factors, is a gradual drive to accumulate things which I like.

I am quite fond of mischief, labeled as fun in my sugar-coated brain. At church, a rich burgundy carpet covers the floor. It begins at the base of the steps, just inside the front door, continues up into the sanctuary and all the way to the altar. Underneath the pews, though, is wood. So of course I create a new game in which we pull ourselves from the back of the church to the front by grabbing the bottoms of the pews and thrusting ourselves forward. On many occasions, our games become contagious, influencing other kids to join in. Their parents quickly snap up their children, scolding them for their misbehavior, more often than not saying nothing to me or my siblings. During this period, I discover I can slip through the claws of reprimand.

I do not remember the first time I saw a comic book or even actually owned one. But after buying my first, I want more. The heroes and villains tantalize my young mind. Each comic, vibrant with color, dialogue and historic flashbacks, finishes with a cliffhanger, usually a new villain rising from the ashes, promising mayhem on the city and the hero. I trade issues with classmates. We talk endlessly of our favorite heroes and villains and of what we believe is to come in the next month. Davie, a friend from grade school, my most knowledgeable friend and fellow accumulator invites me to his house. I sleep over at his house often, but this visit is defining. Davie looks up to his brother, an aspiring comic book illustrator, claiming his brother has in his possession the most brilliant and massive collection in the world. Coming from Davie, I desperately want to see this collection, which makes Davie giddy each time he describes it. We have our chance as Davie's parents and his brother have left us alone in the house.

We move stealthily to Davie's brother's room. Davie pushes open the door. We step softly. The room has posters and drawings and action figures, leaving nothing to guess as to Davie's brother's love. Davie knows where the collection is and goes straight to it. Davie opens the closet door. Suddenly I understand why Davie's eyes grow bright when he talks about the collection. There in front and to the sides of me are piles and piles of comic books. The organization is meticulous. The stacks are aligned perfectly. Issues are in numerical order and have been separated by both heroes and companies. On one side are Marvel Comics and the other, DC Comics.

"Wait till you see this!" says Davie.

"Wooowww," falls from my mouth.

In a trunk, Davie's brother has the rarest issues of his collection. Incredible Hulk #1, Iron Man #1. All of the issues are secured in a clear plastic sleeve. The top of the sleeves are folded over and taped closed, reducing the air exposure, extending and preserving the life of the comic. The comics in the chest have an even heavier plastic sleeve, and inside have a sheet of cardboard which stabilizes the spine of the book. They are sealed completely shut. My mouth gapes open as I touch a copy of X-Men #94, the most important comic book ever minted. We leave Davie's brother's room. An impression has been made on me. "I want" a collection like that. "I need" a collection like that.

4
Stolen Comic Books

I begin to unpack boxes bearing my name on the side. I envision where everything belongs on my side of the room. We are in our new house on Chandler Avenue. In a windfall of luck, Joe and I are granted easily the largest and most attractive room in the house. Mary, Talitha, Mom and Dad take the rooms on the opposite side of the top floor. Joe and I divide our room down the middle, as if splitting up a newly discovered continent. In our negotiations, it turns out that the closet is on my side of the room, so we section off a narrow path leading into the closet on which Joe can walk, so that he would not be trespassing in my area of the carpet.

Invariably, I claim the largest shelves in the closet, a closet so large that Joe and I can both fit inside with space between us, and play. I am drawn to one particular box. I know what is inside. I slide it quickly to the edge of the closet, open the flaps, and place mounds of comic books on a three-foot-wide shelf. I go to a second box after emptying the first. This one reads "Matt's Comics." Joe doesn't realize the first box does not say, "Matt's Comics," but he also does not remember my having so many.

"Wow, Matt. I didn't know you had so many comics," he comments, not so much amazed as suspicious.

"Yeah," I answer, not wanting to say too much. I continue to stack, the comics now bending the shelf. A smell of must fills the closet and seeps into my area of the room. Joe pauses. He notices that most of the comics on the shelf do not have plastic sleeves on them. Not long before, I showed him my collection, having purchased plastic sleeves at the comic book shop in an attempt to preserve my issues as Davie's brother did. Joe deduces.

"Are those the comics from the barn?" Joe asks.

"Yeah," I quickly reply, not looking at him, but continuing to stack. Joe understands what this means. Not even a month earlier, on an afternoon adventure on Heerdink Lane, we investigate a barn many yards behind our neighbor's house. Seeing it many times before, we never dare to even look in a window. It is aged and abandoned. Vines crawl in and out of windows and holes in the wood. It looks a hundred years old, as if we knew what a hundred years looks like. Aware that we are leaving Heerdink Lane for a new neighborhood, we chose to do some of the few things we have not tried before departing. This means entering this old barn.

Every step is silent as we open the door, ready to turn and flee at the first sign of a bat or a monster. The only light comes from hazy window panes. There is not much of interest. An old lamp, old jars, an old chair, everything seasoned by a rust-colored dirt. Joe and I often think in tune, and we communicate to each other, without words, that we should leave. There is a large box which seems to want to be opened. My meddling hands reach down and open the box. Dust and dirt fall down the sides of the box as the top lifts. It is like discovering a great treasure in the dragon's den — rubies and sapphires and gold — in stories that Dad reads to us. But this is more valuable. My eyes, wide and lucid, light the room. Comic books, hundreds of them, all of them older than me. They must have been forgotten. I rationalize. They therefore would not be missed. I think to myself that in one "removal" I could double Davie's collection.

Ecstatic with our find, I conceal my intentions. Joe agrees we have made a great discovery, but we are on someone else's property and these are someone else's comics.

"I don't think you should do it, Matt," Joe begs of me.

"I won't," I promise him.

5
Grounded

"Matthew, we are going to have to ground you," Dad says. He and Mom shift their body weights, looking at me then looking away. They analyze the impact their sentence has on me. I look down at the floor, studying the sensation of this new form of punishment. Their new prototype is more sophisticated and hits harder than mere spankings. They take away opportunity. I am missing out on things now. Every Thursday, across the street at the Carnegie library, down in the basement, Godzilla movies are played. I love Godzilla and will miss him for two weeks. This hurts.

I look up at Dad. I see the concern in his face. There is also something else. His demeanor says, "Don't play with me, my son. If you try to outwit me, you will lose." I review my plan, wondering how I got caught.

Mom doesn't know how many comic books I have. Well, maybe quadrupling my collection in one day was too much. She shouldn't have been in my closet. Nothing to do now but serve my time.

———

My desire to accumulate betrays my desire for freedom. Mom encounters the comic books looming high on the shelf in my closet. She calls the neighbors after twisting a confession out of Joe and me. She returns the comics to the neighbors, surely a surprising gift, for they had forgotten they even owned them. I watch from my window as Joe, Mary and Talitha cross the street to the library. It is Thursday, the first day of my punishment. Joe looks both ways, up and down the street, wary of any approaching cars, protecting his vulnerable sisters walking behind him. They hold each other's hands, less cautious, trusting Joe's judgment. I should be with them. Instead I am isolated in my room. I hurt.

6
Introduction to Sports

I jump, landing in a patch of grass. "Seven feet, three inches." Clarence Fields, my scoutmaster, reads off the measurement of my standing broad jump. He writes the score on a clipboard.

"That's very good, Matthew," he says, containing a smile which wants to extend across his face. I have just scored in the top fifteen percent of all boys across the country in the standing broad jump.

Clarence Fields, a member of Grace Lutheran Church, has unearthed an athlete. He, himself, is athletic for his age. A man in his sixties, he runs in 5k and 10k events. He is tall and dark. His hair is mostly gray. He maintains a well-shaped, short afro. I first learn how to pick the pellet-like knots out of my own afro after watching him groom himself in the basement of the church. He also teaches Sunday School. He is a constant. For those that need consistency in their lives when few things can be counted on, Mr. Fields's being at church on Sunday is assured.

Sometimes one doesn't want to see Mr. Fields though. If your behavior was atrocious the prior Sunday, you will benefit from his reminder. He will greet you, reaching out his hand for a shake. If you forgot that you were a jester last week, you will recall, after he closes his large dark hand around yours and squeezes. As your eyes bulge and your metatarsals grind to dust, you understand that you need to improve on this Sunday. Before falling to your knees he releases your hand, sometimes with a smile at your mother who returns an understanding smile, and says he is happy to see you.

Mr. Fields, familiar to athleticism, encourages Mom and Dad to involve me in sports.

I try all sports and do well at them. My passion becomes football. I love Walter Payton, but the Pittsburgh Steelers have my heart. Terry Bradshaw, Franco Harris, Jack Tatum, Lynn Swann and the rest, excite me in unexplainable ways. Sundays become very difficult for me. Sitting at the dinner table, waiting for others to finish their lunch is almost unbearable, like riding with Mom. Sometimes I just get up, go into the family room and check the score, then return to the table. My message is clear to all at the table that their camel-like chewing keeps me from my game. My temper flares, and I wrestle with it. I negotiate. I ask if we could move a television into the kitchen. I suggest changing the lunch hour. My amendment is vetoed. "Okay, let's pray." Dad nudges the others, winding up the meal. He sees the passion writhing through my body. He wants me to be happy. He does not, though, want a small boy's fire to singe the threads holding firm the family unit. We say "Amen," I open my eyes, and am on the family room floor, a pillow under my head, watching Franco Harris run for the sideline before the first dish is cleared from the table.

7
Moving to the Neighborhood

"What's up, youngblood?" Philip Lawrence greets me. He reaches out to me, but different from what I have seen before. He doesn't crouch down, lowering himself to my line of sight, as many grownups do with small children. Instead he bends his right knee and leans his body to the right, only going as far as he has to. His hand is not vertical as with a formal handshake. It is more horizontal. It is like he is showing respect to a shorter man. I grab his hand while thinking of a reply.

"Uh, the sky?" I say, feeling dumb and stupid. He wraps his fingers around the back of my hand, as if making a fist with my hand inside his, then opens his fist, sliding his now flattened palm across mine, then locks his fingertips with mine.

Dad watches as I shake hands with this black man, the way black men do. Phil understands quickly that I don't know how to "give dap." He chuckles, then begins conversing with Dad.

Mom and Dad move the family to this inner-city neighborhood for several reasons. Dad wants to be closer to his job, as distance, gas prices and the elements, prove to be formidable opponents. Another is so that

Talitha and I can have a relationship with those of our own ethnicity. In my adolescence, I cannot fathom the role of race. I do, though, see a difference. Black people move differently, more lubricated. They talk with a freedom from a language manual's stricture. They dress with a flair which pleases the eye. Not all, but most. I feel a natural attraction to blacks and become friends with many, though always adhering to Mom and Dad's compulsory teachings, that we are all equals. My mind is open to influence, though unburdened with the complexities in life. I have my family, my friends and football. I want to have as much fun as possible, without hurting anyone.

8
Number 23

I have stolen again. I am grounded again. I don't know why this keeps happening to me. I am not a thief. I don't look to steal anything I can fit in my pocket. I don't do it just to do it. But when I see those seductive comic books, I blink once and a plan is already hatching as to how they will become mine.

I lie in my bed and think again of how I got caught. Remorse escapes me. I indulge in self-pity. This time they have taken away television. I drift away into sleep.

"Matthew, wake up! Hurry!" Mom is shaking my arm. I rise quickly as I have not been asleep long. Our walk down the hallway is brisk but delicate, not wanting to awaken, the small pop of Mom's ankles the only sound as we close in on Mom and Dad's bedroom. I see the glow of their nine-inch color television flicker against the doorway. I enter, mildly compunctious. Dad sits upright in bed, under the covers. He looks serious. I do not know what is happening. Had they discovered another one of my "removals"? Are they adding on to my sentence? Mom and I sit at the edge of their bed.

"I thought you might want to see this," Mom says.

I look at the television screen. It is a basketball game, which is peculiar, because they don't watch basketball. It is the 1982 NCAA championship game. North Carolina is losing by one point with less than a minute left in the game. I don't know any of the players, since I only watch professional basketball. My favorite player is Julius "Dr. J" Erving. The good doctor tickles the emotions like a skilled, soulful bass guitar player. He holds the ball like I would a grapefruit. He enervates defenses with spins like a ballerina's and swoops to the basket with length and extension, like a giant condor descending on a corpse. His moves are a variety of the unpredictable, and one can never look away from the television, or risk missing the fantastic.

I lean forward as the commentator introduces the current storyline. I learn as much as I can. The two teams walk out of a timeout. The coaches mask their stress. My eyes are drawn to one player immediately. He is very dark and exceptionally skinny. There is some majestic quality about him, which words can't spell. I like how he walks. His head bobs rhythmically with each step, like a racehorse walking out to the track. There is something about him ... this number 23.

A North Carolina player passes the ball inbounds. They swing the ball back and forth, looking hesitant, but also like they are searching for something. Standing on the left side of the court, number 23 gives a subtle wave of his hand. The ball comes to him, almost magnetically. He rises, his form text book perfection, and releases a shot. It lands clean, into the net. The whole city quakes. Georgetown rushes up the court with only seconds to counterattack. A Georgetown player thinks of passing to the wing, but pulls back as he reads a North Carolina player moving into the passing lane. The charge of the North Carolina player takes him towards half court, out of the play, leaving only four defenders guarding the basket. In what cannot be understood, the Georgetown player then throws the ball to the defender which overran a potential pass, a player whom he shunned seconds before. The North Carolina player catches the errant pass and dribbles away the clock.

My heart flutters. My parents, even though I am grounded from television, allow me to witness basketball history. I say goodnight to them. I walk back to my room and climb under my cool bed sheets. I roll over and turn, trying to find comfort. Once I settle, the reel in my head rewinds and replays the last seconds of that game. As my thoughts slow and I succumb to sleep, I wonder who number 23 is.

PART 2

9
Dad Builds the Basketball Court

Dad decides to build a patio/basketball court in our backyard on Chandler Avenue. I watch him from nearly start to finish. His jutting jaw, overgrown by a goatee, is unchanging. Neither fatigue nor discouragement slow him. I go out to the backyard and observe. As Dad works, he explains each step of the plan, withholding nothing. He digs up the ground. He then measures and sets up his perimeter of about twenty feet by twenty feet by tying twine to small wood posts sticking out of the ground. I return another day and he has leveled off the earth inside the twine. There are piles of dirt in the middle of the yard, probably three feet high. I take a sip of Crystal Lite. Dad's white undershirt is wet in the armpits and in the middle of his back. He wastes no motion. I try to remember stories of his working as a contractor, but cannot. I ask myself, "Does he know how to do everything?" He has already rebuilt the garage, painted and shingled it, and erected a fence around the yard, which keeps pot smokers off of our back steps and corrals our new dog, Lincoln.

It takes less than two weeks for Dad to plant the last slab of limestone.

He smoothes the cement, love in each sweep of the hand, then instructs us kids not to walk on it for at least a day. Mary and Talitha immortalize themselves by scratching their initials in a patch of drying mix. When the patio is finished, Dad puts on his final touches, hanging a basketball hoop on the garage. I percolate with excitement. I lace the new net on the basket and drop a new basketball through the rim, scoring the first goal. As Joe, Mary and Talitha lob up shots, I walk to the other side of the yard, dodging Lincoln's landmines, so I can see what others see when looking over the fence. The court is brilliant.

I put the court to quick use. I practice for hours every day, even when it is raining. My jumpshot changes almost by the month as I rehearse each variation thousands of times. When I watch basketball games, during timeouts I run out to the backyard spouting "Brenard King" and hoisting up as many shots as I can in two minutes, then race back inside as play resumes.

The constant door slamming and bouncing of the ball pound Mom and Dad's and the neighbors' patience as thin as a sheet of aluminum. But Mom and Dad know where their son is, his safety preserved. In the backyard, I am free to create.

10

Pain from Others' Pain

I dribble up the court, moving to the right side. I rise, my form textbook perfection, and release a shot. It lands clean, into the net. The other team rushes up the court with only seconds to counterattack. Time works against them. I score the game-winning basket of the state parochial school championship. I win the most valuable player award. We are the champions of the state of Indiana private schools. I wear number 23, just like Michael Jordan. I hit the winning shot just like Michael Jordan. I am not happy.

I go through bouts of selfishness, as does most any child on the planet. Certain things have to go a certain way and that is final. Certain things are just mine and that is how it is. Kids want to control their environments. Many of us just know how matters are to be, and we impose our will on those who do not yet understand these matters. Sometimes I ignore reason and rationale and simply want my way, regardless of how right or wrong I am. At times it seems to Mom and Dad as if I have an extra bone in my forehead, or maybe in my special nose, which locks out their wisdom and influence, sustaining my hard driving, ostensive willpower in its rawest, purest state. That "bone" already battles furiously with the concept of eternal life and eternal damnation, the clashes continuing deep into my dreams, causing night terrors, my body wet with sweat, me horrified, often waking up after falling from a cliff.

My will is iron, my desire permanent, like a tattoo or a scar. It runs through my DNA, as does the will of a greyhound. You can train one to sit and roll over and be a good dog, but when that door opens, its hind quarters contract, and it becomes a gray streak down the street. When one great will meets another, greatness can be achieved, unless their goals are contrary. Then horns and blades come together, the ringing of blows severe, shooting sparks into the sky.

And so it is with me and Dad. When I need, he provides me. When I want and then take, he acts to stop the taking and tries to reform.

How many times have I rested my gaze on the biggest steak, my pantry clearing appetite spurring my sides, only to have a man eight inches taller and fifty pounds heavier, extend it to me without my asking. Yet, how many times does that same man have to preach into that bone in my face, after catching me drumming on my brother's spine, to correct my flailing knuckles.

"You don't hit! You never hit," Dad roars, his face like an angry fist.

When I want to control the phone and the VCR and the TV channel and my dear sisters and brother, I end up in Dad's office or in the backyard.

"Matthew, look at me. Look at me! Those who think only of themselves are the saddest persons in the world!" Dad drills and pounds and digs at that bone. He wants me to be happy, to be free. Each day at his job, he sees the result of selfish, self-centered obsession. They smash through his door, asking for counseling and services, help and handouts. He listens to stories unravel, like a kite string, in which at the core is a soul that, like a small child, pulls close everything around them and shrieks, "MINE!"

With each lecture, sermon and castigation, that bone fights valiantly to preserve my original nature. My eyes water. My neck burns. I look down at the ground, watching ants work, knowing Dad's mantra now, word for word. After a time, he seems to be pushing through that bone.

I look at a picture of me holding my MVP trophy. I look at my face. I look at the face of the one holding the trophy with me. After winning a championship, he is not happy and neither am I. For the picture, I ask him to hold the trophy with me, for he could easily have won it himself. In the final game, he scores thirty-six points with an array of high-arching, net splattering set shots, closing the mouths of the other team's fans. My expression is sullen because I *feel* him, at a time when I could be absorbed with my own greatness. I ache for him. In this picture, my best friend holds this trophy with me, his face saying "It's your trophy, but I deserved it." I am not happy.

11
I'm Going to North Carolina

"You don't have to worry about paying for me to go to college. I am going to get a scholarship to North Carolina." I say it because I mean it. If I grow another foot, you can forget about it. I bless Mom with my prophecy, who I know will pass on the financial news to Dad.

I back my plan with diligence. Hour upon hour I work on moves, borrowed from Michael Jordan, Larry Bird and Isaiah Thomas. I take little from the "good doctor," though, because most of what he does is impossible for me to replicate. Most days, friends and others pass through our gates to play ball. I shower them daily with raining jumpshots.

"You're only hitting like that because it's your court," say angry competitors in defeat. Their assessment stings, but I do not desist in my work.

At night I work more, this time at the "secret court" or the garage. With a one-speaker boom box blaring "RADIOACTIVE" and "PLANET ROCK," I execute countless dribbling drills and a special jumping program of my design. After finishing with the secret court, I watch a film, decrypting a video tape of Michael Jordan's science. They are the most treacherous, daring and creative moves I can find. I splice together plays of slipped screens, back door cuts, steals and hang time moves, then replay the tape hundreds of times, in my quest to earn a scholarship.

I am a starter on the junior varsity basketball team, in our annual pre-season, inter-squad, Bosse High School match-up called "soap night." Coach Masters coaches my team. Coach Murrain leads the varsity squad. In the previous weeks, Coach Masters has built my confidence, matching my skill to his strategy, in practices against the varsity.

"When the ball comes back to you, split the gap and use the back-board," he whispers quick lessons to me during our half court sets. I listen and they work, as if by magic.

By halftime of the game, I have twelve high flying points. Coach Murrain rages.

"G– – — t! How the h– –are you going to let the reserve team kick your a— like that?!!" In a brash move, he steals me from Coach Masters and inserts me in the starting lineup for the varsity. I look at Coach Masters. I cherish his guidance. His words of knowledge are treasures. He gives me a nod, but does it while crossing his arms. He just lost his best player. In this coaching decision, my new best friend unhappily swaps places with me, going from starting on the varsity team to starting on the reserve team. A huge, emotional, life-altering swing of momentum for two young teens. I see and feel the displeasure of my friend. Our relationship is threatened because I score some baskets. We are now pitted against each other, not just on the court, but off. My varsity career begins, like a new company that grows too fast, outdistancing its support and fundamentals. It is an ascension which I am not prepared for.

12
My First Love

I write and then revise it. It doesn't sound right. I look up to see if my teacher knows I am not paying attention. How could I? I am grappling with this letter. I have to get it right for there will be no second chance to make a first impression. She doesn't know how I feel about her.

I see her for the first time as I sit in the porch, toiling away with my bicycle. I am in eighth grade. It is spring and spring things are happening. Bright colors spread through the park and the yards surrounding it like a beautiful virus, flowers blooming and trees showing green. I look away from the silver spokes which I shine and see a young lady walking across the park. She comes from the direction of Bosse high school, where Joe is a freshman. Before I know what I am doing, my hand is turning the knob of the porch door and I am outside. My vision is clear. She becomes smaller and smaller, before she exits the park and disappears around a corner.

Soon, my routine becomes depositing myself in the porch at around four thirty every day, to see if I can catch a glimpse of her. I see her at least twice a week. When I do not see her, I feel empty. One evening after dinner, I go outside to the backyard to shoot baskets. I hear voices. As I often do, I trot across the yard, to the fence and look over to see who passes by. It is her, jogging. She jogs with a young man, though, and seems pleased with his company. I lower my head as if in defeat. My mysterious dream girl is spoken for.

In my freshman year, I familiarize myself with the student body. I stick close to my friends, and new experiences occur in tandem, two of the blind working our way down a path. Just a few days into the school year, I pass by her at her locker. She doesn't acknowledge me as I hope. Her mind is occupied by other matters. Mine is by her. In the past, I filled the basketball hoop to satisfy my desires to be great, like number 23, and to earn a scholarship. Now, along with my short list of motivations, I do it for her to notice me. This new stimulant makes me extend my hours of practice, and my sweat which was once a trickle now pours.

In late November of my sophomore year, I close my locker and advance to the stairwell for a second period class. My skull is muddled by conflicting thoughts of my abrupt promotion to the varsity basketball team. I climb the first step and feel a hand catch my arm at the elbow. I look up and my world skids to a halt, like Dad's green Toyota truck once did.

"Hi," she says. One word. It was the most amazing sentence to pass through my ear canals. I fear my heart will burst through my sternum and land in her book bag. Her skin is like a creamy dark chocolate. Her teeth are white as Joe's primer and the arches in her eyebrows make my neck prickle. My choirboy voice in transition, I muster a raspy "Hi," then glide up the stairs as if riding a cloud.

My letter is complete. No way I can give it to her. I huddle with two of my closest friends in Box's basement. Square laughs at my plan.

"Man, that letter is weak!" he cajoles. He exposes me, saying out loud what I think in private.

"No, that's not weak. It can work." Box rebuilds me. To be so young, he seems to know more than both of us as to the ways of the heart.

"So you think it will work?" I ask Box.

"Yes, just give it to me. I will give it to her after first period. Trust me," says Box. I pause for only a second, deleting a thought that he may scratch out my name and write his on it. Box wouldn't do that though, which is why I chose him to help me.

The next day Box executes the plan. I know, not just because he tells me, but because two periods later she finds me and presses her own letter in my palm.

"I loved your letter. Mine is not as good as yours. Write me back." She smiles, filling my heart with ecstasy. Days later, she invites me to a dance.

Mom sees the turmoil in my face, which I do not explain to her. I rummage through the short list of dance moves I am familiar with. They all frighteningly lead back to Dad, cutting the rug in his underwear, to a Neil Diamond song. I can't use those. I want to make her laugh, but not at my expense. Dad drives me to the dance in the minivan. Inside, teens mingle. The faster the beat of the song, the harder I press my body against the wall. Great strategy. The hours pass like minutes. The DJ announces the last song. One of the parents calls out to me.

"Matt, your Dad is here." My mood sours. I have not even spoken to her. I don't have the courage. Then, just as that hand grabbed my arm on the stairwell, she does it once more.

"Want to dance?" she asks me, though not so much to ask but to lead. The song is slow and the lights dim. She pulls me close and I follow her lead. Shadows and darkness disguise my bungled rhythm. Her perfume swirls in my nostrils. She pulls me closer. Thinking it impossible, I fall for her even more than I already have. I have a girlfriend.

Weeks turn to months of my spending afternoons at Deandra's house. Letters she writes to me, passed between classes, build up in my closet like the books in Dad's office. Well into my second year with her, the fragrance of love diminishes and the prevailing call of my instincts grows loud in my head. My focus on her is still intense, like the focus Lincoln has on escape from the backyard, but it is not what it once was. My grades slip, like a mailman on an icy patch of sidewalk. I see less of my brother, sisters and friends. My attendance at her house soon feels obligatory if I am to hold her attention. Suitors are everywhere: from men younger than me to men in their forties. Her beauty attracts with the strength of a black hole.

I sit in the bleachers at Central stadium, where all of the city's major track meets take place. Deandra, the best in the state at what she does, competes for a city title in the 100-yard dash. She reaches the finish line many lengths ahead of the second place competitor. I hear an older man's voice behind me.

"Man, do you see the legs on that girl? I mean, do you see that?" The fluctuation of his voice underlines his interest. I bristle, unthrilled by what I hear, but say nothing.

"What's her name?" the same man asks the other man with him. His interest grows legs.

"Man, chill! That's his girlfriend," says the other man. I recognize the voice. It is Charles, a graduate of Bosse, who lives a couple blocks away from me. I turn around.

"Man, it's cool. I hear that all the time." I say to the man eyeballing my girlfriend, excusing his statements. I look back towards the track where Deandra is putting her sweat pants back on.

The more time I spend with Deandra, the more time I also spend in Dad's office. This is not coincidence as the line of curfew drawn by Dad fails to compare with the demand of time I must spend with her. Whose will is greater? Dad relieves me of my burdens by giving me a two-week vacation, rather, a grounding, for not respecting the line he has drawn. I thank him in my mind.

"I want a quarter-pounder with cheese, no onions." Square places his order. Though he jeers me at my new job, I find comfort in his efforts. He drives across town, not for a burger, but seeking out a friend he now rarely sees. We no longer meet at six in the morning to practice our moves at Bellemede park. We don't hang out on Friday nights, crashing parties with Box and Big Jake. We hardly see each other. I have a girlfriend.

I hear his order before the ticket comes to the McDonald's printer in the kitchen. I begin lining up his burger patty as he sails jokes about my uniform over the counter. Before I close the lid of the box, I take a fistful of onions and press them on the steaming meat. Square falls to the floor in laughter, after he checks to see if his minimum-wage-earning grunt of a friend remembers to exclude the onions. Something has to change.

13
Rage

"The score is TEN to EIGHT!" I exclaim, as sure as an actuary. I argue with Greg, our all-state center. He glares down at me, his ten inches of advantage and John Henry–like back and shoulders intimidate, but I stand firm.

"It's NINE to EIGHT, you little punk!" he snipes back. His dark brown features are squeezed and his words venomous.

I name off each basket, every play recorded in my mind.

"Jake scored on the lay-up. Square hit the jumpshot from the corner. Moses got the tip in. That makes ten!" I am beyond irritation. My temperament begins to sizzle like bacon strips on a hot skillet. I feel it coming, but this time greater than before. I used to see it in another, every Friday night.

They slap him around and pound on his back as he pleads with them to stop. They continue their assault, tremendous blows to his body, until … until his iris turns white, his gamma-ray-inflicted skin green. His shirt splits, ripping off his back.

I have it, that Hulk-ish rage. I don't know where it comes from.

Maybe from being abandoned by my birth mother. Possibly from being called a nigger time and again. Was it the tiring of Joe's and my being chased home by bullies? Could it be the needling from friends, jeering me and my white-capped pimples, my baseball-glove-sized nose or my mixed bloodlines? Was it all of this together?

"Mr. Blite, Mr. Blite, three-fourths white," they say. "Nose-stradamus." As with each joke, there is both a hint of truth and a pinch of ill intent. I take everything in, even as I laugh, each jest leaving a mark. I don't vent. I just internalize, the fires inside me building up like steam in a coffee pot. I don't know where it comes from.

"It's NINE, EIGHT punk! Check ball!" Greg ends the argument, then walks to a water fountain behind the far basket, cooling his heat.

If I turn my head too fast, the tears welling up at the edge of my eyelids will fall over onto my cheeks. I won't let them see me cry. My face is red, my hands shake, and my thinking murderous. Dad tells me to never hit. Fright comes over me for a split second. Not fright of Greg. Fright of my immense, putrefied, boiling wrath. I do not fight it, though. I let it grow.

I check the ball into play as ordered. On the return pass to the point man, I slip into the passing lane and steal the ball. I speed-dribble to the other end, where I encounter ... HIM. Greg turns away from the fountain and sees me coming at him at high velocity. A storied leaper, his calves like footballs, he lunges forward, back onto the court, wanting to swat the ball down my neck, to muffle any further bad score-keeping. Seeing HIM, my eyes go blood red with malice. I crouch, pronate and explode. My head rises above the rim. I feel Greg's body climb with me as he terribly wants this block. I am too high. My arm comes down, like a hand axe did on the necks of Dad's chickens. My middle and ring finger crash into the front of the rim, as the ball crashes through the rim. Everyone in the bulldog gymnasium collapses, as if mowed down by gunfire. If people were jailed solely for their thoughts, I would be done for life, for I am thinking of killing. I follow Dad's words, though. I don't hit.

14
Dinner

One after another I put forkfuls of food in my mouth. I wish I could use my hands. It would be faster. I don't look up. I keep my eyes to myself. I don't want anyone to try to engage in conversation. In between bites, each of which Mom liquefies, she reaches out to me.

"So, Matthew, how was your day?" Mom asks. I shrug.

"Are you going out with Deandra this weekend?" Mom tries again. My sister's ears perk up.

"I dunno. Maybe." I keep my head down, hoping she will end her probing. She looks across the table at Dad, talking to him with her eyes. They agree.

Six minutes into dinner, I finish. I put my salad bowl on top of my plate, along with my silverware. I push them towards the middle of the table. I fold my arms, putting them where my plate was, and drop my head in my arms. I lose myself in my teenage thoughts:

What is my girlfriend doing? Does she really love me like she says, or am I only a checkmark on her "to do" list of accomplishments? Why are guys always trying to talk to her as soon as I turn my back? They know she has a boyfriend. I'm either very happy with her, or my stomach screams with jealousy. I'm always at her house. I keep getting in trouble because I come home late. I spend all that time with her when I could be practicing. I didn't know it would be like this. Coach Murrain was right. I don't need a girlfriend. Should I break up with her? I'll ask Dad.

I sigh. I lift my head and see that Mom is still eating. I lower my head.

Why won't coach Murrain let me shoot the ball? I kill these guys all summer, then in the real game I score eight points. He always wants me to pass the ball to Greg, Chip and Square. I might as well be sitting in the bleachers. I should've stayed on the JV team. I would be scoring thirty points a game. I wish coach Murrain would stop yelling at me. It's like it's his job to hold me back. He's always telling me I am not Michael Jordan. What's wrong with trying to be like the best? I see why Johnnie went after him that time.

Man, I'm tired. I need some sleep. I'm tired of school. I'm tired of taking out the trash and singing in the choir. It seems like all I do is what other people want me to do. Why can't everyone just leave me alone? It is always "we decided" and "you need to." I just want to be left alone.

"Let's pray." Once again, Dad brings an end to my silent suffering.

15

Escaping the Box

I feel boxed in. Rules. Homework. Others' expectations on my life. People always demanding something. Concerned for me? Or concerned for their personal agendas? Why can't I do what I want to do? It is always about other people's needs. Those who think only of themselves are the saddest people in the world. Always thinking of other's needs before mine does not make me happy. I brood. School. Assignments. Papers and reports to complete. Practice after school. The yelling and cursing. A girlfriend that needs me by her side or on the phone so she can feel complete. I want to be left alone. There is no more peace that I know of than the streets of Evansville late at night. I need peace.

A geography assignment is jammed down my throat. Mom stands over me. "You sit here and do not move until you finish!" Mom is at the end of her wits with me. This is what my life has come to. Her concern is that I will fail to graduate, scheduling struggles later in life. I care much less than she does. My moods darken. Later on that night, after all have turned in, I fix my regular midnight snack: A small frozen pizza, two packs of ramen noodles and a bowl of sherbet, all from the Schwannman.

I devour the food, barely chewing. I am still not satisfied. Not on this night. I walk outside to the basketball court. Lincoln escorts me, sensitive to my brooding. I walk to the edge of the fence. I look over. The park is beautiful in all its silence. The streets are empty and inviting, as they demand nothing from me. Lincoln whines. I search for the reason.

———

"What's up, Milk?" My head snaps towards the voice. It is Big Jake. He's roaming. He's free.

"What are you doing out here?" he asks.

"I can't sleep," I answer.

"Why don't you come with me?"

"Where are you going?"

"Over to Tony D's crib to watch a movie."

"I'll pass, man. I don't want to get in trouble again."

"Man, you get grounded more than anyone I know." We laugh.

A feeling rips through me; a feeling of loss or losing. No … missing. I am missing out, confined by a wooden fence and a parent's law of curfew.

"Don't you have a curfew?" I ask.

"Naaaw, man." His eyes brighten, his mischief compounds.

"What about tomorrow night? What are you doing tomorrow?" I inquire.

"We can go to Tony D's tomorrow. What time do you want me to come by?"

"Twelve."

"Awright man." The orange-headed giant moves into the night. I am not the only one seeking solace in the quiet streets, looking to escape the pressures. I conceive a plan.

I hear a pop. Then another. The sound comes from the side window by my bed. Joe, a deep sleeper, moves under his covers, and is now awake, as am I. I lift up the blind, looking down toward the street. It is Jake, hurling pebbles at the window. On time as he promised.

"C'mon, man!" he whispers, nearly loud enough to awaken a hibernating bear.

I hold up a finger to let him know I am coming. I open the window to the left of my bed and simply walk out onto the roof. I climb down, toeing the ledge of the porch window. I touch down in grass. Free. Why didn't I think of this before? Jake and I walk. After an hour of nothing except wandering through the night, drowsiness makes my eyelids droop. I return home. As often happens, plans evolve. With each walk out onto the roof, I brim with new ideas and modify my escapes into the night. I make my bed up showcasing pillows with a cap, making it appear that I, so fatigued, collapsed, with a brimmed head. I also remove the screen on the porch window, making it easier to climb up on the ledge and pull myself up onto the roof, upon returning. I replace the screen the next morning. I descend out into the night at least twice a week, Joe grinding his teeth until I come back. One night I come home, after not missing out, and pull on the screen latch. It doesn't respond. I pull harder. The latch snaps against the window pane. I freeze. Seconds pass. Nothing. I climb up onto the roof. I stand there, looking out across the land, absorbing the moment. Suddenly, there is movement to my right. A white man walks around the corner of the house and looks up at me.

"Can I help you?" the man asks. For a brief moment, Dad does not recognize me. Then he does.

"Into my office, NOW!" He barks. I climb in the window, weighted with dread, and walk to the bedroom door. Judging from my demeanor, and that I don't dive immediately into bed, Joe knows something is wrong. I go to Dad's office for sentencing. Grounded ... again.

16
Trip with Dad

"Over here, Dad. Our seats are in this section." I direct Dad. He can surely find his seat for himself, but he lets me guide him. He absorbs my electric zeal. We find our seats. We are at Chicago Stadium to see number 23.

"Where did we sit last time, Matt?" Dad asks, remembering our history.

"We were over there," I point. I then consult Dad, spitting out records and statistics like a wood chipper. Dad listens intently.

The players jog out to warm up. I see him. He runs differently. He glides, his grace and ease, splendid. Jordan takes shot after shot, banks and fade-aways, most of them with a string of dribbles and spins preceding them. He is part dancer and part salesman, peddling silky deceptions. A teammate guards him. He jab steps, shot fakes, the defender buying, then dips his shoulder, his entire body nearly below the waist of the stopper. He slips down the baseline, agile as a cat walking the back of a couch, and dunks.

"Did you see that, Dad?" I look to him, smiling hard, amazed.

"Yep," he answers, more impressed with my happiness than the man with the long wristband.

The game begins. Jordan trots around the court for most of the first half, looking almost uninterested, as if he were a decoy. Then with about a minute left in the half, Jordan acts. He takes a pass in the right corner, standing upright with his back to a Milwaukee Buck defender. Then, quick as a lightning strike, he pivots towards the baseline, dribbling once. I jump out of my seat for I know what is to come. Jordan launches with a beauty and explosiveness unseen by me in person. He cups the ball, just like the good doctor, extending above the top of the white square. Then there is an awful sound, like a sack of bones dropping on wood. A Milwaukee Buck player catches Jordan in midair and slams him to the ground.

I gawk in disbelief. Michael Jordan is on the ground. He's not moving. He was just getting started. I knew something like this was going to happen.

Last time Dad and I came to see him, he didn't even play. This time, somebody tries to kill him. Jordan squeezes at the wooden floor in pain.

"Come on, Michael, get up! Get up, Michael!" a woman two rows in front of Dad and me cries out for Jordan, like he were dying. She stands up, then sits down, then stands up again.

"Girl, sit down. He's just faking," says the man next to her. His hands are folded above his stomach, his elbows on the arm rest. His head is cocked, not looking at Jordan writhing in pain, but at the chair in front of him. He is experiencing a pain of his own, the lady with him, in a state of despair, over a man she does not know. I understand his pain. I understand Jordan's pain as I have injuries of my own. I have a new pain.

Dad is reaching out to me. When we are on our personal trips, it is like every bad thing I have done is forgiven and forgotten. I don't feel tired when we go on these trips. I don't have to appease my friends or my girlfriend. Nobody yelling God-something at me. We stick to the plan.

We explore. We carve up enormous steaks together. He lets me order whatever I want. But for the second time, as much as I enjoy my time with Dad, my mouth tastes bitter.

At the end of the game, I push my way down to the court and snap pictures of Jordan, hobbling off the court, his leg wrapped from his hip down to his socks. He scores more than forty points in nine consecutive games. I come to the tenth game, and he scores 11. He hurts, and so do I.

17
Not Good Enough

My high school basketball career is over. I feel the change. Once our service ends, so does our utility. So does much of the adulation. Perks once extended are withdrawn. No longer can I walk the halls without a hall pass. We are evicted from gyms for reasons of liability, gyms we could play in only weeks before, without consequence. The look in the principal's eyes is different. They now say, "You're just like the rest of them now. You're not special." I no longer have the puffiness in my chest. I now face reality. Coach Murrain wants to see me in his office.

I knock on his door, which is partially open.

"Sit down, Matt," Coach says. "I have a few offers that you might want to look at." He pulls out a file, looking to be mine—mailers sent from different colleges. "North Dakota is interested, DePauw in Greencastle still wants you. Morehead State is also interested. What do you think?"

I turn my face away, scowling, then look back at him for a brief second. My dissatisfaction fills the room. Coach Murrain has seen it before. Each time we are out of agreement, that look, falls over my face. Each time he curses at me, he sees that look.

"Don't give me that look now, son. I have another one that is interested in you. They are trying to decide on whether they want you or this other kid that is in junior college. It's a school in Florida. I believe, Florida Atlantic University."

"Florida Atlantic?" I ask, as much out of disgust as curiosity, as I have never heard of them.

"Yeah, Florida Atlantic," Murrain says. "Their coach saw you at camp last summer."

I look at Murrain's desktop, searching for that letter from North Carolina, which I know he is hiding from me. My anger flashes. He sees it.

"G– – –t, Matt, you're just not good enough. You just didn't get better after your sophomore year. You're not tall enough," he growls.

I tell him I will think about Florida Atlantic.

"See you later, Coach," I say.

"Good luck."

I walk from his office. My stomach is no longer churning. My sides no longer throb, hurting from the rib punches of reality. I now feel sorry for myself.

I go home to look for Dad. He knows what happened. He knows I was good enough. He saw the work I put in that others wouldn't and didn't. I tell Dad. His voice is encouraging. I hear the disbelief in his voice and see it in his face. He knows the moves that I had, looking many times like the very same ones on my highlight tapes. I was shut down. He also knows, though, that I would back down and let others be better than me, for they needed it more. That is what separates me from number 23. That play was not in my highlight reel. Stomping down an opponent or competitor/friend every single time they got back up. Unrelenting tenacity. I miss that part. I worry about how others feel, taking my foot off the gas pedal when I feel I have dished out enough punishment. I reserve my true abilities for when I became angry and didn't display them immediately. Why? I know it is lonely at the top and I am afraid to live in that universe. I fail to deliver on my promise to earn a scholarship. I hurt.

PART 3

18
College in Florida

I sit in the backseat, arm curled around a basketball. *Welcome to Boca Raton*, a sign reads. I am grouchy, sad and unsatisfied. My dream is crushed and my goals are unmet. Dad turns slowly into Florida Atlantic University parking lot.

I am going to play college basketball, but not on scholarship. Not at North Carolina. Not like I planned years prior, dribbling and jumping at the secret court. I look to blame others and excuse myself. Many kids across the world would kill for a chance at college. I pout because my parents have to pay. What happened? Too short? Though 5'7", I jump as well as anyone in the country. Was I too slow? I ran the second leg on our 4x100M relay team, which took second place in the State Finals track meet. Was it that blasted left hand, that lifeless limb? It could have been better, but I worked hard. Too many hours on my girlfriend's couch? I righted that ship. We drifted apart as I continually missed dates with her, choosing instead the playground courts in the Lincoln projects. Was it my coach? My final conversation with Coach ended with his say-ing, "You're just not good enough." Not good enough? That came after his prediction during my sophomore year that I could become the best player ever to come out of the city. He was the coach. Was I not taught well enough? Must have been the injuries. I missed four games late in my senior year. I was playing the best basketball of my career, when a player from University Heights intentionally dove squarely into the side of my knee, straining my knee ligaments. My left leg atrophied, becoming so thin that it didn't look like it belonged on my body. I never regained my form for the rest of the season. In my last opportunity to impress college scouts, I pinched a nerve in my neck in a post-season all-star game. After a quick start, scoring two three-point baskets, I ended up leaving the gymnasium, looking as if I had suffered a stroke. Was I an unpopular troublemaker? My record-setting groundings aside, I was not. I was voted "Most Likely to Succeed" in my senior class, as well as homecoming king and team captain on the basketball team. So what happened? The question spins around my mind for the entire sixteen hour drive to Florida.

We empty the van. Mom and Dad help me take my things to my room. I hug them both. They drive away, my heart feeling hollow and dead. I fight tears. I told Dad I wanted to be left alone. I finally got what I wanted. I was alone. I hated it. What happened?

19

"You're not Michael Jordan!"

"You're not Michael Jordan!" A biting observation turned verse, from the mouth of the coach. I am at a new school in a new city with a new team and a new coach, and I hear the same line I heard in high school. I poorly mask my fury. I try to understand this resentment of my wanting to be good. My new teammate places a caring arm around my shoulders.

"Shake it off, Rook. Don't let that piece of crap worry you," Leonard quips, drawing a smile from me. I immerse myself into college life. The school fell short of what I had envisioned. Lacking a football team, and being a commuter campus, the parking lot drained on weekends, leaving the small lot of us isolated with the owls. My teammates and I make the most of the situation. We play sand volleyball, drive to clubs in Miami and Ft. Lauderdale, listen to music, argue about basketball, wrestle and pull pranks on each other. Leonard regularly cooks curry chicken and stew peas, which easily becomes my favorite cuisine. My roommate Daryl and I spend many nights talking about the day's events and evolving philosophies before drifting off into sleep. My academic work begins brilliantly. Soon, though, I discover that if I miss class, there is no call home to parents. Well into my second semester, it dawns on me that I have gone weeks without attending class. Once my first season ends, there is nobody requiring my attendance.

I have finally found freedom. It was perfect at first. I stay awake all night. I sleep through class, getting up only to eat. In the evenings I go to the gym to work on my game. I then engage in horseplay with my teammates, before they send me away so they can attend to their responsibilities. Not caring about my own, I return to my room and watch recorded basketball games. Before long, the dark clouds gather. Bad interest is accruing. I know what comes next. Final exams are approaching and I have not been to class for over a month. As the duress increases, I soon cannot sleep, even when I try. I know I have to study. I know I have to go to class. I choose to do neither. I miss home. I miss my family. I miss church. I miss my friends in Indiana. The seasons never change in Florida, exacerbating my depression. I thought I wanted to be left alone. Now I am and I don't like it.

20
My First Drink

For about thirty minutes I work my way out of bed. I yawn. I stretch.
I don't hear any talking or movement about the house. I don't smell
breakfast. I descend down the steps. The house has emptied. I decide to
attack the fridge. I pull bacon and eggs out and apply heat to them. As
I scramble and flip, I look over at the counter. I see an envelope with a
Florida Atlantic letterhead. It has my name on it. I open it. "Academically
ineligible." My heart shatters. I want to cry. I want to blame someone.
*It was the coach's fault. He drove and drove me into my Floridian depression. He said
he would give me a scholarship and never did.* How would I face my parents?
They spent hard earned dollars on an education that was never tended to.
Gripped by the fear of facing Mom and Dad, and the humiliation from
my siblings finding out that their brother was flunking in Florida, I go
out to the backyard. I begin to shoot baskets, hoping all will magically
correct itself.

———

In a summer of perpetual groundings, allowed only to work delivering
pizzas and assisting youth at the YMCA, I secretly cherish my isolation

from my friends. My relationship with my girlfriend slowly fizzles away, like the fuse on a dud firecracker. The downs became overwhelming and unbearable. My heart hardens, walling itself off from the pain of my romance. I focus on my remaining love, basketball. I toil away in the backyard. CJ, Big Jake and Tapper stop by regularly, often watching my repetitions before announcing their presence. I have my excuse from joining them in unproductive activity.

"I wish I could, but Big Walt shut me down," I lament, though quietly content with Dad's punishments. In the summer humidity, my game grows strong.

Entering my second year at FAU, I have a new focus. I attend classes. I need to regain my eligibility. My scholarship is not granted, the reason being my inadequate academic performance. I would not let that wobbly excuse stop me this year. My dead limb of a left hand was now alive. My speed with the ball has become blinding. My shooting range is extended. My court awareness opens up. I rebound ferociously. I am going to get a scholarship. Coach, the man with the tie, seems to acknowledge none of my improvements. He soon stops using my name, only referring to me as "you" and "him." I had seen him break a teammate of mine the year before, splintering his mind. The player withdrew from the team because of a nervous breakdown, no longer able to bear the psychological battery. It soon seems that I may join the list of those folding their hand. After one particularly brutal Saturday practice, I return to my room and stare at the wall. I wonder if playing basketball is worth the torment. I wonder if my love for this game can carry me.

I decide not to waste away the evening and go to my teammates' suite. I walk through the doorway. Leonard had finished cooking, which is always exceptional. Shane "Wonder" and Morshee flip around a basketball, also flipping the usual insults at Leonard, which he swats back at them, referring to them as different sizes and shapes of crap. They pause as I fall into their suite, shoulders sagged, looking like a wounded soldier, dragging my suffering with me like a bag of soiled laundry. They took to me as those do a little brother, having been steamrolled by a parent.

"Don't worry about it, Rook. Dat mon is a fool." Shane says. Shane grew up in the Bahamas. His rich, cutting voice made everything sound wise and official, as if having the omniscience of a philosopher much older than himself. He had quickly become one of my favorite players to watch. At 6' tall, he was truly the micro version of number 23. His moves were bionic and aerial, causing those watching to grab their skulls in disbelief each time he ascends to the heavens.

Morshee, one of our overabundance of point-guards chimes in, "What you need is a drink."

Leonard, the watchdog, explodes. "Leave dat man alone!!" he barks in his piercing Jamaican accent. "The last thing he needs is a drink. You sound like you have been drinking, you piece of crap!"

Morshee responds "You see how coach treats him. He should be starting over Smith [the starter]. He needs a drink!"

Nothing new in this suite. Debate over everything and all. I sink deeper and deeper in my chair, watching my teammates decide my path.

"Well, maybe you're right" finishes Leonard.

Morshee, always fond of a last word, harpoons Leonard. "You're dang right I'm right!" He contorts his body, dodging a punch from a laughing Leonard.

"Let's go, Bunny [Leonard's nickname]," says Shane.

We all move in formation, in search of something for me to drink. We drive to the convenience store across from the campus. We walk straight to the alcoholic beverages. I look around for a short time, wanting something economical, finally selecting two 16-ounce cans of Schlitz Malt Liquor, and hand them to Leonard. He pays. We go back to the suite. The beer has an unusual flavor, far different from the little sips I would take from Dad's cans of Old Milwaukee when I was small. The taste scolds my tongue, as my taste buds prefer sweetness. I take big gulps and try to ignore the bitterness. I finish my first can in silence, then crack open the second. My teammates talk loudly, with opinions from Jamaica, the Bahamas and Florida meshing in a fresh debate. They are unaware of the transformation taking place in the corner of their room, as they each coddle their own drinks. After listening to the others talk, then reviewing my own personal problems, I flatten my second empty can into an inch-high aluminum disc. My teammates stop in midsentence, as I insert my own opinion into the debate.

"Man, that wasn't nuthin'," I announce. I surmise that the beer is ineffectual and a waste of money. Their eyes widen and their mouths hang open. Leonard looks at Shane and then at Morshee, then back at me, trying to see if they heard the same ludicrous words that he did. They all know that malt liquor is far from "nuthin'" as I have deduced. I stand up, though unsure why. I return immediately to my seat, or fall, as if asked to do so by a pastor during a service. The sensation is marvelous. I feel light in the head and numb in my body. Though I do not hear any buzzing sound, I know this is the condition that I have often heard of. I feel a new boldness in my spirit and a growing sense of humor. My problems have fled my mind. It is great! My teammates rush over to me, ensuring that I have not hurt myself. "Git off me, chicken necks," I say. They throw back their heads, laughing at the ceiling. I smile, my rosy cheeks stretched, my beady eyes turned to minus signs, with my forehead glistening as if it has an early morning dew on it.

"Look at Rook, he's drunk … you piece of crap." Leonard chops the air in his high-octaved chortle. I cut them off and in my best "captain of the ship" voice, I proclaim that we need more beer. I get up again, my legs shaky, like a newborn colt's. I slam open the door, sending shock-waves through the walls, which startles others in adjoining suites. Our seven foot German center fills the doorway, his head ducked down, to see what shook the building. "What's going on, dudes?" His voice of deep German bass fills the room. He looks at my shiny red face and quickly understands, as he has seen that "look" in his own mirror. "I'm drunk, Ingo, let's get some beer!" And so it begins.

21
Walking Lincoln

"Matt, Lincoln needs to go out," Mom says. Lincoln has become one of my new responsibilities. I sigh, as if this is yet another thing to burden my life, even though I agreed to do it.

Lincoln often seems like one of my truest friends. He never mocks me. He doesn't make fun of my nose. He doesn't lust after my girlfriend when I turn my back. He doesn't judge me. After every one is asleep, I watch television. Lincoln has a rug, full of colors, half of which is in the kitchen and half in the family room. He knows he cannot come any farther into the family room than the edge of that rug. Late at night, though, when I am on my back, stacking thoughts of bitterness and resentment, I feel a nudge at my shoulder, a wet snout at my ear, whiskered sniffing. Lincoln sneaks into the family room to comfort me. I scratch his neck and behind his ears. I put my arm around him. I watch TV. He only watches.

I walk through the kitchen and open the basement door. On a wall which leads down the steps is a hook, holding an assortment of leashes. I choose my favorite leash, a chrome chain, and close the door. Lincoln hears the jingling of the chain and trots over to me, bumping my leg with his head to let me know he is there and ready. He pants, anticipating.

I snap the latch of the leash onto his collar and we move to the door. We go down the back steps, walk across the patio, and to the back gate.

"Open the door, Lincoln," I urge him. He rises up, plants his front paws on the gate, then comes down. I look at him. He yips and gives a few small barks, twirling with energy. He wants to run, but also seems to hide his secret as to how he opens the gate. Sly dog.

I open the gate and we turn into the alley. Lincoln tries to dictate the pace, charging at the street. I pull back on the leash and check for cars. Slobber appears at the corners of his mouth. His breathing strains as the harder he pulls, the tighter the leash is on his windpipe. We cross the street and trot into the green grass of the park. It is dark.

Is this what it is like to be a parent? Is this what it is like to be my parent? Is this how Dad feels? He strokes your side, cools you when you are hot, feeds you when you are hungry. He builds a fence to protect you. He takes you to the doctor. He teaches you. He gives you boundaries. He gives you slack. And what do you do? You sneak out, bust out, climb out. You trick him, run from him, create scandal in the alley, leaving a trail of garbage and ravaged garbage cans, not caring or understanding how these deeds damage relationships not only between you but with others in the community. And when you tire and are hungry again, oblivious and uncaring of your transgressions, having pooped and peed and eaten everywhere, you go back to him and he takes you in. Smoke pours out of his ears, upset by your shenanigans, but he still takes you back and still loves you. And you act as if that is how it should be.

Lincoln stops to sniff, runs, stops, digs, pees. There is no pattern to what he does. No direction. No outline. He follows instinct. I wait on him patiently, his stops and starts. I am the mature one. Lincoln now wants to run. I run with him. His speed increases. The hair on his body flies backwards and his eyes squint. He is in a full gallop. I hear the wind in my ears. Our hearts pump and I enjoy the spirit-lifting sprint. He darts to the right, then straight. He angles left,… then my consciousness goes white.

I am on my back. I look up and see a huge tree that was not there seconds before. Lincoln, so clever, is gone. He is free.

22
Frustration

I look down inside my cup. It is large, like a blue barrel. Pieces of fruit bounce into each other. On the side of it reads "Florida Atlantic University." I lift it to my lips. I sip. The Carlo Rossi bites the back of my neck, before draining into my stomach. I say I will never drink alcohol. I never promise or swear to anyone. It was only something I felt unnecessary in my life. Now I feel it is.

The perpetual sun and unchanging seasons of South Florida grind at my sanity. My "Midas touch" deserts me. With an idea, some planning, and my obsessive effort, I was once able to accomplish, while others languished in mediocrity.

I sip. Mom and Dad are on a plane, flying back to Indiana. I couldn't look Dad in the face. He cannot discover all of my failings, my missed classes and squandering of the money that he and Mom send to me. He saw enough at the game. Why did they cancel tomorrow's game, my redemption? They may never see me play again. How did I miss that lay-up? Dad has watched me pull the rim down in the backyard, as easily as a bibbed two-year-old tosses a carrot across a table. Was I meant to fail in his eyes? How do my five thousand hours of practice and study amount to a missed lay-up? Will he believe me unworthy of a scholarship, as does my coach?

Why did that serpent in a tie try to manipulate my parents' thinking, like soft clay on a turning wheel? Does he think they don't know the other side of things?

"Matthew is doing fine. He is doing well. He just needs to put in a little more work in the classroom and he will be fine," he tells them. I will put in more work in the classroom when you pay for it.

All of my friends have scholarships. Am I the runt of the litter? I may be the smallest, but only those with demise in their hearts would seriously try to challenge me.

I sip. I stand up. The gravity in the room has tripled. My eyes feel pressure from behind them. I walk over to my desk and pour more wine in my cup. I look up at my dorm room wall. Jordan, with his palm on Spike Lee's head, looks down at me. My pity exacerbates. Why me?

I feel something. I look up to the corner of my room. Nothing. Something was there.

I sip. Sadness swells in my abdomen. It rises up, engulfing my defeated back, up to my shoulders. It rises, pressing on my brain, finally leaking out through my eye sockets, dripping on my wrist. My lips quiver. I press them tight, trying to contain this sadness. I can't.

Why do I have to work during the summer, when others play? Where is the fairness? Why do my parents have to pay, when far lesser players' parents don't? The questions recycle, each generation more rancid.

My legs are heavy. I stagger. I reach for support, which is not there. I fall. Wine and pieces of orange splash on my shirt. I smile, through the sadness, at my ineptness.

I hear a knock at my suite door. A swoosh of pressure change slams shut my bedroom door. My door reopens. A head appears.

"Rook, let's go … what da — —?" Leonard frowns, then laughs at me, collapsed on the floor, still holding my cup. He understands my condition, for he plays for that man in a tie. He understands that coach has a system. He also understands my need for creativity and self-expression. He feels the voltage crackle between us, knowing his intercession necessary, or I will never get off the bench.

"You can't let that piece of crap get to you, dude. Look at you. You're drunk. I can't believe you started without me." His voice goes high, his words consoling. He reaches down and pulls me off of the floor. He does not encourage me to drink. He knows I will do it with or without him. He only cares that I not damage myself. He provides the little cheer that I have in my perspective. He is the crowbar, trying to crack open a closed, beaten spirit. I sip.

23
"Scobbing"

"He'll be back from school with the rest of y'all, drinking forties on the corner with Greg!" says C. Everyone laughs. I turn left on Lincoln Avenue. I feel the cool of the beer, which is locked between my legs as I drive. My friends and I are "turning blocks" which has become our nighttime routine.

"There's Will!" spouts someone in the back seat. I look to my left and see a young man, his skin dark, his short arms holding a bag with a bottle, standing and talking in the liquor store parking lot.

I turn my steering wheel and pull in next to a car.

The five of us jump out, charged emotionally. We surround Will.

"Aww, lookie here, okay, okay," says Will. C steps up to Will, with three inches separating them. They then circle each other, looking up and down at each other's anatomy, almost as if they were doing a strange, exotic dance. C draws the first blood.

"Your momma rides a goat with five star rims on it!" We all crumble into piles of laughter.

As we ride through the night, nearly every night, turning blocks aimlessly, drinking to our fill or unconsciousness, we look for moments like these, battles between the top "signifiers" in the neighborhood. Though they are not as skilled and poetic as the old heads and ancestors, their one-liners can make your face and stomach hurt with laughter. Though these are jokes, what lies at the core of the activity is the humiliation of your fellow man. Very little is off-limits, as anything from clothes to body features, and even mothers can become targets in what we call "scobbing."

Will strokes his chin. He regroups after C wallops him, reaching into his disturbed genius of metaphor and analogy.

"Aww, is that right. So you wanna scob?" says Will. They circle more. His countermove is a barrage.

"Your momma is so poor, she has a chandelier with fireflies in it. When she wants to turn the lights on, she smacks it with a rolled newspaper!" He doesn't give us a chance to catch our breath. "Your momma tried to get into the club with a bag of instant winner caps!" he continues. "Your momma went to pay her gas bill with a sack of pennies!" With that, C is done. After farewells and hand claps, we climb back into the car and turn more blocks.

24
The Black Cloud

I open my eyes. My head hurts. I feel a pulse, only it is in my right temple. I am in the backseat of a car. The car is mine. Street lights pass by, each glowing lamp making the pulse in my temple ache. I look to my left. My friend CJ slumps against his door, still sleeping. His left hand covers his eyes. An empty bottle of cheap wine rests on his shoe. I look over the front seat. K-Dog is driving. He talks in a soft voice. His flattop haircut blends into the night. I look in front of me. I hear Dinky's voice. He laughs. K-Dog laughs with him and they clap hands the way black men do. I lean forward.

"What's up, fellas?" I muster. The smell of alcohol from my words spreads around the back of the car. My voice cracks as the only moisture in my throat is phlegm.

"Milk, you're awake!" says Dinky, almost excited. "You and CJ have been out for over two hours."

"Two hours?" I look at the clock on the dash. It is three in the morning.

"Yeah, you and CJ tried to drink a second bottle of Cisco and passed out."

I look down by my feet. There is one empty bottle by my right foot, and another, nearly full, by my left foot. The last thing I could remember was being in the parking lot of the liquor store, listening to C and Will scob.

"Milk, look at the gas hand," orders K-Dog. I look. The needle is past full. I think for a minute how this is possible, since I only put two dollars' worth of gas in the tank at a time.

"We rode to Henderson and stole it while you guys were sleeping," he confesses.

"Wait 'til you see the trunk!" says Dinky. He giggles, proud of himself.

I look over at CJ. He starts to move. My intestines groan.

"Man, pull over. I don't feel good," I say.

K-Dog turns into an empty lot. Foot high weeds congest it. A walking path cuts through the middle, like a part in an afro. K-Dog turns off the engine. He and Dinky get out. They walk to the back of the car. I hear a key go into a lock, and hear the trunk door open.

"Milk, come here, look!" says Dinky. I open my door. My legs do not move, though my brain orders them to. I topple over, falling out of the door. My neck, shoulders and elbows mat down a tuft of weeds. I can't move. Dinky comes to me and pulls at my arm.

"STOP! Give me a minute!" I bark. The earth spins. I brace my body so as not to fall off of it.

"Take me hooome," comes a muffled moan from inside of the car. It is CJ, crying. "I wanna go hoooome. Take me hoooome." He sounds like an old hound dog, wailing at the stars.

I find more order in my head. The spinning stops, and I slowly pull myself and my dead legs out of the car. After three minutes or so, I am on my hands and knees. Dinky, having lost all patience, lifts me up, grabbing me under my arms. He drags me to the back of the car, as if I were a hobby doll.

"Look," he says with a giggle. I look into the trunk. Thirteen cases of soda weigh down the back of the car to ten inches from the ground. I look at K-Dog, who nods his head up and down smirking as if he just looted Fort Knox.

I smile, bleary-eyed, and clap hands with them. We deliver CJ to his doorstep.

K-Dog parks the car in front of Dinky's apartment building. We open the trunk. Something moves in the shadows, at the end of the block. We freeze. We see nothing. We lift Dinky's share of the heist, resting it on the lip of the trunk. The car bobs. K-Dog helps Dinky carry the soda to his back steps. I wave at Dinky and climb into the front passenger seat. K-Dog gets in seconds later and starts the car. I slump down in the seat, my head leaning against the door, the door lock boring into my head. K-Dog talks about the heist in detail, he the star in his story. We drive. He looks in the rearview mirror, once, twice. His body tightens.

"It's the cops!" He stomps on the gas pedal. I fear the cops, but this time I feel no squirt of adrenaline. I feel nothing inside. I only look back over my headrest and see indeed that the cops are in pursuit, their fruit cocktail of lights illuminating the sides of houses.

"If I can get to my sister's house, we'll be straight." K-Dog leans forward, his eyes wide, his competitive mind taking control. Our lead on the cops lengthens. We are close to the projects. He turns hard to the left, forcing me against the door, then another right, into an alley. He speeds, then slams the brake while cutting the lights. We made it. K-Dog smiles. Breathing heavily, his belly expands like a bag pipe, then contracts.

In an instant, police cars come from all directions. They surround us, as if we were bank robbers. I see guns. I wonder what else K-Dog and Dinky did while I was sleeping. I move my hands away from my body so they are visible. A female officer comes to my door. My window is already down.

"Can I see your identification?" she requests. I oblige her. She looks at it for a moment.

"Why did you guys run from us?" she asks. We both understand it is an obvious sign of guilt.

"Because you're the cops. Why were you chasing us?" I volley back. Their chase was a sign of something not so obvious.

"We saw you unloading something at 912 …" I don't wait to hear the rest. I realize they were already watching Dinky's house before we even pulled up. They knew of Dinky's occupation. They thought they saw drugs being moved.

"Can we see what you have in the trunk?" she asks.

"Yeah." I take the keys out of the ignition and hand them to her. She opens it. Officers gather around the back of the car. The car moves as they rummage around the trunk. Minutes later, she returns to my window, handing me the keys and my ID.

"Where did you get all of those sodas?" she asks, feeling she knows the answer.

"They bought them while I was sleeping," I say. My temple hurts again.

"Do you have a receipt?" I look over at K-Dog, as if I were asking him where it is. He shakes his head.

"He doesn't have it."

"Since you don't have a receipt, we will have to confiscate it."

"Go ahead. It's not mine," I say in truth, wanting to make an issue of officers taking something from me just because I don't have a receipt. I didn't have a receipt for the wine bottles in my back seat or for the tennis shoes on my feet, but they didn't seem interested in that. They release K-Dog, who goes into his sister's house. In a glitch of insanity, they allow me to drive home. I swallow saliva, tasting the sweet burn of the wine.

I park the car in front of the house. It is four-thirty in the morning. I walk slowly, as if I were in my nineties. I open the porch door, then try to put my key in the front door lock. I keep missing the hole. The door magically whips open. Mom, in her bathrobe, crosses her arms and glares at me.

"I am getting sick and tired of your coming in at this hour!" Her fury surges upward with every word. Her anger is rolling. I look at her, deadness in my eyes, and do not answer.

She pauses, turns her head to the side, like a parakeet, and looks into my eyes. A glaze covers them, like cream cheese on a bagel.

"Have you been drinking?" she asks, with discovery in her voice.

"Yep." I give her my most matter of fact answer, rife with frosty condescension. With the back of my forearm, I push her out of my way. I walk through the foyer and up the stairs, my legs still weighted with intoxication. I open the door of my bedroom and slam it behind me.

Mom, smacked with insult by a visitor in her own house, close behind me, blasts the bedroom door open. No one wakes, for all in the house are already awake.

"I don't appreciate your coming in my house drunk!" she yells, her blood at a boil.

"I don't appreciate your disrespecting Joe like that!" I shoot back, as if I have the authority and the leverage to contend with Mom. My rage swells up and I no longer see Mom, but an adversary, challenging me. My eyebrows arch and bush, my face a snarl. Mom sees someone who could not possibly be her son. She backs down, turns, and stomps to her room, slamming the door behind her.

I lie down in my bed, fully clothed. I wait for Dad to kick the door flat and rain blows on my head, his having warned me in the past to *never, ever,* yell at my mother again. He does not come. I hear a snicker. It comes from a corner of the ceiling. It is evil. A darkness, like a black cloud. Sleep escapes me. After some minutes, I feel inside of me something like a chemical reaction. Components of wrath and wreckage mixing; fronts colliding and moving into a swirl. The black cloud speaks: "Destroy something."

I sit up, but not by my own choice. I feel as if I am in a body, which is under the control of something else. I feel nothing. I only ride along in this cadaver as it moves down the stairs. I become reconnected with my body, and see that I am in the family room.

"Destroy something." The black cloud has followed me, it hovers, moving up and down in the corner, like a large male mosquito.

I obey. My rage manifests. I throw over the desk. I smash books on the floor and topple the bookshelf. My wrath is mindless. I am the Hulk, thrashing about without reason.

When there is finally nothing else to destroy, I stop. My breathing is heavy. The room is leveled. A figure appears in the doorway. It is Dad. His face and his mouth say nothing. He steps forward, reaches out and hugs me. My levy breaks. My body heaves and convulses. I soak his shoulder, crying a baby's squall. His squeeze tightens, pondering what forces have turned his child into such an angry young man.

25
Leaving Florida

"Matt, you can't wear those," says Coach B. I look down at my socks. I am wearing footies. "You're gonna have to go back to your room and change your socks." I problem solve. If I walk the third of a mile back to my room, I will hold up the team photo shoot for at least thirty minutes. I remember the new shipment of socks in the equipment locker. I deduce that I could borrow a pair, take the picture, then return them. I offer my resolution to coach.

"We don't freakin' need you!!" he screams. "You can take the next freakin' bus back to Indiana! We don't freakin' need you!" Coach B, his cheeks red like Jonathon apples, erupts. The gymnasium stops. My teammates, startled by the outburst, stand still as statues, trying to understand this arousal. I lower my head, deciding whether to take on the challenge physically, or whether to be smart and follow orders. I turn and walk across the basketball court, incensed, but veiling the signs.

Sun rays needle my scalp as I trudge across the parking lot towards my dorm room. I know my solution was sound. I think coach's response is foolish, to berate the team captain in front of the others.

My pace quickens as scenarios of payback spin through my mind. These thoughts are not fresh, as my desire to stay in Florida has been whittled away by that man with the tie and Coach B.

They continue to toy with my emotions, promising scholarships, then do not deliver. They sing my praises, then tear me down like a condemned building when they see the lack of agreement in my face. For more than two years they have dangled the scholarship carrot in front of me, jingling it just out of my grasp. I keep jumping for it, believing them, while they grant scholarships to far lesser players. I did what they asked. I rid my forearm of my Air Jordan wristband. I arrive first to 5:00 a.m. practices. I become the best player the man in a tie has ever coached. In return I get seven dollars for post game meals, shoes that are two and a half sizes too big, and tongue lashings, which I replay nightly as I stare at my dorm ceiling. I sense the black cloud, hoping the Carlo Rossi will change my fortunes.

I slap open my dorm room door and curse at the walls. I find my socks, then turn right around and walk a third of a mile.

I structure a plan. *Know the rules of the game that you are playing.* In order to change programs, one needs the blessing of the former coach in the form of an athletic transfer. Without the transfer, one may possibly end his career, stubbing his toe on a mountain of grudges. Leaving on good terms may allow a transfer to be placed in one's hand, along with a letter of recommendation. I choose to flunk out of school intentionally but believe that I can cloak the fact since my academic record is nothing to build a reputation on. When I emerge at another institution, they will gladly sign, feeling it to be the least they could do, especially after receiving my services without spending a dime for it. You don't need me? The die is cast, and I work my plan, like a trainer works the back muscles of a prize fighter. Am I sure I want to do this?

———

Barry University players resort to the desperation chapter in their playbook.

They will not win, not because the deficit facing them is insurmountable, but because of one of the characters they face. Winning has an anatomy, and I have calculated the mathematics of each step of the last two minutes, all the way to a checkmate.

A Barry shot attempt misses and I rise high for the rebound, snapping the ball, a pop sounding off the leather. I am fouled immediately. I stroll without worry, towards the other end of the court, to shoot free throws. In my periphery, I see the Barry coach motion to a player, who runs to him. This oak tree of a young man, poor in skill, but wealthy in his brutish physique, runs to the scorers' table and is buzzed into the game. Instead of walking to the scene of free shots, he walks in my direction. He throws his shoulder into my body, his action foul with conspiracy. His coach crosses his arms, watches and waits for his player's action to bear fruit, then flails his arms when I react.

As I move past the thug, without looking, I rifle the ball at him, tit for tat. I fail to consider, in my mathematics, the third official behind me, who disqualifies me on a technical foul, my fifth. I walk to the bench, past the fuming man in the tie, who is unaware of the plot. I sit on the bench and join my face with a towel. It dawns on me that I was targeted because I had the mathematics.

The game changes suddenly, like the mood of one with bipolar disorder. Barry shooters ignite, inciting panic, narrowing the lead, three points at a time. They finally miss a shot. Bixby, a transfer from Clemson University, rebounds the ball. Yeager, a sophomore with pogo sticks for legs, is down the court, envisioning a mind-splintering slam dunk. Instead of making the two-inch putt of a pass, Bixby reaches for the mustard, launching the ball from behind his back. A Barry player intercepts the pass and drops a three pointer through the net. The armpits of the man in the tie grow wet and his face pink. Time finally expires and we pull out the win. FAU fans have witnessed the drama of the week.

We shake hands with the Barry players, then return to our locker room. Coach teaches, redressing our errors in the last minutes of the game. He incredibly passes by the felonious error of Bixby, with his choice of passes, and turns to me.

"… and you!" He stops talking, his eyes dark as a raccoons, draws his fist back nearly to the Bahamas, and plants it into my chest plate. My teammates' jaws drop open, like the doors on mailboxes. The three percent of indecision flies out of my back and into a locker. I am now sure of what I want to do.

I watch my last game at Florida Atlantic University from the stands. My academic strategy works as administrators dismiss me from the team and the university. Players miss timing plays and throw the ball into the bleachers, as if by design. They need Jordan. The man in the tie turns around, looks up at me in my seat, and shakes his head. I look back at him, never having received a scholarship, and think to myself, "You said you don't need me."

I drive out of the Florida Atlantic parking lot, sobbing.

26
In the Streets

My bedroom door opens. I release a memory of the last words spoken to me by Talitha, before she and Mom move away from Evansville for good. "You need to get a life," she quips, a hand on her hip, contempt ruling her countenance. She looks down at me flattening couch cushions, paralyzed with depression. She and Mary used to look down at me from their bedroom window, proud to be my sisters, as I shot baskets, aiming for the heavens. Now I was gunning for the streets. C used to joke, as one of the athletes from our neighborhood left town for college, "He'll be back in two months. We'll have a case of 40s waitin' for him when he gets back." His calendar was often correct as person after person returned home, unable to meet the requirements. Talitha endures these jokes about me, the condescending tone in people's questions, "What happened to your brother?"

I look up and see Big Jake, crouching in the doorway, a menacing goon, coming to resolve a fabricated beef with an old friend. Standing upright, he is six foot four, with pecan skin, spattered with freckles and domed by a fiery orange flat top afro. He grits his teeth, gums exposed, sinister as the black cloud, his breathing sounding like an Indy car engine revving at the starting line. He is now his alter ego, "the spider," inching sideways like a crab, towards my bed. I stare at him, his disturbing features and arachnid gait, and like a desert scorpion, cautious and defensive, I wait for the spider to pounce. He strikes. We clash, like Inspector Clouseau and his butler Cato in the Pink Panther movies. We roll on the ground, crashing into a chair, into a table. I seldom win our wrestling matches, but never lose in big fashion, which brings Big Jake creeping through the door each morning, for he finds delight in the competition.

"Jaaake!" Big Bill, Jake's father is resting before work at the steel plant. He bangs on the wall, ending our fiasco as we have the house rumbling. "You guys knock it off in there!" We catch our breath.

"What's up, man?" asks Jake, starting a conversation as he always does.

"Nothin', man," I say, my back glistening with sweat.

"What time do you have to go to work?"

"Eleven."

"Want me to drop you off before I go to school?" he asks, through a fiendish grin.

"Yeeaah," I answer, getting down in my stance again as Jake wants one more battle before a breakfast of chili-squetti.

I live with Big Jake and his parents. Mom and Dad are living in Valparaiso. Dad accepted a tenured position at the university there, moving his career in a forward direction. My life is moving opposite. Goal setting and ambition are no longer a part of my life. I feel discarded and abandoned, similar to what my biological mother did. I have my hometown, but not a home. I engross myself in a mind-altering existence, shielding my soul from pain. As one walks across a tiled kitchen floor with damp socks, picking up dirt and hair and germs, so do I walk the streets, picking up habits that will leave me in poverty, incarcerated and destitute. I slowly push myself away from Big Jake and his family not intentionally, but because they are moving forward in life also and our agendas negatively attract, naturally. Though I work at the Country Buffet, and owe them no agreed-upon debts, I offer them no coins of thanks, yet ravage their food supply and keep hours that even Big Bill and his wife cannot condone. I soon drift from house to house, hosts taking me in with a smile, then smiling when I finally leave, many wondering how I stayed in school as long as I did.

I am soon a hood rat, nibbling at anything, lacking discretion. I am without direction, living void of rules, having the freedom I thought I wanted. Big Jake no longer takes me to work, so I hitch rides with friends who sell drugs, whose consistency and punctuality are incongruous with a good employee's schedule. Partying stretches late into the night and the thirty dollars that I earn for a day's work lack priority, as my friends make that in one hand-to-hand transaction. During a "scobbing" session, Will says that my paychecks are direct deposited to the liquor store. Soon afterwards, that joke is invalid as I quit my job and earn money cleaning my entrepreneurial friends' houses and cars. Each night in the street presents the unpredictable. Listlessness, fighting, unscrupulous women, gunplay, crack smokers and police.

The police know my face, somehow believing me to be a drug trafficker. They search my person numerous times, finding nothing, but promising to "catch me later." They oppress, though doing their job, by being predatory. When I see them, alarm rushes through my veins as I feel neither protected or served. They have wanted me ever since my incident at the record store and would love nothing more than to place a bulging, guilty, zip-lock bag of Columbian cocaine on the hood of their car, next to my face, as they fold me over and handcuff me.

I now live with Dinky and his aunt as the police have raided our other friends' houses. We keep our same hours, staying out until five in the morning, then babysit Dinky's aunt's six children, mostly by sleeping off brain-bending hangovers. Without dealer stipends, we resort to drinking ninety-nine-cent bottles of Golden Dragon from the bottom shelf.

I have a dream one morning. I am in my backyard on Chandler Avenue. The yard is alive, slithering, full of pythons and anacondas. The basketball court is missing. I hear a vehicle approaching the house. I go out the front gate to meet the vehicle. It is Dad. He is parked at the curb in his green Toyota truck, as if he no longer lives there. I am happy and run to Dad.

"Hi, Dad!" I hug him, bubbling with affection for him.

"Get in, Matt, and let's talk," he requests. I get in.

"Are you doing alright?" he asks.

"I'm okay," I say. He looks me over. His face has a look of concern and anguish. My clothes are rugged and soiled. I smile at him with a lying mouth.

"Why don't you come with me?" Dad says.

"No, Dad, that's alright. I am staying with my friends." I motion with my head in the direction of the backyard. He understands. We say goodbye and I get out of the truck. I watch Dad's tail lights shrink away into the darkness. I am overcome by feelings of folly. I lower my head, wanting to change my decision. I walk to the gate, open the door, and rejoin my friends inside.

There is a knock at the door. Dinky and I are back in a bedroom, talking. Dinky's aunt answers the door. I hear a multitude of voices yell "Merry Christmas!" Dinky and I look at each other, then jump up in synchrony. We walk into the living room and see fifteen or more college-age white men. They hand Dinky's nieces and nephews gifts, wrapped in bright-colored wrapping paper. They explain, as Dinky's aunt listens in joy, that they are passing through the neighborhood, giving gifts to underprivileged families as part of their fraternity charity work.

I look at each of them, as does Dinky, my eyes passing face to face. I stop at the one speaking. He stops talking and stares into my face, quizzical.

"Meat?" He is as astounded as I. He remembers my old nickname, given to me for my complexion.

"What's up, Steve?" I ask. He is Steve Simmons. We attended the same grade school. He was a class behind me. We won the state basketball tournament my eighth grade year. He is stunned, as he's aware of how I was raised and never expected to see me in an impoverished home. He tries to hide his embarrassment, but the pink splotches on his cheeks give him away.

"Man, you got tall!" I say, trying to relax him. I reek of beer. "I have been following your quarterbacking career at U of E. You're doing really good." After a few more words and puzzled looks by Steve's fraternity brothers, they return to the snow and back to where they came from.

"You know him?" asks Dinky.

"I went to grade school with him." I answer. Dinky laughs, now understanding Steve's edginess. As we reach again for our bottles of Golden Dragon, I know that I must move forward.

27
Keys Locked in the Car

I drive south, down 34th Street, six blocks, and turn into the liquor store parking lot. My plans are mapped out for the end of the day. I am off tomorrow and want to drink for a few hours before going out with friends. I open the car door, get out, then close the door behind me. I leave the engine running as my gas tank is empty. I know that I can coast to the end of the block to the gas station if my engine sputters and quits. I take three steps towards the store, then whip around.

"D– —t!" I curse. I just locked my keys in the car. My anxiety rages as I realize the knot I have tied myself into, a tale I couldn't invent if I tried. My spare car key is at home. It is quarter to five on Saturday and the apartment office is closing in fifteen minutes. The office is closed on Sunday. I can't make up the six blocks in this time. I won't be able to get into my house all weekend. If my car runs out of gas, it will damage the engine. I am screwed. I am a mental wreck and cannot think clearly. I call Mom, collect.

"Mom!"

"Hi, Matthew." She says, I hear the warmth in her voice. She is happy to hear from me as my calls are less than monthly. I spoil her surprise.

"I locked my keys in the car. It is running and I am out of gas. My spare key is at home and the office is about to close. What should I do?!" I am frantic. Negative thoughts compound upon themselves and the muscles in my neck and shoulders grow tight. Mom laughs.

"It's not funny, Mom!" I snap at her and feel myself growing angry.

Mom laughs because nearly every time we talk, I have discovered a novel way to handicap myself. I am comedy. It now seems that with every forward step I take, I move two steps backward.

"Where are you?" she asks, her voice calm, which slows my funnel cloud of emotions.

"I'm at the grocery store." I lie to her.

When I talk to Mom on the phone, she believes about half of what I tell her. I earned this over the years. She guards herself, fighting back her motherly instincts. I am usually requesting money, having spent mine or given it to others, leaving myself with nothing.

"Hey, Matt, why don't you go to Butler with me?" My sister has a well of happiness which she draws from. I can't seem to find one of my own, so she lets me drink from hers. During one of the lowest times of my life, when I am the most damaged as a person, she asks me to live close to her, so she can nurse her dear brother back to health.

I move to Indianapolis to attend Butler University. I wanted to be in school to appease my parents. I also believed I could be a walk on, on the basketball team. The players on the team felt my presence. I harrowed many of their dreams at night, their fearing I was coming for their positions. I was not out to take anyone's job, but I was coming, as threatening as an incensed bull. But I hear rumors of poisonous inferences planted by players around the coaches' office. "He can't shoot." I would hear. After my team won the intramural championship, the innuendo changed. "He drinks and he is a thug." Another person or persons hampering my process. My fortitude had the strength of wet toilet paper. The trauma from former coaches pounding away at my desire to be great, soon became a psychological abomination which I nourished and fed on my own. I would fold my hand as soon as someone stepped in my path, impeding me. Jordan once said "Sometimes you have to step over people to get where you want." I now step out of the way of people so they can get where they want.

"Can you call your office and ask them to open your door for you?" Mom asks.

"No, Mom, they won't do it." I reply.

"Well, how do you know?" she asks, tiring of my closed mind.

"They won't!" I insist, with the crankiness of a child in a tantrum.

I lay in my bed during the walk-on tryout at Butler. Self-defeat. Guys come to my dorm room, inquiring why I was not there. They all knew I would easily make the team as I was as good or better than anyone on scholarship. I concoct a reason.

I flunk out of Butler in a near repeat of Florida, rarely seeing my sister Mary who lives right on campus with me. I am a horrible older brother to her after she delivers a life raft to me, which is something else to feel bad about. I go to Valparaiso for Christmas. Mom learns of my repeating patterns as she opens a letter from Butler Student Records. Her face shatters. I dread even more Dad's finding out. Each time I see him, I want to show him the diamonds his good son has acquired. But when I open my hand, there are only cinders.

"Well if you don't want to at least call them, then I don't know what to tell you," she says, finished with my pungent attitude.

I lie around the house, staying out of sight during the day, then descend in front of the television at night after Mom and Dad are in bed. Lincoln is dead and is not there to comfort me. I haven't any ideas as to what my future will become. Dad gives me a date for when I must be out of the house, unless I secure employment. I rarely see him so serious. I fill out not a single application nor ask for a ride in which to do so. When my time is up, I sit with Mom and Dad and describe what my life feels like.

"It is like there is a black cloud over my head, following me everywhere I go," I say. I dissolve in a rain of tears, completely frustrated, but also hoping for a merciful extension of time. The extension eludes me.

"Where do you want me to drop you off?" Dad asks. As he drives his pariah of a son to Indianapolis, I look over at him and the indomitable steel wall of resistance he has placed between us in the front seat of the minivan. The vehicle points in one direction and the outcome is absolute.

"You can drop me at a friend's." My answer is small and dry. He takes me to my destination. We hug, but it lacks the love I have felt in the past, which I now crave more than sugar. It is more a hug of finality. I hurt.

"Mom, what should I do?!" I ask, close to a shout. I hear a car horn honking. I look over my shoulder and see Glen, in his car, next to mine. We work together at Outback Steakhouse. I tell Mom I have a ride and hang up. Glen drives me to my apartment office, where I, two minutes before they close, get the key to my apartment. I retrieve my spare key, ride with Glen back to the store, and open my car which is still running. For saving me, I buy Glen a bottle of liquor of his choice. I believe I saved him also, for his face looked as if he wanted to borrow a few dollars until payday. I buy my beer and return home. Did Mom send Glen, or was it someone else?

PART 4

28

My Move to Atlanta — the End of a Dream

I am homeless, but I feel free as never before. I know what I want to do. I attend Talitha's graduation from Spelman College in Atlanta. She is far different as a person than when she told me I needed to get a life. She is still hot with ambition but is kinder in her judgment. Now she accepts me, school or no school, job or no job.

I never would have thought my little sister, who brought me so much joy when she would bite and pinch me as a baby, would be the one leading me in my adulthood. She helps me. She suggests that I attend Morris Brown College, a school in the Atlanta University Center which is known for accepting underachieving students and giving them second chances, or in my case, a fifth. I take a chance and apply, and they accept me. Mom and Dad agree to pay my tuition … again.

I also have the opportunity to revive a dead basketball career. As shrewdly as Dad used to be during our monopoly games when I was a child, I piece together my strategy.

My roommate in Indianapolis, fatigued by my late nights and posse of friends, turns in his keys to the apartment office and terminates his lease. My name is on it, but only as an occupant. The owner of the complex, flanked by two apartment managers, walks into my housing.

"What are you doing in here?" the owner asks me, the bass in his voice authoritative, as if anything he says is law.

"I live here," I answer, murky as to what the problem is. I have moved Mick into my roommate's old bedroom. My friend from Butler had been put out of his apartment the day before.

"Not anymore you don't," he says, his line sounding like something out of an old movie. "You have to be out of here by five o' clock or I'm calling the sheriff."

"But I am on the lease," I say. I look at the manager, in whose hands I have placed many rent checks. She looks at the floor. She is a black woman who wants to keep her job and is unwilling to stand up for a rogue resident to a boss who wants me out.

"No it's not, I checked it. Out by five." He looks at me, ensuring that I understand the brevity of the circumstances. The sheriff will be called.

I move my possessions to Public Storage, where I rented a spot days earlier, believing something like this could happen. Mick shares the storage with me. After moving our things, we plop my old couch down on the grass in front of my apartment. We buy beer and grill chicken and hot dogs, and hoot and holler, late into the night, laughing at our plight.

I adjust, as people do. The bill collectors no longer have their claws in me, which is liberating. Dad once told me, "You are your reputation; guard it with your life." I cannot change my reputation in the minds of those I've met in the past. But I do not let anyone know that I am sleeping in my car. I wake up in the morning and go to Hardees. I wash off the smell of beer and eat breakfast/lunch. I go to the library and make photo copies of sections from books on basketball which I place in a binder and name "the basketball book." Then I travel to the YMCA, where I practice on my game for hours, dribbling, shooting and lifting weights. I wish my friends from home could see how good I am. Scary good. Professionally good. After showering, I go to work. Sometimes I cut my hair in the basement of my new job. After work, I go to a pool hall operated by my former manager at Outback Steakhouse. Possibly the hardest working man I have ever seen, he was accused of stealing by the owner and fired. As he feeds me free beers in exchange for my ear, we trade lava-hot stories of injustice. When the hall closes at three in the morning, I drive two blocks to my old apartment parking lot and sleep, then repeat the process. I do not care because I am going to Atlanta.

I check into my dormitory at Morris Brown, which is like a twin high-rise apartment building, right in the heart of the city. I can see the skyline of marvelous buildings and the Georgia Dome. I drive around the West End and through downtown, wanting to learn my new home. Never have I seen so many black people. I have to readjust my small-town thinking, in order to comprehend what I see. At twenty-five years of age, living with much younger students is often invigorating. It also wears on me, hearing their immaturity day to day. Kids cut the lunch line and sit on the front steps of the dorm, wasting time. But I slacken my judgment, for that was me for many years. All that matters now though is that I have a fresh start.

I begin classes with one thing in my mind. I know all the steps I have to take in order to play basketball. I need good grades. I need to practice. I cannot be seduced or distracted by anyone or anything. I stop drinking. I receive occasional visits by old friends, intrigued by my stories of the city. After my first semester, I have a 3.14 grade point average. I am executing the plan.

My summer is filled with incidents. I total my car on my birthday. I am evicted unlawfully. I have my television, CDs, clothes and stereo stolen by a crack-smoking neighbor. I still call Mom and Dad with my problems, but I do not falter as before, caving in with the earliest sign of trouble.

I enter my second semester with a building determination. I study more. I work out harder. I work with Mom's efficiency and Dad's relentlessness. I am on course. The day of the tryout arrives.

My thinking is clean. I am prepared. I look in my mirror. I look at my abdomen, smooth cobblestones of muscle. My triceps are like they have been chiseled and sanded by Joe, now a professional sculptor. I glance at some pages in the basketball book. Then, I walk to the gymnasium.

The doors leading to the court are closed. More than twenty young men, nervous but hopeful, sit, stand and pace in an area outside the doors. I walk into the area, radiating with confidence. They wish. I have been a team captain and have scrimmaged with NBA players. Others look at me, standing still, with my arms crossed, undaunted by any of them. I have it all figured out.

The coach swings open the doors to the court. He looks to be in his seventies. His skin is dark and he walks with a forward lean. He is solemn and about his business. He makes an announcement.

"Everybody pull out your transcripts." he demands. Transcripts? I didn't know anything about transcripts. Yet, every other kid pulls out papers from thin air. Everyone knew but me. I walk the campus every day and nobody said anything about transcripts. I talked with the coach and the athletic director and there was not one word of this requirement. I walk over to the coach to try to deal with him.

"Coach, I don't have my transcript with me. I didn't know we needed it. I can get it right after the tryout." I reason, just like I reasoned with Coach B years ago, over the socks.

"Don't waste your time, son," he says. Does that mean don't waste my time getting the transcript because I didn't need it to try out, or because I won't be able to try out? It sounds like the latter, so I clarify, no, beg.

"But I could just—" He cuts me clean off, like a straight edged blade slices through stubble on a man's chin.

"I said don't worry about it!" He glares at me over the top of his glasses, his words more like the warning growl of a Doberman Pincer. Don't worry about it? That is how my dream ends. An old man tells the answer to his prayers and a twenty-win season, the author of the most fantastic plays he will ever witness, one who can jump over the moon and shoot from the parking lot, the best player he will have ever coached, his first NBA draft pick, the holder of the mathematics, and one who has spent the last seventeen months of his life readying himself for this hour, not to worry about it. Can you believe it?

I sit in the bleachers and watch the tryout. It looks like a bunch of third graders in gym class being introduced to a new sport. The final part in my plan was to throw down one monstrous, impossible dunk to get everyone's attention, then pick out my locker and get measured for my shoe size. The athletic director comes to me in my seat.

"Why aren't you out there?" he asks, confused as to why I was in the bleachers. We had multiple conversations in the past. I told him of my intentions. I gave him my background. He knew I was a starter and team captain in Florida. He knew I helped beat Morris Brown when they traveled to Florida for a holiday tournament years before. He remembers the comeback led by me, after trailing by twenty points at the half, against Clarence "Big House" Gaines, to win that tournament.

"He wouldn't let me tryout because I didn't have my transcript." I tell him. Preposterous to send someone away because of a piece of paper. The athletic director turns and walks away, shaking his head.

I leave the gym and walk slowly home. The dark cloud wins, it bobs up and down, a meter above my head. Instead of turning right onto the street on where I live, I continue straight, and walk into the convenience store across from Popeye's chicken. I open the cooler door and select a bottle of malt liquor.

29
Dad's Wake-up Call

I walk down the sidewalk. With me is a young Mexican man. We step quickly for our schedule is tight. We need to be early in case our deal does not go through and we need to resort to another option. I walk up to a window and give the woman sitting behind it, my last name.

"Wangerin," I tell her. Nervous runs laps around my body.

"Could you spell it please?" she asks me.

"W-A-N …," I begin.

"I found them," she cuts in. She hands me an envelope. I take it from her and look inside. Sure enough, he did it. Two tickets and two post-game passes for the Boston Celtics versus Atlanta Hawks game. My back straightens and my chin elevates. I pass one ticket and one pass to the Mexican man walking with me. He is my employee, whom I work with. He looks at me with a broad smile.

"You didn't think I was lying did you?" I ask him.

"No, Mateo! I believed you," he answers.

I call Calbert Cheany's hotel and leave a message for him, requesting tickets. He is on his yearly tour, playing basketball for a living. I had been warned for dreaming too big, as I was likely setting myself up for disappointment. I was given the odds of my chances of playing pro basketball. My odds were even smaller as I never grew to be six feet six inches, according to my original plan. I top out at five feet nine inches, even though I eventually ate my vegetables. I no longer play basketball or the "what if" game either. When I did, though, I wondered if I should have just kept the wristband.

"Calbert, this is Milk. I was just calling to see if you could leave me some tickets for the game tonight. I am trying to bring an employee of mine. If you can't do it, I will be at the game anyway. By the way, I'm gonna need you to do somma that 'All American time' for us. You know, how you used to do it. I'll talk to you later." I hang up.

When I used to play with Calbert, on *his* secret court, we would play a game called "21." Each plays for himself. If you score a basket, you are allowed to shoot up to three free throws. A free throw counted as one point and a basket two. Whenever someone was close to winning, Calbert would say, "It's All American time!" His demeanor changes and his game ascends, becoming high caliber, leaving us mere mortals with only moral victories.

We walk inside Alexander Memorial Coliseum. We check our tickets for the section and seat number.

"Over there, Mateo," directs my friend. We find our section, then our seats. Once we settle in, hands filled with popcorn and soda, I go to my favorite thing: basketball analysis.

"See that guy right there?" I ask.

"Yeah," says Israel.

"That is Kenny Anderson. He was once considered the best point guard to ever come out of New York. He played in this gym when he was in college." Israel nods.

I put seventeen years into the game of basketball. Somewhere, I made a wrong turn, creating a great strife in my life. Did I believe in the odds somewhere in the back of my mind? What are the odds of five of my friends from a small town in Indiana playing professional basketball?

Two of them, both lottery picks, last more than ten years in the NBA which is nearly as difficult as making it. Square doesn't stick in the NBA, but during his efforts, he played with or against Jordan, Bird, Magic Johnson and Shaquille O'Neil. Kevin Hardy, an All American linebacker, made it to the NFL, winning defensive rookie of the year. Andy and Alan Benes became Major League pitchers, with Andy being the number-one draft pick. I played my first game of basketball in their backyard as my brother and sisters took piano lessons from their mother. Though not as players, Chris Lowery and Brad Brownell are moving to the top of the college basketball coaching fraternity. All of this from little old Evansville. Did I believe a little *too* much in the odds?

Two Giants walk out onto the court. They nip at each other, playing a lax defense, working on their shot.

"That's Calbert right there. He is the one that left us the tickets," I say, pointing. "The one guarding him is Walter McCarty. He is also from my hometown. Can you believe it, Israel? Two guys from my town are on the same NBA team." I shake his shoulder, trying to rub some of my excitement into his body. He laughs.

When Calbert reaches high school age, his mother moves their family to the East side of town. She is moving forward. Somehow Calbert receives criticism for leaving the inner city, where he grew up. As I recall, he did not have a job, so he himself did not pick up and leave. Walter remains in the inner city, and those same criticizing mouths never move against him. Is this what we do to our own? When we try to better ourselves, why are we considered traitors, sell-outs and incredibly, not credible? Have I been so influenced by this mentality that I now look for the negatives in the behavior of others and hate when they move forward?

The game starts and both Calbert and Walter watch from the bench.

"Did you know that Calbert once scored twenty-eight points against Jordan in the playoffs?" I ask Israel. His eyes go wide as if he were on a downslope on a roller coaster.

"On Jordan? Really?" A look of awe climbs his face. Though too young to truly understand the essence and impact of Jordan, he knows enough, as the Air Jordans on his feet attest.

I ask Calbert what it was like to battle "Black Cat," the man who covered my walls when I was younger, the one on whom I modeled my game, my walk and my talk. It was his wristband that drew the ire of my coaches when I pulled it high on my forearm.

"He is like a computer. Regardless of what you throw at him, he is always calculating and is one step ahead," says Calbert.

"When I was in Florida, we used to call him 'the robot'," I reply.

Calbert is living his dream, and I now live mine through him. He dodged, ignored and insulated his being from the persecution and made a career for himself.

To find my career, I take a different path. When hopes of a basketball career were finally put to rest, reality was waiting at my door to speak to me. Mom and Dad did everything in their power to give me an education. I tuned them out, not believing education to be a type of dividing line. I saw some cheat and connive their way to a degree and I lost respect for "the paper." Since then, many deem me insufficient and insignificant, as I have not completed my studies. It is as if I were a leper. But my true studies never stop and life does not end because there is no document confirming a formal education. I must move forward. I understand this after calling Dad some years back.

"Hi, Dad," I say, my voice unsteady, deceit seeping into the receiver.

"Oh hi, Matt! How are you doing?" he asks.

"I'm alright … well, no, not really." I hesitate.

"What's the problem?" Dad asks with caution, wary of my ways. He knows me.

"Well, I am not working right now. I don't have either of my jobs. My rent is due and I only have fifty dollars." I reach into my pocket and rub the bills, as if to show Dad that this is indeed factual and true. I am in a large city, alone, and fending for myself. The dirty South rips away at my clothing, tearing into my flesh, traumatizing his son. If he could help me just this one time, I would never ask him for help again. Strange how, ever since I announce I am going to get a scholarship, declaring my independence from him and Mom, I have been asking for his help. They try and try. As much as I disturb their sleep and bring malfeasance to their doorstep, they try. I use their love, tamper with it, play on it like it's a lyre. They still try. I did it to myself, and again, I need help.

"Matthew, as much as I would like to help you, I am going to have to say no." I don't believe what my ears tell me. I stand in silence at the pay phone, pressing the receiver against my head.

"Now I am going to have to say goodbye." Dad hangs up. I am cut off. I want to feel sorry for myself. I want someone to pat me on the back and tell me it's not fair. I wait for a sensation to cause tears to trickle down my face. But as I look around, I feel not sad, not mad, but … free.

When I was a baby, Dad would toss me into the air. Each time I would go up like pizza dough, Dad's hands, like a pizza maker's, were shaped for release. As I descend, with the wind swooshing around me, my smile is as long as the Ohio River. His hands move together into a cradle to catch me, his love and affection and my safety guaranteed. But now, as my limbs have elongated and my mind is my own, that crib of hands no longer form to catch me, only to release me. Dad severs my umbilical cord of dependence which was entangling, tripping, strangling and choking me. He unwraps it from around my neck and cuts it. I am now truly on my own.

Calbert gets into the game. In his second possession, while on the left wing, he waits for a cutter to curl over a screen at the free throw line. The defender guarding Calbert looks over his left shoulder, wanting to cheat and steal from him. He turns back to Calbert, who has gone down the baseline for "All America time."

30
Freedom

I pace around my apartment. I turn on my television. I turn it off. I have looked over my whole life and cannot think of anything to talk about. I pick up my phone and call Joe.

"Hey, Joe!" I say.

"Hey, Matt! How's it going?" he asks, happy to hear from me. I am happy also. In all of the thinking that I have done this afternoon, aside from my parents and the love of my sisters, Joe has been my truest friend. He has always been there for me. In my blindness, I did not see it.

"Man, I am having trouble thinking of anything to talk about," I tell him.

"Yeah, me too. Well, I was thinking, what if we told stories about the old neighborhood and how they relate to Dad and his legacy?" says Joe.

"I think you're on to something," I say, my mind racing through story after story, every one fresh in my mind.

After years and years of being self-involved, I pull my head out of the sand and I look around. Many "friends" have come and gone, several donning the moniker "best" in my mind. Many of them leave my circle, with my money lining their pockets. As I came of age while living on Chandler Avenue, I dashed past Joe on my way to play with new friends, figuring he would always be there. I took him for granted. It wasn't until I went to see him at his home in Minnesota that it dawned on me that I had a big brother. I am both fortunate and lucky that he never forgot me. He asked me to be his "best man" when he walked the aisle in marriage. His lines are still straighter than mine. The man in the tie once told us that when the dust settled, we would be able to count our true friends on one hand. Now, the dust has settled, and I know I have at least one.

"Remember when Dad was flashing my flash bulb at those guys drinking in front of the house, when he was in his underwear?" Joe asks, snickering.

"Yeah," I answer. We laugh.

After looking over my life, I believe I know now how I will do it. The black cloud is vanquished. I wash my clothes and pack my bag. I take a long shower. I pick up my bag, my wallet, and my plane ticket. I open my door, then shut it behind me. I am going to meet Dad in Colorado.

I stand on stage, in Colorado, looking down at a sea of faces, which are eager to hear what I have to say about "legacy." Sitting behind me are Joe and Dad. I can feel the energy from their support and love at my back, which is warm, like Dad's gas-powered fireplace back in Indiana. My public speaking is rusty and I fight down my nerves as I try to draw from memories of watching Dad preach. After I finish, Joe, Dad and I leave the stage. I move to the back of the crowded room. As I stand, person after person congratulates me on a job well done. I look over at Dad, who is surrounded by people, and realize that he truly loves me, despite my multitude of mistakes. He continues to believe in me, even after my years of deceptions, negativity and squandering of opportunity. In this moment, I feel triumph.

———

The answer is "both." I put many of the wrong ingredients in the slow-cooking stew I call my life. I also have many of the right ingredients in the wrong proportions. Every day we are met with decisions. Often we will make the incorrect ones. Many times the correct ones are the toughest and require the most effort, which is why many experience great frustration and cannot seem to shake that "black cloud" hovering above them. How does one untangle oneself? How does one become "free"? Without Mom and Dad, I don't know where I would be. Many don't have parents that help them. Was I lucky? Definitely. But I also undermined myself for many years, because I was lucky and somehow became ashamed of it. My thinking turned negative, and I watered those weeds. I only wanted to fit in. Much of my trouble was self-created. My knowledge and hard experience have taught me that when you have set a goal and face decisions related to that goal, ask yourself this: "Am I helping myself or hurting myself? Will this put me closer to my goal or further from my goal?" Do I have all the answers? Of course not. I do know that I created the hole I was in, and once I made the decision to get out of it, I received a great deal of help and found the freedom I was yearning for.

Matthew Wangerin

Share Your Thoughts

With the Author: Your comments will be forwarded to
the author when you send them to *zauthor@zondervan.com*.

With Zondervan: Submit your review of this book
by writing to *zreview@zondervan.com*.

Free Online Resources at
www.zondervan.com/hello

 Zondervan AuthorTracker: Be notified whenever your
favorite authors publish new books, go on tour, or post
an update about what's happening in their lives.

 Daily Bible Verses and Devotions: Enrich your life
with daily Bible verses or devotions that help you start
every morning focused on God.

 Free Email Publications: Sign up for newsletters on
fiction, Christian living, church ministry, parenting, and
more.

 Zondervan Bible Search: Find and compare
Bible passages in a variety of translations at
www.zondervanbiblesearch.com.

 Other Benefits: Register yourself to receive online
benefits like coupons and special offers, or to participate
in research.